ROCK BREAKS SCISSORS

Also by William Poundstone

ROCK BREAKS SCISSORS

A Practical Guide to
Outguessing and Outwitting
Almost Everybody

WILLIAM POUNDSTONE

 Little, Brown and Company
New York   Boston   London

Little, Brown and Company
Hachette Book Group
237 Park Avenue, New York, NY 10017
littlebrown.com

First Edition: June 2014

Little, Brown and Company is a division of Hachette Book Group, Inc. The Little, Brown name and logo are trademarks of Hachette Book Group, Inc.

The publisher is not responsible for websites (or their content) that are not owned by the publisher.

The Hachette Speakers Bureau provides a wide range of authors for speaking events. To find out more, go to hachettespeakersbureau.com or call (866) 376-6591.

ISBN 978-0-316-22806-0 (hc) / 978-0-316-37149-0 (int'l ed)
Library of Congress Control Number: 2014931470

10 9 8 7 6 5 4 3 2 1

RRD-C

Printed in the United States of America

It is clear that one thing which human beings find it almost impossible to do is to behave unpredictably in the simple matters of life.

—*J.J. Coupling*

[The] power of accurate observation...is commonly called cynicism by those who have not got it.

—*George Bernard Shaw*

A good magician never reveals what he does for a living.

—*Dan Guterman*

Contents

Contents

ROCK BREAKS SCISSORS

Prologue
The Outguessing Machine

The outguessing machine began with a messy laboratory accident. Dave Hagelbarger was a gangly kid from Ohio, by way of Caltech, who worked at Bell Telephone Laboratories in Murray Hill, New Jersey, in the 1950s. The lab had a strict rule requiring its engineers to wear neckties. Hagelbarger, who worked around drill presses, wore bowties — to prevent a messy accident.

He was trying to devise a new type of computer memory. A vacuum tube had to be heated at 400 ºC over a weekend. Hagelbarger returned Monday to find a gloppy mess. A careless assistant had left a pair of vinyl gloves in the oven with the precious vacuum tube. Months of work were ruined.

In frustration, Hagelbarger took off a few days to read and think. He decided that his next project would be a machine to read minds.

That idea came out of the pages of *Astounding Science Fiction*. The November 1950 issue had a towering mushroom cloud on the cover. Inside, author J.J. Coupling speculated that a computer might be able to create music by analyzing the statistical patterns of existing compositions and churning out similar though novel ones.

Coupling supplied some chance-derived music of his own, created with dice and a table of random numbers—a year before John Cage would initiate similar experiments with the *I Ching*. Coupling observed that randomness was not so easy to achieve. "One may, for instance, ask a man to produce a random sequence of digits," he wrote. "Statistical studies of such sequences have shown that they are anything but random; it is beyond human power to write down a sequence of numbers which are not in some way weighted or connected."

Hagelbarger found these ideas intriguing. But unlike most science fiction fans, he did something about it. He built a

machine to predict human choices. It played the old-time schoolyard game of "matching pennies." Two players conceal coins in their fists, either heads up or tails up. They reveal the coins in a simultaneous showdown. It's agreed beforehand that one player will win if the coins match, and the other will win if they're different.

The outguessing machine, as Hagelbarger called it, was a clunky rectangular box about three feet high. Its front had two lights and two buttons labeled + and -. Those were the options, corresponding to heads and tails. The machine took the role of the matching player, meaning that its circuits had to predict what its human opponent would do. The human selected + or − and said his choice aloud. Then he pressed a button and the machine revealed its prediction by illuminating one of two lightbulbs.

The business about announcing the choice was merely good theater. The machine could not possibly understand human speech with 1950s technology. It had already made its prediction before the word left the player's lips.

The optimal strategy was to play randomly, choosing heads or tails with a 50 percent chance of each. This much was known to any child who played the penny game. "The strategy of the machine is based on two assumptions," Hagelbarger explained.

(a) The play of people will not be random. They will be influenced by training and emotions so as to produce patterns in their play. For example, some people after winning twice, say, will tend to "stick with their luck." Others will feel they should not "push their luck" and change. In either case, if they are consistent, the machine should catch them.

(b) In order to make it hard to beat, the machine should [try to predict] only when it is winning and play randomly when it loses.

Part (a) is playing offense. The machine gradually learned an opponent's unconscious patterns and used them to predict. Part (b) is defense. Should the machine encounter a player it *couldn't* outguess, it would simply revert to random play and win 50 percent of the time.

Over the next weeks, Hagelbarger became an office pest, pleading with coworkers to play the machine. He needed a lot of data to prove that it worked. To boost the machine's appeal, he added two rows of twenty-five lights across the top. Each time the machine won, a red light came on. When the human won, a green light came on. The challenge was to light up an entire row of lights before the machine did.

One scientist spent his lunch hours with it. Another had the system of asking himself a "random" yes-or-no question, such as "Did I put on a red tie this morning?" The yes-or-no answer would be translated into heads-or-tails and thereby make his play more random. After recording 9,795 plays, Hagelbarger was able to report that his machine had won 5,218 times — 53.3 percent of the time. Though the machine's advantage was small, its victory was statistically conclusive.

One of Hagelbarger's supervisors demanded to play the machine. The boss beat it easily. As one colleague noted, "No scientist or engineer will fail to recognize the well-known syndrome of an experiment that refuses to work in the face of upper management."

At a place like Bell Labs in the 1950s, brilliant people were always tossing off sparks of genius. John Pierce had a special job — catching the best ideas in a basket and pressing their originators to follow them up. A Caltech-educated engineer, Pierce juggled the roles of instigator, motivational speaker, and life coach. His hardest case may have been Claude Shannon. It was a running joke: "You should do something on that," Pierce would say to Shannon.

"Should?" Shannon would reply. "What does 'should' mean?"

Shannon, in his late thirties, had wavy hair and handsome, rather angular features. At Bell Labs he came in when he pleased and left when he pleased. He was welcome to do that because he had published work of such phenomenal value to AT&T that it would have been petty for anyone to complain. Shannon was the godfather of our digital universe.

His MIT master's thesis described how symbolic logic could be encoded in electrical circuits, and how those circuits might compute using binary 0s and 1s rather than decimal digits. This was one of the founding documents of the computer age.

Shannon spent a fellowship at the Institute for Advanced Study, Princeton. His first wife, Norma, poured tea for Albert Einstein, who "told me I was married to a brilliant, brilliant man."

That was before Shannon published the work for which he's most renowned, "A Mathematical Theory of Communication." The 1948 paper established the science of information theory. In Shannon's revolutionary vision, information is one of the world's fundamentals, on a par with matter and energy, and subject to laws of its own. These laws became the foundation of the Internet and all digital media.

With information, Shannon had invented a new lens. When he turned that lens back onto human behavior, he found some surprises. One was that human actions are often highly predictable.

For instance, Shannon found that all natural languages have many redundant and predictable elements. As we listen to a speaker, we silently anticipate what comes next, and attend most carefully to whatever is unexpected. That's roughly what today's dictation apps do as well.

Shannon's interest in language inspired Pierce. He wrote about it in a column for *Astounding Science Fiction,* under the pseudonym J.J. Coupling. There he also outlined his ideas on computer-generated music. Since then, theorists of music have proposed that the listener is constantly anticipating the next few notes based on the past few notes. The experience of music rests largely in how the music conforms to or departs from the listener's expectations.

A garden-variety genius might have spent the remainder of his career tilling the fertile field he originated. Shannon all but dropped information theory after his magnum opus. His interests veered toward computing machines and, to some extent, the human mind. "We hope," Shannon once wrote, "that research in the design of game-playing machines will lead to insights in the manner of operation of the human brain."

Shannon spent much of his time building outlandish machines. In 1950, he created one of the first chess-playing machines, and years later a pair of robot arms that could solve a Rubik's cube. Shannon's THROBAC was a desktop calculator that worked in Roman numerals ("*TH*rifty *RO*man numeral *BA*ckward-looking *C*omputer"). His best-known contraption was Theseus, a mechanical mouse that could thread its way through an aluminum maze. Theseus became a media celebrity of sorts, and Shannon himself starred in a short film demonstrating it.

Then there was the Ultimate Machine, created around 1952. The curious observer was invited to push a toggle switch to turn it on. A mechanical hand popped out of the machine to turn the switch off and slink back into its trapdoor. This exercise in surrealism was destined for memehood. Try Googling *ultimate machine* or *leave me alone machine*. Scores of homages and rip-offs are marketed or displayed in science museums. There's a YouTube video of an ultimate machine made of Lego blocks.

Like many shy persons, Shannon had an exhibitionist streak. He was known for riding a unicycle down Bell Labs' corridors, sometimes while juggling. For a period he explored pogo sticks as an alternative means of interoffice transport. To the uninformed eye, Shannon was segueing from scientific genius to prop comic. But in his way he was exploring profound issues. One of them was: How complicated does a machine have to be to outwit a human? As colleague David Slepian said of Shannon, "My characterization of his smartness is that he would have been the world's best con man."

Dave Hagelbarger was one of the few Bell Labs people Shannon sought out. They often had lunch in Hagelbarger's lab, full of interesting contraptions to play with. Hagelbarger once hooked Shannon up to an electroencephalograph to determine whether his brilliant mind would be evident in its traces. Hagelbarger didn't see anything unusual. Then they hooked the outguessing machine to the EEG. Its waves looked like Shannon's! It turned out that an internal motor was spinning at a rate approximating the alpha waves of a human brain.

Shannon was of course delighted by the outguessing machine and resolved to build one of his own. His outguessing machine was not a mere copy but an improvement. In long sequences of plays against the same person, Shannon's machine was correct about 65 percent of the time. Its superiority was quickly evident, and it became the water-cooler sensation of Bell Labs. A stream of brilliant and egotistical scientists, engineers, and mathematicians passed through Bell Labs in the 1950s. Shannon's outguessing machine was the sword in the stone. Anyone with pretensions to being smart could hardly leave without matching his genius against it. Few could resist the challenge, and few left without sacrificing a bit of ego. To add to the mystique, Shannon alone was able to beat his outguessing machine.

Shannon described his device in a March 18, 1953, Bell Laboratories memorandum with the title "A Mind-Reading (?) Machine." There he noted that the matching game had a distinguished and somewhat literary history. It was "discussed from the game theoretic angle by [John] von Neumann and [Oskar] Morgenstern and from the psychological point of view by Edgar Allan Poe in 'The Purloined Letter.' Oddly enough, the machine is aimed more nearly at Poe's method than von Neumann's." The hero of Poe's psychological detective tale solves crimes on the premise that people are predictable when they try not to be.

In this day of chess- and *Jeopardy!*-playing supercomputers, it's no big deal for a human to be outwitted by a machine. In the early 1950s, the machine's success was almost magical, and Shannon's use of the phrase *mind-reading machine* captured a common reaction. The longer one played Shannon's machine, the better it got at predicting one's thoughts.

Bell Labs' Manfred Schroeder wanted to show off the machine to visiting mathematician Fritz Hirzebruch. Hirzebruch won the first thirteen times in a row. Had Shannon's machine met its match?

No. The machine won its fourteenth match. It won all but one of the next seventeen matches, by which point the machine was ahead of the famous mathematician. Hirzebruch kept playing, to no avail. He never managed to pull ahead of the machine thereafter.

Having come across scattered mentions of Shannon's outguessing machine over the years, I wondered whether it still existed. I knew that Shannon had been a packrat, filling his homes with toys, machines, and memorabilia. After his death, Shannon's family donated a trove of material to the MIT Museum. I checked on the museum's website and found it there, cataloged as a "penny-matching machine."

Despite the machine's considerable status in the history of artificial intelligence, it is not normally on display. To see it, I had to trek to the museum's storage site, a Costco-size window-less brick box in Somerville, Massachusetts. Inside, the build-ing is a curiosity cabinet of inexplicable inventions and relics of collegiate practical jokes. An outsize can of Jolt Cola hangs from the ceiling beams, like a stuffed crocodile in the wun-derkammers of old.

Shannon's outguessing machine is a Lucite box, about a foot on each side, with an opaque black top angled toward the player for visibility. With nerdish humor, the square top forms an abstracted face. There are two lights for eyes, a button for a nose, and a red toggle switch in a black slot for the mouth. Though much heavier than any laptop, it qualifies as luggable. A sturdy handle on the left side allowed it to be transported.

The Lucite case permits a glimpse of the workings from all sides. I was also able to turn it over to see the open bottom. A thicket of wire is neatly braided, as in an old-fashioned AT&T switchboard.

Shannon bettered Hagelbarger's rows of lights with an amusingly steampunk scorekeeper. It employed the same physics

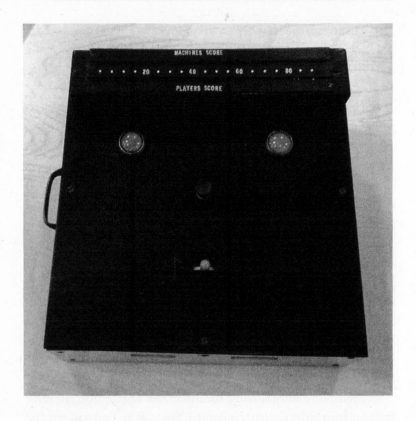

as a "Newton's cradle," the desktop toy consisting of a row of suspended steel balls. Each time the machine or player won, a steel ball shot into one of two glass tubes. The ball transferred its momentum to a row of identical balls, sending the ball at the far end of the row into the win column. Every victory must have been punctuated with a satisfying *click*.

"To give an idea of how much intellectual activity to expect from the out-guesser, consider that a man has 10^{10} neurons, the very dumbest army ant has 200 neurons, and this machine has less than 100 relays." That was Hagelbarger describing his machine. Shannon cut the number of relays in half. His machine had only 16 bits of storage. That's 2 bytes, or 0.0000000018 gigabytes. It was nonetheless enough to beat a human, as much as that player schemed and pondered, second-guessed, and double-crossed.

On Shannon's machine the two choices were labeled *left* and *right*. On its first play, the machine guessed randomly, using a rapidly spinning commutator—think of it as an electrical roulette wheel. Thereafter the machine gradually learned its opponent's inadvertent patterns. It was a triumph of record keeping over code. Imagine a chess master who tabulated how Garry Kasparov responded to the Blumenfeld gambit each time he encountered it. That would enable predictions about what Kasparov would do the next time the gambit occurred.

Both Bell Labs outguessing machines broke the penny-matching game down into eight basic situations. I'll give one. Suppose you win twice in a row with the same choice. What would you pick next? You could stick with the choice that's been winning—or you could switch, perhaps on the grounds that three times in a row wouldn't be "random."

Each time a particular situation occurred, the machine archived what the player had decided. Every decision was encoded as a 1 or 0 and slotted into one of the machine's 16 precious bits of memory. For each of the eight given situations, Shannon's machine cataloged the last two decisions only. That filled the machine's 16 bits.

When the machine needed to predict, it looked at what the player had done the last two times that same situation had occurred. Whenever the player's response had been identical both times, the machine predicted that the player would do the same thing once again. Otherwise, it guessed randomly from its ever-spinning roulette wheel.

The main difference between Shannon's machine and

Hagelbarger's was that Shannon's was simpler. Hagelbarger's machine kept track of a percentage of outcomes for each of the eight situations. The higher the percentage, the more likely Hagelbarger's machine was to predict a repeat of the past. This may sound more reasonable and nuanced than Shannon's all-or-nothing approach, but in practice, Shannon's device was the better predictor.

When confronting a new opponent, both machines took a while to hit their stride. They had to build a digital dossier on the opponent. Fritz Hirzebruch must have been lucky on the early trials, for Shannon's machine would have been guessing randomly on most or all of them.

Like kids fighting a war with toys, Shannon and Hagelbarger decided to pit their machines against each other. They built an "umpire machine" to supply an identical sequence of random choices to both machines. "The three machines were plugged together," Shannon said, "and allowed to run for a few hours to the accompaniment of small side bets and large cheering." Shannon's machine won 55 to 45 percent, to its creator's delight.

When Hagelbarger came to publish an article on this work, AT&T objected that the name *outguessing machine* didn't sound serious enough. Acronyms were big at the time, so Hagelbarger rechristened it SEER, the *SE*quence *E*xtrapolating *R*obot. I'll leave it to you to decide whether that sounds more serious. That, at any rate, supplied the title for a 1956 article in the *IRE Transactions on Electronic Computers*. There Hagelbarger posed an obvious question.

> Why build such a machine? The game it plays is really not a very exciting one and probably has little or no commer-

cial value. By relabeling the panel of the machine we can change it from an adversary to a servant which is trying to please the operator.

A digital servant that could anticipate the user's needs or desires would be useful! He gave this example:

It is possible, if not probable, that it would be economical to design a telephone central office to measure traffic and adjust itself accordingly. It might observe that most calls from the business district occur during the day and more calls from the residential section during the evening, and connect its apparatus accordingly, yet it would be able to readjust itself if a large fire occurred in the business section during the night.

Perhaps in an extremely complicated situation it might be easier to design a machine which learns to be efficient than to design an efficient machine as such.

This was a prescient description of just what did happen with the telephone business and every business. Designing machines that learn to be efficient is a twenty-first-century credo.

The outguessing machine is a commentary on the human soul no less than on the powers of technology. All of us are constantly trying to predict the actions of others, while reserving some unpredictability for ourselves. The outguessing machine presents a caricature of our scheming, one in which humans are oddly "mechanical," having short memories and little subtlety. Strategic decisions are based on what worked or failed the last time, and the time before that. The machine's success was proof that this précis wasn't too far off the mark.

Hagelbarger and Shannon's key realization was that humans have a hard time being spontaneous. A right-brain counterpart to the outguessing machines was Andy Warhol's "screen tests." Warhol pointed a silent black-and-white movie camera at icons of 1960s coolness—Bob Dylan, Susan Sontag, Allen Ginsberg, Yoko Ono, and Dennis Hopper, among many others—and instructed them to do nothing at all. It was the actor's nightmare, with no lines and nothing to do. Watch the results and you'll see that almost everyone resorted to the same threadbare bag of tricks. Warhol's subjects swallow, blink, purse lips, and brush already perfect hair. Most struggle to look unselfconscious. A few take the opposite approach and mug for the camera or gesture emphatically. That eats up a few seconds... then what? They default to the standard nongestures of unease. In trying to be cool, they were uncool in much the same ways.

Bell Labs' scientific superstars had equally few tricks for counterfeiting randomness. Once they used them up, they had no deeper well of spontaneity to draw on. They were powerless to prevent the machine from anticipating their choices.

Except for Shannon, that is, the one man able to outguess the machine. He revealed his secret in his 1953 memo. Like a Zen archer, Shannon *became* the machine.

He had to mentally emulate the machine's operation, figuring out the machine's prediction. Then he did the opposite. "It is extremely difficult to carry out this program mentally," Shannon coyly admitted.

Given the machine's design, a perfect emulator could win 75 percent of the time. (It's not 100 percent because sometimes the machine plays randomly.) Shannon managed to beat the machine about 60 percent of the time.

It's said that some Bell Labs visitors were given a quick description of the machine's operation before they played, and even this did not help much. Odometers giving cumulative scores appear on the Lucite front of Shannon's machine. They are labeled in humble pencil on paper tape: "Player" and "Machine." A final score, frozen for posterity, is Player 3507 — Machine 5010.

When I looked again at the machine's face, I realized a gag I'd missed before. The red toggle switch is a tongue. Shannon's machine is sticking its tongue out at humankind.

Today outguessing machines are all around us. You may have one in your smartphone. Talking apps like Apple's Siri seem more human than they are because humans are more mechanical than we think. Siri is able to anticipate many user requests by drawing on constantly updated statistics about what people are asking their phones and in what situations. This enhances the illusion that Siri understands the user. (Siri takes its name from SRI International, the former Stanford Research Institute, once notorious for its CIA-funded psychic research.)

The most important outguessing machine is the one known as Big Data — the all-embracing algorithms that track our every digital move in order to predict what we can be persuaded to buy next. Shannon's and Hagelbarger's devices were arguably the first to use "cookies" — archives of past human choices that are employed to predict future choices. Shannon's little machine with a face offered a game you could play or not; faceless Big Data's predictions are hard to opt out of.

One Minnesota man learned that a few years ago. He stormed into a suburban Minneapolis Target department store, demanding to speak to the manager. "My daughter got this in the mail," the man explained. The manager took a look at what the customer had brought. It was a Target mailer, like millions sent out every year, addressed to the man's daughter. This one looked harmless enough, with pictures of adorable infants, baby furniture, and maternity wear.

"Are you trying to encourage her to get pregnant?" the man sputtered. His high school–age daughter was unmarried.

The manager apologized and said he'd look into it. When he did, he learned that Target was using *predictive analytics*. It aggregated the information it had on its customers — from visits to the website, purchases in bricks-and-mortar stores, calls to customer support, and use of coupons or rebates. Software parsed this haystack of data in order to find needles of pure gold. This enabled the retailer to make specific, actionable forecasts of individual customers' future behavior.

One secret initiative was to predict which customers were pregnant. Expectant mothers have to buy a lot of products that they may never have purchased before. With novelty comes indecision. This makes mothers-to-be receptive to advertising, discounts, and anything else that might nudge them in the direction of buying at Target. A customer who comes to depend on Target while expecting a baby may decide to do her grocery shopping there — for decades to come.

Target's pregnancy predictions were much more accurate than random guessing, though of course not 100 percent certain. A few wrong guesses were acceptable. The awkward exception is when a customer gets really, really upset by a wrong prediction.

A few days later, the manager called back the irate customer to apologize a second time.

"I had a talk with my daughter," the customer said. "It turns out there's been some activities in my house I haven't been completely aware of. She's due in August. I owe you an apology."

Witness the new human condition. A department store's software can guess that a woman is having a child; her own father can't. Should we marvel at how clever our algorithms are, or at how bad we are at listening to and understanding our fellow beings?

The pitch for predictive analytics says that software can find correlations in large datasets that no mere human would ever notice. These correlations may have no obvious rhyme or reason. Target's pregnancy-prediction algorithm was based on purchases of twenty-five products, among them scent-free lotion and soap; calcium, magnesium, and zinc supplements; cotton balls; and hand sanitizers. None of these items means much by itself. A fifty-year-old bachelor might buy a zinc supplement. But a female customer making several purchases out of the twenty-five is highly predictive. Target is able not only to guess which customers are pregnant but also to pin down the delivery date to within a week or two.

Predictive analytics is indeed a kind of mind reading, though the goal is not to leave you mystified. The organizations using it would just as soon you never knew you'd been out-guessed and manipulated. It's said that Visa is able to predict which of its married credit card holders are most likely to divorce and factors that into its projections of default. Need-less to say, it wouldn't be tactful to inform the ill-fated couples of that.

"With the pregnancy products," as one Target executive explained, "we learned that some women react badly. Then we started mixing in all these ads for things we knew pregnant women would never buy, so the baby ads looked random. We'd put an ad for a lawn mower next to diapers. We'd put a coupon for wineglasses next to infant clothes. That way, it looked like all the products were chosen by chance. And we found out that as long as a pregnant woman thinks she hasn't been spied on, she'll use the coupons. She just assumes that everyone else on her block got the same mailer for diapers and cribs. As long as we don't spook her, it works."

Consumer behavior is a sequence of impulse buys fitting an envelope of economic necessity. We don't always know what we're going to buy much before we do so, and we're bewildered by the notion that someone can predict our purchases. No one complained back when shopkeepers knew their customers and offered recommendations. One difference is that today's digital recommending comes from an algorithm that we know is relatively simple. It serves as an uncomfortable reminder of how mechanical our desires and decisions can be. The new predictors challenge notions not just of privacy but also of freedom. In a consumer society, shopping is the supreme expression of free will. Am I less free because a website can guess what shoes or movies I'll like? At the end of the day you can have your tastes or you can have total, existential freedom. You can't have both.

At thirty-five, Mark was boy-band handsome and worth about $5 million. He'd married his college sweetheart from the University of Michigan and had two kids in a trophy home in Greenwich, Connecticut. With all that going for him, he might have been arrogant. He wasn't. Mark was smart, outgoing, and instantly likeable. Maybe his only demon was a touch of father issues. But Mark felt especially lucky today, and he was about to do something to get the old man's attention.

It was November 10, 1999. United Parcel Service was having an initial public offering of 109.4 million shares. Traders across the globe were frantically trying to outguess one another. No one really knew what UPS shares should sell for. In the coming hours the market would have to invent a price. There were fortunes to be made in that confusion.

Mark was seated at a terminal at his office, staring intently at the passing numbers. His job was being a highly paid mind reader, predicting what the crowd was going to do before it knew it itself. Prior to the offering, shares of UPS had been valued at $25.50. The first trade, at 10:03, was for $65. An hour and a half later it topped $70.

Mark believed that the stock would continue to shoot upward. This counted for a lot because—as yet another token of his invincible luck—he happened to be the son of his firm's owner. Mark entered a trade for a large block of UPS stock, for the company's account.

He was not buying stock to hold it. Mark was in the firm's proprietary trading division, where the goal was to sell quickly for a little more than was paid. The market was not cooperating. No sooner had Mark bought UPS than its price began to sag. Mark soon had a staggering loss.

His reaction was *it was a great buy before, and it's a better buy now.* He doubled down by buying more UPS stock.

The price kept falling. A crowd gathered—bonuses and summer homes were riding on this gamble. Mark had become the star of a little drama, and the spotlight is bad for decision making. He vowed to keep buying, if necessary, to prevent the stock from plunging further. He would move the market all by himself.

Word got around to Mark's dad. There was a hush as Bernie shut down his son's computer.

It's alleged that Mark's trading had lost Bernard L. Madoff Investment Securities over $4 million. Bernie, white-haired and focused, began asking questions. It was Bernie Madoff's good name that was at stake, not Mark's. "Maybe we could use this on the seventeenth floor," he thought out loud. The seventeenth floor was where Bernie ran the secret project that he didn't talk about. "Yes, this is actually okay," Bernie announced. "This could be *good*—for the seventeenth floor."

Somehow, through Bernie's wizardry, the $4-million disaster was wished away into that cornfield. It never haunted Mark again. Mark's lucky streak resumed, lasting until the awful day nine years later when he and his brother turned in their father for running the largest Ponzi scheme in history. Two years after that, the unrelenting scandal drove Mark to end his once-perfect life.

It seems such a simple thing to predict the random walks that determine our fates. It's not, and one reason is that our intuitions about close-to-random sequences often fail us. Misprediction can be the stuff of tragedy.

In recent decades psychologists have explored a subject that, on first encounter, sounds incredibly abstract: *human perceptions of randomness*. They've studied how we generate random or arbitrary choices, and how we predict events that defy prediction (such as the stock market, basketball tournaments, and "the future"). This subject turns out to be of great practical importance. One way or another, we are all in the business of predicting. It can be as simple as playing rock, paper, scissors to pay a bar tab. Rock breaks scissors. The better predictor wins. Anticipation of other people's thoughts and actions is crucial to winning an argument or a game; getting a date, a promotion, or a fortune. Personal and business success is often a matter of guessing a little more accurately than the next person.

This book will show you how to use psychology to improve the quality of your own predictions. Specifically, it will focus on predictions of other people's choices when they are trying to be unpredictable. It will take a hands-on approach, describing how a few simple principles can apply to many everyday situations. You'll learn that outguessing is easy, fun, and often profitable. Here are a few examples:

- *Multiple-choice tests.* Test makers try to put the correct answers in random order. Most don't succeed, and that makes it possible to get an edge when you have to guess.
- *Office pools.* When your coworkers bet on football, NCAA brackets, or the Academy Awards, their picks are moderately predictable. You can often win the pool by forecasting how others will bet and strategizing from that.
- *Games and strategy.* From tennis to poker to rock, paper, scissors, almost every game has elements of second-guessing. The player who anticipates an opponent's strategic decisions can win points and games.
- *Detecting financial fraud.* White-collar crime is all about made-up numbers: padded expense accounts, phony profit and loss statements, crooked tax returns. When people make up numbers, the numbers fall into predictable patterns. Those who recognize these patterns can get a quick check on the credibility of financial figures.
- *Investments.* The investor or homebuyer who recognizes that market valuations are predictable over very long periods can beat the crowd and the market averages.

All of this book's applications are founded on one simple idea. When people make arbitrary, random, or strategic choices, they fall into unconscious patterns that you can predict.

Part One

The Randomness Experiment

One

The Zenith Broadcast

Commander" Eugene Francis McDonald Jr. favored checked suits and a cocktail made of gin and pistachio ice cream. He resided on his 185-foot yacht, the *Mizpah*, docked in Chicago's Lincoln Park Yacht Harbor. As the chief executive of the Zenith Radio Company, McDonald lived as swashbuckling a life as any titan of industry could hope for. His interests ranged from Arctic exploration to searching for pirate gold.

McDonald's primary contribution to American business was the publicity stunt. In 1934 he sent a telegram to every US tire and oil company: WATCH ABSENCE OF PEOPLE ON STREET BETWEEN ELEVEN AND ELEVEN THIRTY DURING PRESIDENTIAL TALK. The streets were indeed deserted during Franklin Delano Roosevelt's fireside chat. A follow-up mailing touted the power of radio. The B.F. Goodrich Company agreed to sell Zenith's radios through its chain of 1,200 tire dealers. Many radio shops had gone bust after the stock market crash, making this a lifeline for Zenith.

McDonald supplied Zenith radios to Hollywood movie

sets, inventing product placement. From 1929 into the television era, Zenith radios appeared in films ranging from Busby Berkeley musicals to *Night of the Living Dead*. They're in war pictures, screwball comedies, film noir, and Three Stooges shorts. In one, Curly gets hit over the head with a Zenith radio—which must have been how regular moviegoers felt. McDonald didn't pay for the plugs. Zenith sent along two radios to each production, one for the property manager to take home as swag and the other to appear on-screen, preferably in a close-up.

McDonald's biggest publicity stunt of all involved network radio at the peak of its influence, in 1937. In May of that year, a few words from NBC announcer Herb Morrison were sufficient to destroy an industry. "It's burst into flames," gasped Morrison as he watched the *Hindenburg* disaster unfold. "Oh, the humanity!" Thereafter no one wanted to fly a dirigible. In 1937 Arturo Toscanini picked up the baton of the NBC Radio Orchestra, and the young Orson Welles took over as the voice of *The Shadow*. But nothing on the 1937 radio dial was as peculiar as the show that "Commander" McDonald cooked up.

Across the nation, Zenith dealers began handing out complimentary decks of cards. A free pack of cards was hard to pass up in those Depression years, but these were not cards that anyone could play a normal game with. The backs shimmered with a hypnotic design containing the Zenith logo and the words *DEVELOPED IN PARAPSYCHOLOGY LABORATORY AT DUKE UNIVERSITY.*

The cards were promoting a new Sunday-night radio series. It was McDonald's plan to capitalize on the nation's craze for ESP (extrasensory perception). During the mid-1930s, Joseph Banks Rhine commanded the nation's attention with his psychic experiments at Duke University. He claimed success in demonstrating telepathy, clairvoyance, and telekinesis. With piercing eyes and a dramatic sweep of steely hair, Rhine—a botanist by training—was a compelling advocate. He received mostly favorable attention in publications ranging from the *New Yorker* to *Scientific American*. As one journalist condescended, Rhine made ESP "the brief rage of women's clubs all over the U.S."

On a balmy June night, Rhine and his wife had dinner aboard McDonald's yacht. McDonald sketched his idea for a nationwide test of ESP by radio. Listeners could test their own psychic powers. It would be the biggest experiment ever, providing the best possible proof that telepathy was real.

Rhine was not sure that his newborn science was ready for prime time. Skeptics suspected that Rhine was reporting successes and ignoring failures—that some of his telepaths were cheating.

The skeptics didn't worry McDonald. As one of his associates put it, "nothing stops a crowd on a street like a fight." McDonald played Mephistopheles, tempting Rhine with plans to monetize telepathy. He said he'd have his attorneys look into copyright and trademark protection for the cards that Rhine used to test ESP. This was the so-called Zener deck, named for a colleague, marked with five symbols (circle, cross, wavy lines, square, and star). Rhine would get a royalty on every pack sold,

McDonald promised, and they'd put them in five-and-dime stores.

Rhine was ambivalent about the show. He agreed to let his name be used as a "consultant," on the understanding that other psychologists would supervise the experiments. McDonald agreed.

The half-hour series debuted as *The Zenith Foundation* on NBC's Blue Network on September 5, 1937, at 10 p.m. Eastern time. By design, the show's name didn't give the slightest clue to its subject matter. It was teased as "a program so DIFFERENT—so STARTLING—so INTERESTING—that it will become a regular habit with people all over the country." The word *Foundation* evoked grand philanthropy on the scale of Rockefeller's, but McDonald saw no reason why public service couldn't coexist with profit. A flyer sent to dealers spelled it out: "The broadcasts of The Zenith Foundation have been planned to help you sell more Zenith Radios....Make the best of this opportunity. Get behind it and push."

McDonald was concerned that the word *telepathy* might deter the more hardheaded listeners, so the first broadcasts said little or nothing about it. Early episodes took up the theme of great thinkers whose ideas had been unjustly ridiculed. Over a period of weeks, the program eased into a template that remains familiar in today's cable TV universe—dramatizations of allegedly real psychic phenomena with commentary by a motley group of "experts."

The novel element, McDonald's telepathy experiment, was introduced on the fourth broadcast. A panel of ten "senders" in a locked Chicago studio attempted to broadcast their thoughts to the nationwide audience. Listeners were encouraged to write down their psychic impressions and mail them in.

In the first test on September 26, the senders transmitted a random sequence of the colors black and white. To forestall any trickery, the choices were decided during the broadcast by the spin of a roulette wheel.

> *Narrator:* It is best to write down your impression as soon as you receive it. Do not think about it or try to reason it out. Write down your impressions in consecutive order—as rapidly as you get them. The machine is now ready to select number one.
>
> SPIN... STOP... BELL... INTERVAL... BELL
>
> *Narrator:* That was number one. The machine will now select number two....

Almost as soon as the audience responses started pouring in, it was apparent that something remarkable was going on. There were five black-or-white choices to be guessed. The majority of the radio audience was correct on all but one. Rhine must have felt pleased, and relieved, at this favorable result.

After that first test, Woolworth's department store sold out of ESP cards and had to reorder. The card symbols were used in several of the later tests. It's said that 150,000 packs were printed during the show's run. They still turn up on eBay.

The next week the choices were drawn from five vegetables: carrots, beans, peas, corn, and beets. This made it harder, as there were five possibilities for each of five places in the sequence. Two times out of five, the choice that got the most listener guesses was correct. That was twice what might be expected from chance.

On the following two broadcasts, the testers again used

black and white as the choices. On October 10, the majority's guess was correct four out of five times; on October 17, five out of seven times.

For the October 24 broadcast, the choices were circle and cross. The transmitted signals were OXXOX, and the majority's guess was right on every single one.

That's not to say that every individual listener guessed so well. But somehow the majority choices were amazingly accurate—a telepathy of crowds? In many ways the aggregate results were more impressive than any individual's could have been. Given that parapsychology was a game of statistical significance, the Zenith experiment was like a more powerful microscope or supercollider, able to discern smaller effects with precision. During its fifteen-week run, the series collected over a million individual guesses, making it the most ambitious test of ESP ever conducted. On many of the broadcasts, the statistical significance of the audience's correct guesses was fantastically high. The Zenith Foundation later put out a report claiming that the odds against the results being just a coincidence were 10,000,000,000,000,000,000 to one. The radio audience didn't need that suspiciously round number to feel that it had participated in something uncanny.

Zenith retained several distinguished psychologists to design and carry out the experiment. Behind the scenes, they were fighting tooth and nail.

As Rhine preferred to keep the show at arm's length—easy to do from his Durham, North Carolina, lab—the hands-on role went to two Northwestern University psychologists, Robert Harvey Gault and Louis D. Goodfellow. Gault, a few years from retirement, had a longstanding interest in telepathy experiments. Goodfellow was a young psychologist in Gault's department. He wore donnish spectacles and parted his hair down the middle. Both shared McDonald's conviction that the radio show was a unique opportunity to test whether telepathy was real.

It was easy to replicate Rhine's experiments, requiring only a deck of cards and a grad student with an hour to kill. Those psychologists who did so were generally disappointed. The inability of colleagues to confirm a finding is supposed to be fatal in science. In reality, it's never that simple. Rhine's thesis was, or came to be, that telepathy is a delicate thing. It is not 100 percent accurate, nor can it necessarily be summoned by anyone at any time. A failure to repeat Rhine's results might simply mean that the subject(s) lacked the "gift."

Goodfellow and Rhine bickered at long distance over details large and small. Gault was exasperated with both of them. After the first few broadcasts, Goodfellow realized something that infuriated Rhine. Goodfellow could predict the radio audience's guesses!

It wasn't telepathy. In a way, it was *better* than telepathy. Goodfellow had a simple way to predict what the American public was going to think before they knew it themselves.

Interesting as this was, it was not what Rhine or McDonald wanted to hear. Goodfellow's opinions were a threat to their increasingly profitable ESP industry (oh, the humanity!). Goodfellow was branded an enemy of the paranormal and dismissed from the show. Meanwhile, the ESP program's novelty wore thin, and the ratings trailed off. In early 1938 McDonald canceled the show.

Goodfellow independently published an analysis of the Zenith results in the *Journal of Experimental Psychology*. He offered a convincing explanation that did not involve ESP. *Time* magazine wrote that Goodfellow "pricked Telepath McDonald's iridescent bubble." For good measure, Goodfellow debunked some of the tales discussed on the program. In one, a psychic detective was said to have led police to the body of a murdered woman, buried in a woodshed. Goodfellow found court records showing that the body had been located on a tip from a boy who peeked through a knothole.

After that, the parapsychologists' feud got really childish. Goodfellow, who did not entirely live up to his name, penned an attack on Rhine under a fake name.

Cadaco-Ellis, a Chicago-based publisher of popular board games, introduced a new game called Telepathy. It was created by a certain "Dr. Ogden Reed," and the instructions slighted Rhine's science as "full of loopholes." One criticism was that the ink used to print Rhine's ESP cards caused the paper to shrink.

Those royalty-bearing cards had brought Rhine no end of grief. In the interests of cost cutting, the cards had been printed on such thin paper that amateur psychics could see through them. Psychologist B. F. Skinner "guessed" twenty-three out of twenty-five cards, to the hilarity of his students. This made Rhine a laughingstock even though he had nothing to do with the cheap cards and they weren't the ones used in his lab.

It did not take telepathy for Rhine to guess that "Dr. Ogden Reed" was Dr. Louis Goodfellow. "Is it proper," Rhine wrote to Goodfellow, "for an academic man to use a surreptitious approach (in this case, an assumed name) to avoid having to meet the responsibility for the things he is expressing?"

McDonald was furious. He told Rhine that he should sue the toy company over the game and promised to foot the legal bill himself.

"Rhine and Goodfellow keep me supplied with carbon copies of their love letters," wrote Gault, the show's senior psychologist, to McDonald. "I'm not surprised that R. is up on his ear. Between you and me and the gatepost, I don't care what kind of spanking he administers to G. The latter is an excellent technical man in the laboratory and in that capacity he is useful to me. But in some other respects he is a damn fool."

As that indicates, Goodfellow did not have an inside track on tenure at Northwestern. He left during the war to become director of the air force's Technical Training Command. Afterward he joined the psychology faculty of his hometown school, Penn State Altoona. He spent the remainder of his career in that comfortable backwater, teaching and doing good works in the community, though achieving little of note to the outside world. Today Goodfellow is remembered almost entirely for the Zenith experiment. He is a hero to the skeptic movement, almost on a par with Harry Houdini or James Randi. But Goodfellow did more than debunk. In demonstrating that the radio show's mindreading was fake, he discovered an authentic form of mind reading.

Goodfellow was not even trying to do what the show's listeners were trying to do — predict the senders' transmitted thoughts. Those thoughts, determined moments before by roulette wheel, were truly random, as Goodfellow himself had made sure. Instead, Goodfellow was predicting the audience's *guesses* about the random sequences.

On the first broadcast, the psychologists had played a trick on the listeners. The audience had been led to believe that seven choices were transmitted. Actually, there were only five. For the third and seventh transmissions, the panelists were instructed merely to count rapidly to themselves and *not* to think of black or white, the two allowed choices.

That was good science. And no one in the radio audience

realized the deception. Had there been any authentic telepaths out there, they could have written in to say, "Hey! I didn't get any color for #3 and #7, just someone counting." No one did.

This foreshadowed Goodfellow's key finding. The transmitted sequences were random; the audience's guesses were not. In aggregate the guesses were similar for *every* broadcast. They followed some simple patterns.

For instance, when the choices were heads and tails, most people chose heads as their first guess. This was not a trivial effect. Nearly four-fifths picked heads. Goodfellow was able to confirm this by doing his own survey experiment with Northwestern University students, supermarket shoppers, and town businesspeople. Each volunteer was asked to invent a five-item sequence of heads or tails. (Telepathy was never mentioned.) Seventy-eight percent picked heads as their first choice of the sequence.

Goodfellow found that 66 percent chose "light" rather than "dark" as the first choice when those were the options; "white" was favored over "black" by a slim 52 percent majority. This meant that someone schooled in these preferences could guess someone else's first "random" choice with greater-than-chance accuracy.

Goodfellow discovered that 35 percent picked the circle as their first choice when devising a sequence of the five Zener card symbols. Someone who knew this and predicted "circle" would be correct much more often than the expected 20 percent. Six of the Zenith experiments used these Zener symbols.

Goodfellow also found that some sequences of responses were greatly preferred over others. For most broadcasts there were five two-way choices. I'll use H and T as shorthand, with H representing the first-picked choice, whatever it was. The *least* popularly guessed pattern was HHHHH. No mystery there! The audience had been told to expect a random sequence. Five of the same thing is the least random-looking possibility.

This brings up the distinction between "random" and "random-looking." HHHHH (and TTTTT) is just as likely to show up in five fair coin tosses as any other sequence. You can't say it's any less random—though it sure looks less random. Perceptions of randomness are based on how mixed-up a sequence is. The Zenith show's most frequent guesses fit the pattern HHTHT. This is H and T back and forth, with one extra H thrown in to mix it up. That syncopated rhythm was characteristic of all the popular responses.

The public liked the split between heads and tails to be as even as possible. With five choices, the closest you can come to fifty-fifty is to have three of one and two of the other. *All* the most popular answer patterns were three/two splits.

Well-shuffled patterns (like HHTTH or HTTHT) were preferred to oil-and-water patterns like HHHTT or HHTTT. But shuffling could be taken too far. The least popular three/two split was the perfectly alternating sequence HTHTH.

The radio audience guessed HHTHT almost thirty times as often as TTTTT. This was true throughout the show's run, regardless of the sequence being transmitted. Though individuals might have sent in different answers for each broadcast, the overall popularity of patterns remained fairly consistent. The guessers were picking the same sequences, again and again, without realizing it.

This analysis accounted for the results without any need to assume telepathy. Whenever the correct sequence happened to start with a favored symbol and thereafter follow a favored pattern, there were lots of direct hits. When the patterns didn't look so random, America's amateur telepaths went off their game.

On November 21, using circles and crosses, the correct sequence was OOOOOX. The majority of the audience guesses were wrong on four of the six choices. It seemed evidence of "negative ESP."

On December 12, the choices were heads and tails, and the correct answer was TTHHH. Because a lopsided majority picked heads for the first pick, there were few perfect scores.

Goodfellow showed that ten of the fifteen transmitted sequences happened to be popular ones, and five were unpopular ones. That accounted for the high rate of successful guesses. It could have just as easily gone the opposite way, with more unpopular responses.

What no one, not even entrepreneur McDonald, appreciated was that there might be value in what Goodfellow had discovered: a way to predict what the public will think and do.

The random, the arbitrary, and the made-up are all around us and sometimes take on great importance. We are all currently engaged in a Zenith experiment, and the stakes are our privacy, our wealth, and our very identities. I'm talking about the passwords that lock and unlock our digital lives. The computer user believes that she has utter freedom to choose a password. For practical purposes, she doesn't. She is limited by the way her mind works, and by the fact that her mind is not so different from anyone else's.

It's not just that many use those common passwords we've all been scolded not to use. The deeper issue is that even prudent users favor the same patterns of obfuscation (such as adding "123" onto the end, alternating capitals and lowercase letters, and other schemes only a bit more clever). This cuts the exponentially vast range of potential options down to manageable size. Password-cracking software does what Goodfellow did, only billions of times faster.

*   *   *

For a time, AT&T's vision of a wireless future did not rule out telepathy. Thornton Fry, head of Bell Labs' mathematics division and the man who hired Claude Shannon, was in that diehard minority of scientists who believed that J. B. Rhine might be onto something. About 1948, Bell Labs built an ESP machine. It was a device for generating random sequences that a would-be psychic would attempt to guess. By taking the place of Zener cards, the machine could exclude the possibility of cheating or unconscious signaling that had dogged Rhine's research. Rhine himself saw the machine on a visit to Bell Labs and fell in love with it. He immediately wrote to the president of Duke University, hoping to get Bell Labs to build him one, too. It never happened. Today, random generators are free on the Web, but back then this was expensive hardware.

In 1953, the year of Shannon's mind-reading machine, Bell Labs focused on a more modest goal: designing a push-button keypad for the telephones of the future. It assigned the task to the famous industrial designer Alphonse Chapanis, who happens to be of some importance to our story.

Chapanis is known as a founder of ergometrics, the discipline of human-based engineering. In a famous tale, Chrysler chief executive Lynn Townsend once pulled Chapanis aside to ask what he thought of a sporty new model. The steering column had a decorative boss—a spike—extending an inch or two beyond the steering wheel.

"Mr. Townsend, do you know what you've designed here? You've designed a spear aimed at the driver's heart."

Townsend's reply was "Doc, it'll sell."

In at least modest ways, Chapanis invented the world we live in. He figured out which controls should work which burners on a kitchen range. His durable keypad design is still used on smartphone touch screens. Chapanis did not believe in telling clients or consumers what they should want. His concern was to find out what worked. He tested every reasonable design for range controls or telephone keypads to see which produced the fewest errors. His approach was experimental, using the methods and statistical tools of a psychology lab. An important part of that was randomized trials. Testers would be assigned to designs at random, to eliminate various sources of confusion or error.

You can't randomize without a random sequence, and Chapanis noticed that it was not so easy to invent such sequences. In 1952 he performed an innovative experiment. He asked twelve volunteers at Johns Hopkins University to write long sequences of random digits. They were given four sheets ruled into squares and told to write a number in each square.

> Use all the numbers 0, 1, 2, 3, 4, 5, 6, 7, 8, and 9 in a random way. By random, I mean that each number should be written down about an equal number of times, but there should be no regularity or order in the way in which the numbers are written down. A random series of numbers is a completely scrambled one with no system to it.

The subjects each produced 2,520 digits, a demanding task that took over an hour. As Chapanis expected, the volunteers weren't very good at counterfeiting randomness.

Some digits were chosen more often than others, despite the instructions. The least chosen digit, for just about everyone, was 0. Otherwise, digit preferences varied. One volunteer consistently overused 3s; another liked 8s.

When Chapanis looked at consecutive pairs and triplets of digits, patterns were pronounced and often consistent across subjects. The ten least popular pairs of digits were (in order of descending popularity):

66   99   00   11   33   44   88   22   77   55

All are same-digit pairs.
Here are the ten most popular digit pairs:

32   43   21   76   65   10   31   87   86   54

See the pattern? All but two are decreasing pairs in which the second digit is one less than the first.

There were similar patterns for triplets. Same-digit triplets (like 888) were rarely used. This meant that streaks of the same digit were fewer and shorter in the volunteers' worksheets than in truly random sequences. Decreasing triplets (like 987) were popular. Increasing sequences like 34 or 234 were popular, too, though to a lesser degree. The volunteers may have felt that decreasing sequences looked more random than increasing ones. The pattern in 321 does not jump out at you so quickly as the one in 123.

These made-up digit sequences were unrandom enough to be predictable. Chapanis computed that just by knowing a person's previous digit choice, he could guess the next digit 17 percent of the time. That's much better than the 10 percent chance you'd expect for random guessing. By using the two last digits, he could guess correctly 28 percent of the time. That's almost three times better than could be expected. Were you able to guess the numbers in roulette with this accuracy, you could make a quick fortune (well...you could get quickly banned from the casino).

Chapanis divided his volunteers into "sophisticated" and

"relatively unsophisticated" groups. The sophisticated group, with strong math backgrounds, was somewhat better at counterfeiting randomness but subject to the same types of errors as the others.

The most striking finding was that strings as long as eight digits might be repeated exactly, thousands of digits later in the sequence. One volunteer wrote the sequence 21531 four times and 21924 three times. Another repeated 43876538 and four other eight-digit sequences. These coincidences can't be explained by chance. They have the quality of amnesia or sleepwalking. The subjects fell into mental ruts and repeated themselves without realizing it, like a dotty grandparent who tells the same joke every Thanksgiving.

Chapanis's study was a "randomness experiment." That term is now applied to one in which volunteers are asked to make up random sequences. The point is usually to examine how humans fail to be random.

Of the many such experiments done in psychology labs, Chapanis's had particular relevance. It involved decimal digits, the kind of numbers that make the world go round. When a fraud artist fabricates financial data, he must make up a series of numbers that look normal and unsuspicious and random. We now know that fraudulent numbers usually have fingerprints of just the sort that Chapanis described. In recent years the idiosyncrasies of invented numbers have become a valuable clue in authenticating expenses, sales figures, tax returns, election results, and other important data.

Chapanis did not envision this application, however, and for complicated reasons his randomness experiment did not get the attention it deserved. He described his experiment in a slide lecture at an academic conference; an eight-paragraph abstract of that talk appeared in a 1953 issue of the *American Psychologist*. Then Chapanis got very busy with ergometrics, and with playing James Bond.

He had a double life as an American spy, traveling to Soviet bloc nations for design conferences and reporting back to his handlers. In this he was aided by his Russian-speaking wife. Chapanis never got back to publishing his random-number work until his retirement. The full report on his 1952 experiment appeared in 1995, in *Perceptual and Motor Skills*. By then there was a substantial, still-growing interest in the randomness experiment and its applications.

A proper history of the randomness experiment would begin with Hans Reichenbach's *The Theory of Probability*, a 1934 textbook published in English in 1949. Reichenbach, a distinguished philosopher of science, was apparently the first to articulate two key points. One was that "persons not acquainted with mathematics...are astonished at the clustering that occurs" in a true random sequence. In tosses of a fair coin, strings of consecutive heads are longer and more common than most expect. Reichenbach's second point was that people "asked to construct artificially a series of events that seems...well-shuffled" create too many alternations. When inventing a sequence of coin tosses, people tend to switch back and forth between heads and tails, neglecting to include enough streaks of the same choice. This was amply demonstrated in the Zenith broadcasts and in Chapanis's study.

By 1972 W. A. Wagenaar of the Netherlands' Institute for Perception could review fifteen publications on the randomness experiment. Wagenaar complained, "There is no way of combining details of the results...into one coherent theory." The researchers came to this peculiar subject with diverse agendas. Their volunteers were asked to simulate random sequences of coin tosses, die throws, digits, letters of the alphabet, or nonsense syllables. They wrote their answers down, or said them aloud, or pushed buttons. In some experiments subjects could consult a running list of their previous choices; in others they couldn't. Though all the subjects were explicitly told to be "random," the instructions did not always define that word. (A mathematical or philosophical discussion of the meaning of *randomness* could fill a book much bigger than this one.) The experimenters used different and incompatible methods to evaluate their results.

Despite this Tower of Babel, there were areas of consensus. Nearly all the papers supported both prongs of Reichenbach's claim. The randomizing was poor with just two choices (heads and tails, say) and worse with many choices (decimal digits or letters of the alphabet). When attempting to write strings of random letters, subjects overused those letters that occur most often in words (the vowels and *M, N, R, S,* and *T*). Consecutive occurrences of the same letter (*FFF*) were avoided, but volunteers favored pairs of letters that are adjacent in the alphabet (*AB* or *FE*). This parallels Chapanis's finding about digits in ascending or descending order.

To be random is to be unpredictable. Turn that around: Any human action that fails to be random is, in some measure, predictable. For years, mathematician Theodore P. Hill performed a classroom randomness experiment. He assigned the homework of flipping a coin 200 times and recording the results. About half the class (those whose mothers' maiden names began with the letters *M* through *Z*) was told to skip the coin flipping and merely fake the data. Either way, the data had to be submitted at the next meeting.

Hill astonished his students by glancing at the reports and

suavely sorting them into two stacks. His accuracy in distinguishing real from faked coin flips was close to perfect.

Hill's main tip-off was that a run of six consecutive heads or tails in 200 tosses is almost certain to occur with genuine random data. Few fakers dare to invent a sequence of that length, though. Hill could spot streaks of six at a glance, so he didn't need to count. The faked data just *looked* different.

There are now Web apps that perform the same stunt. You enter real coin toss results in one box and a made-up sequence in another. The app "reads your mind" and tells which is which. Because it can run several mathematical tests at once, it requires only about fifteen tosses in each box to achieve high accuracy. It's surprisingly difficult to fool the computer—even for those who know the giveaways and try to correct for them.

Outguessing is founded on the semipredictability of human choices. The *semi-* is the hardest part of that idea to accept. We have been led to think that predictions must be certain in order to be useful or even legitimate. The truth is that we make predictions of human thoughts and actions every day, and even a small statistical advantage can be valuable.

Mentalists were among the first to make a living from not-so-certain predictions of arbitrary choices. A mentalist is an entertainer who pretends to read minds. Much of mentalism is fake. Like regular magic, it uses sleight of hand and outright deception. There's a part of mentalism that isn't fake, though, and it's the more interesting part. When a mentalist tells you to think of a number or a color, you reflexively try to make it hard for him to guess your choice. That is, you try to pick randomly. In fact, you make a choice that fits your mental stereotype of randomness. This is more predictable than you think. Mentalists play the odds and usually have ways of sneaking in a few more guesses, should the first one not hit. They accept a chance of failure. J. B. Rhine unwittingly helped out there by promoting the credo that telepathy is never 100 percent. Audiences, who are often uncertain whether a mentalist's powers are "real," take the occasional miss as a badge of authenticity.

I'll describe a mentalism effect I witnessed that illustrates some of the tactics that we'll be using throughout this book. It goes by the name of Terasabos. The performer calls an audience volunteer onstage and positions him at one end of a table with five upside-down teacups in a neat row. He asks for a personal object, like a watch, and the volunteer supplies one. The mentalist says he is going to turn his back and let the volunteer hide the watch under any one of the cups, ranging from one to five. He demonstrates the action—lift up a cup, put the object under it, and replace the cup.

Then he turns his back. There doesn't appear to be any possibility of his peeking, not with everyone in the audience watching him. The volunteer chooses a cup (say, #4) and hides the watch under it.

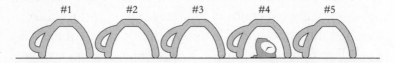

The performer turns around and instructs the volunteer to concentrate on the location of the watch. He says he has to eliminate the four cups where the watch *isn't,* and to zero in on the one where it *is.* For a few moments he stares intently at the cups.

Then ultimately the performer lifts cup #4, revealing the hidden watch.

The name Terasabos and its brilliantly optimized form were invented by mentalist Rick Maue, who drew on a number of traditions of mental magic. The most amazing thing about this effect is how real it is. The performer is guessing where the hidden object is, using the psychology of choice. He's usually right. Properly done, the accuracy is said to be about 90 percent. Understand that, and this simple trick takes on cosmic dimensions. It is about free will, here revealed as the greatest illusion of all.

Start with the basics. The performer stands a 1 in 5 chance of being right. Right?

That's what you're supposed to think. Having read this far, you should know better. Whenever there is a set of options, you should expect that some will be more frequently chosen, even when none offers a clear advantage. This is true of ESP card symbols, lottery numbers, passwords, and just about everything else.

When presented with five objects in a neat row and asked to pick one "at random," most people avoid the choices at either end (#1 or #5). Those prominent positions, at the beginning or end of the line, seem less typical and less random. That is despite the fact that a truly random chooser would pick one or the other end position 40 percent of the time.

Eliminating those two leaves three of the five options as credible choices. But the one in the center is also atypical because it's in the center. That makes it a choice to avoid, too. Eliminate it, and we're left with options #2 and #4.

There are other mentalism stunts that make use of this preference for positions 2 and 4 out of five. Terasabos enhances the basic 2-4 effect with further psychology. Anything that singles out one choice to the volunteer's attention makes it less "random" and, thus, less likely to be chosen.

You'll recall that the volunteer is made to stand next to cup #1, and the performer stands next to #5. The mentalist casually mentions that the cups "range from one to five," touching those two named cups in the process. He takes the offered object itself and places it under cup #1, supposedly to demonstrate how to do it. All of this foregrounding of #1 and #5 decreases the chance that they will be chosen. Touching is especially potent. Touched options are like baby birds returned to the nest, doomed to be rejected. In fact, cup #1, which had the object under it in the demonstration, is so radioactive that it motivates the chooser to pick a cup as far from #1 as feasible. As there are only two or three likely choices, this boosts the chance that cup #4 will be chosen. In practice, about 40 percent do choose cup #4. Less than 10 percent pick #1.

No performer would want a trick that works only 40 percent of the time. That's where the safety nets come in. Before picking up cup #4, the performer says, "Concentrate on the cup you've chosen...I am going to eliminate the empty ones...and zero in on the right one." He waves his hand over the cups and then, with great deliberation, lifts #4.

About 40 percent of the time, the object is there. The audience goes home talking about a feat that utterly defies logical explanation. (So it appears!) Otherwise, #4 is empty and the performer announces without missing a beat: "I have eliminated the first empty cup!"

He goes on to lift up the other cups in order of least likely to most likely to hold the object. The next cup to be revealed is the very unlikely #1. Before lifting it he announces, "I believe this cup is empty, too."

There is a small risk of disaster here. Despite all the precautions, the object may be under #1. In that case the performer mentions, for the benefit of any who haven't heard, that true mentalism is never certain. He segues to a more foolproof trick.

Usually the object isn't under #1, and the performer continues by announcing that #5 is empty, too. He lifts up #5. Provided it's empty, he's home free.

It's now down to two cups, #2 and #3, with #2 being more likely to hold the object. "This is the moment of truth," the performer says. "It is time to reveal the location of the object."

He reaches for cup #3. As he begins to lift it he says, "Here is..." If cup #3 is empty, the sentence ends "...the last empty cup." The performer immediately lifts up cup #2 to reveal the object.

Should the object be under #3, the sentence becomes "Here is your object." In that case, the performer doesn't lift up #2. The audience is left to conclude that, when it got down to the last two cups, it would have been anticlimactic to show the empty one, so naturally the performer cut to the reveal.

The Terasabos effect is an interactive drama in which words, actions, and not-so-random choices form a garden of forking paths. The goal is to convince the audience that whatever plotline they witness was precisely the one preordained. Rick Maue explains the effect's name (but never in his act), and it could apply to some of the stratagems in the chapters that follow. Terasabos stands for "This Effect Requires Acting Skills And Balls Of Steel."

Two

How to Outguess Rock, Paper, Scissors

In 2005 a flagging Japanese economy convinced Takashi Hashi-yama, president of the electronics firm Maspro Denkoh, to sell the corporate collection of French impressionist paintings. This included a major Cézanne landscape and lesser works by Sisley, van Gogh, and Picasso. Both Christie's and Sotheby's gave presentations to Hashiyama touting their expertise and ability to achieve the highest auction prices. In Hashiyama's judgment, the presentations were equally convincing. To settle the matter, he proposed a game of rock, paper, scissors.

"The client was very serious about this," Christie's deputy chairman Jonathan Rendell said, "so we were very serious about it, too." The money was serious, too. The Maspro Den-koh collection was valued at $20 million. Both Christie's and Sotheby's quickly agreed to the game.

In case you never had recess, rock, paper, scissors (RPS) is a schoolyard game as popular in the US as it is in Japan (where it dates to the eighteenth century at least). On a signal, two players simultaneously make one of three hand signs, chosen at will: rock (a fist); paper (an open hand, facedown, with fingers together); or scissors (a partial fist with the index and middle finger extended). An easily memorized rule determines the winner: "Rock breaks scissors, scissors cuts paper, paper covers rock." In other words, a player who chooses rock beats one who chooses scissors; scissors in turn beats paper; paper beats rock. This yields a winner whenever the two players choose differently. When they choose the same sign, it's a tie.

"There was some discussion" of strategies, Sotheby's Blake Koh said. "But this is a game of chance, so we really didn't give it that much thought. We had no strategy in mind."

In contrast, Kanae Ishibashi, the president of Christie's Japan, began researching RPS strategies on the Internet. You may or may not be surprised to learn that an awful lot has been written on the game. Ishibashi had a break when Nicholas Maclean, Christie's director of impressionist and modern art, mentioned that his eleven-year-old twin daughters, Alice and Flora, played the game at school almost daily.

Alice's advice was "Everybody knows you always start with scissors." Flora seconded this, saying "Rock is way too obvious.... Since they were beginners, scissors was definitely the safest."

Both girls also agreed that, in the event of a scissors-scissors tie, the next choice should be scissors again — precisely because "everybody expects you to choose rock."

Ishibashi went into the meeting with this strategy, while the Sotheby's rep went in with no strategy at all. The auction house people sat facing each other at a conference table, flanked by Maspro accountants. To avoid ambiguity, the players wrote their choices on a slip of paper. A Maspro executive opened the slips. Ishibashi had chosen scissors, and the Sotheby's representative had chosen paper. Scissors cuts paper, and Christie's won. In early May 2005, Christie's auctioned the four paintings for

$17.8 million, earning the auction house a $1.9 million commission.

In college I knew a guy who had made a study of rock, paper, scissors. He assured me that the game was not as trivial as it seemed, and as proof he taught me a rather diabolical trick for winning bar tab bets with it. Good RPS players do what the outguessing machine did. They attempt to recognize and exploit unconscious patterns in their opponents' play. That is anything but trivial. A World Rock Paper Scissors Society holds tournaments in Toronto. Though the media inevitably slots it under "news of the weird," the coverage is usually deep enough to acknowledge the psychological elements.

The strategy for playing RPS depends on how skilled your opponent is. Let me start by giving a basic strategy for playing against a novice player (which is to say, 99 percent of the public).

First of all, the throws are not equally common. The World RPS Society reports these proportions (for tournament play, with mostly expert players).

	Percent of tournament throws
Rock	35.4%
Paper	35.0%
Scissors	29.6%

Though the names of the throws are arbitrary, they inherit cultural stereotypes. Rock is the testosterone choice, the most aggressive and the one favored by angry players. The majority of participants in RPS tournaments are male (is this a surprise to anyone?). On your first throw against an inexperienced male opponent, the best choice is paper because that will beat rock.

It's said that women are most likely to throw scissors. You can supply your own psychoanalysis, but there aren't enough women in RPS tournaments to make scissors as popular as the other choices.

Naïve players don't like to repeat the same throw more than twice in a row. They can't accept that as random. That means that a player who throws rock...rock...is more likely to switch to something else on the next throw.

This is a big deal in a game that's nominally luck. The counterstrategy is to choose whatever sign the doubled sign would beat. Should your opponent throw rock...rock...you'd want to choose scissors on the next throw. Given that the opponent is unlikely to play rock again, scissors would be unbeatable. In case of paper, scissors wins; should the opponent choose scissors, it's a tie.

As in the outguessing machine's game, RPS players mentally categorize their throws as winners and losers. A player who loses is more likely to switch to a different throw the next time. Some players unconsciously "copy" the sign that just beat them.

Expert RPS players have many other techniques. "I went in scripting only my first throw in my head," 2008 USA Rock Paper Scissors League champion Sean Sears told me. "Then, depending on if it was a win, loss, or tie, I had the second throw scripted as well." Like chess masters, good RPS players generally plan their openings and then quickly switch to improvisation. Sears uses "pattern recognition" of the opponent's moves as well as perceptions of his emotional state and likely strategies.

Trash talk is allowed in most tournaments, and honesty

can be the most Machiavellian policy. Announce what sign you're going to throw, and then throw it. This trips up the naïve player who figures you *won't* go through with it. It's the old mentalist trick of emphasizing an option in order to steer someone away from it.

Most good players believe in tells, or at any rate the possibility of tells. You should watch your opponent for any facial expressions or gestures that might betray the next move. Monica Martinez, 2008 winner of the World RPS Tournament, credited her victory to reading faces. "I didn't worry about what I was going to do, I just did what I thought they were going to do." Jonathan Monaco, winner of the 2009 USA RPS Tournament, wears dark sunglasses to make it harder for opponents to read his expression.

Players begin by *priming,* pumping their fists to a count of three. The throw usually comes on the fourth pump. Take note of whether the tip of the thumb is tucked in the crook of the index finger. Sometimes this is a giveaway. The tucked thumb often forecasts rock.

A really good player will know all of the above and will be thinking a step ahead ... or not. This is the hall of mirrors that every serious strategist faces.

In "The Purloined Letter," Edgar Allan Poe's detective C. Auguste Dupin is trying to find a hidden blackmail letter. He recognizes an analogy to the game of "even and odd," strategically identical to matching pennies. In Poe's analysis the complete "simpleton" tries to be unpredictable by alternating. He'll choose even, then odd. This allows the smart guesser an obvious counterstrategy. But "a simpleton a degree above the first" does a double-cross. Instead of alternating, he repeats the first choice. Dupin reasons that, since he's dealing with a criminal mastermind, he can expect a double-cross. Poe inaugurated the tradition of detective stories in which the culprit is the least likely suspect and the paradox that he is, to an extent, predictable on that basis. (The French literary theorist Jacques Lacan did a seminar on Poe's "The Purloined Letter" in which he challenged his students to invent random sequences. Lacan was inspired by the Bell Labs outguessing machines.)

In detective fiction and elsewhere, it's important to know what degree of simpleton you're dealing with. That is the inner game of competition-level RPS. The RPS player can concentrate on playing randomly, so that his own throws will not be guessable, or he can try to predict what his opponent will throw and deliver the winning countersign. The best players switch between these modes as the situation demands. "If I was behind, I would play what I considered to be the conservative/defensive throw, while if I was ahead I would play the aggressive/offensive throw," Sears explained.

This opportunism resembles that of the outguessing machines, which defaulted to random play when they were unable to predict. There are impressive RPS-playing apps on the Web, which outguess the player much as Hagelbarger's and Shannon's machines did (and more accurately). RPS is good preparation for the strategic outguessing in more serious sports and games. The next few chapters will give some examples.

If you play RPS as a grown-up, it's probably as a fair(?) way to decide who pays for drinks or gets an advantage in sports. You might want to remember this little flimflam that I learned from my college friend. When a suitable situation arises, you say, "Hey, let's do rock, paper, scissors for it!" Without waiting for an okay, begin pumping your fist. *One... two... three...*

There's a good chance your partner will join in. Then you throw paper.

The usual preference for rock is greatly enhanced when the player doesn't have time to think. For the best odds, you should try this only with a male.

The safety net: In the event you lose, immediately start priming for the next throw. You're going for two of three, of course.

Recap: How to Outguess Rock, Paper, Scissors

• Scissors is the least popular choice, and men favor rock. Both are reasons to choose paper in a one-shot match.

• Announce what you're going to throw and do it. Most players figure you won't go through with it.

Three

How to Outguess Multiple-Choice Tests

Our fates in school and beyond are decided by pop quizzes, final exams, drivers' exams, SATs, and professional exams. Test makers try to make it hard for someone who doesn't know the material to guess the correct answers. In the case of a multiple-choice test, that means that each of the allowed choices should have an equal chance of being correct.

Making up a test is thus a real-world randomness experiment. The answers to a multiple-choice test are usually arrayed in a vertical list or a horizontal line. You would expect that test makers would unconsciously favor some choices over others, and that the sequence of correct answers would fail to be random.

At one point or another, most teachers have probably been warned of these issues. Journal articles and textbooks instruct educators to vary the location of the right answer randomly, though rarely does the literature acknowledge that this is easier said than done. Test makers would need to use software, dice, or coin flips to randomize effectively. They're not likely to do that unless they're aware that there is a problem and they have the time to correct it. Are they aware, and do they bother?

That's what I tried to find out. Universities now post online archives of old tests with answer keys. A staggering variety of other tests are available on the Web, too. I crunched statistics on a sample of 100 tests, 34 from schools and colleges and 66 from other sources, with a total of 2,456 questions. The tests included middle school, high school, college, and professional school exams; actual and practice drivers' tests from ten states (including New York, Pennsylvania, Georgia, and California); the US Naturalization Self Test; licensing exams for firefighters and ham radio operators; newspaper quizzes on current events, sports, and celebrities; a *Cosmopolitan* quiz ("50 Guy Phrases"); and safety quizzes for electricity, condoms, and food poisoning. I looked for strategies that would aid a guesser and computed how helpful they might be.

Every test maker is different. Some worry about randomizing their answers, while others never give it a thought. A student who will be taking tests from the same professor might want to save several tests (or get them online) and examine the pattern of correct answers to learn that professor's idiosyncrasies. My aggregate data suggest, however, that you can bet on some widespread patterns even when going into a test cold.

Let's start with true-false exams. A teacher uses true-false tests because they're the easiest type of test to make up and the fastest to grade. The test maker who resorts to a true-false exam is cutting corners, and from the strategic guesser's perspective, that's good.

Two patterns were evident. One is that "true" answers are more common than "false" ones. The average split was 56 percent true and 44 percent false.

This isn't hard to account for. True statements come more easily to mind. Recalling a fact is quicker than inventing a falsehood. Test makers follow the path of least resistance and produce tests with an excess of trues.

The other finding is that, as expected, there is more true-false-true-false alternation than in a properly random sequence. For example, here's the answer key to a twenty-item test from a college textbook (Plummer, McGeary, Carlson's *Physical Geology*, ninth edition): FTTFTFFTTFTTFTTTFTTF. I'll display it as a series of black and white squares, with white representing true items.

This is not as random as it looks. One way to judge randomness is to count how many times a correct answer (true or false) is followed by the same correct answer. This occurs just seven times out of nineteen (the twentieth answer has no successor). To put it another way, the chance that the next answer will be *different* from the present one is 63 percent. That's more than the expected 50 percent for a random sequence.

You won't be guessing on every item, let's hope. For the most part you will know the correct answers to the questions before and after the difficult ones. That permits this true-false test strategy:

• Go through the entire test, marking the answers you know, before attempting to make any guesses.

• Look at the known correct answers of the items before and after the one(s) that's left you stumped. When both neighboring answers are the same (both false, let's say), guess the opposite (true).

• Should the before and after answers be different, guess true (because true answers are more likely overall).

Example. You have to guess on an item that is surrounded by items you're sure are true. You're better off guessing false.

When one neighboring answer is true and the other is

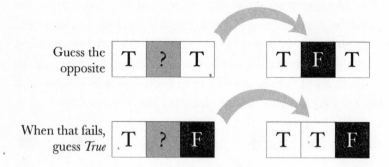

false, the alternation rule gives conflicting signals. You should default to the more common answer, true.

There is a rich folklore on multiple-choice test guessing. I remember being advised to pick the center choice. Based on my data, that tactic wouldn't do much good. On tests with three choices (call them A, B, and C), the options were about equally likely to be correct. With four options, the second answer (B) was favored, being correct about 28 percent of the time. That's compared to the expected 25 percent for four answers.

With five options, the last answer (E) was the most commonly correct one (23 percent). The middle choice (C) was the *least* favored (17 percent).

It appears that test makers intuitively get the proportions right for three choices but have trouble doing so when there are more than three. This is in line with experimental findings that the quality of randomizing decreases as the number of options increases.

A better guessing policy would be to pick the second answer (B) on four-choice tests and the fifth answer (E) on five-choice tests.

Another popular bit of test-prep advice is "never pick never." You should avoid answers that include *never, always, all,* or *none*. These universal qualifiers almost inevitably convert a true statement into a false one, in our wicked and complicated world. This tip is easy to accept, the more so when you consider what a slog it is to create multiple-choice tests. The teacher has to think up several believable wrong answers for every right one. Quick recipes for falsehoods must get used over and over.

I found one notable exception to this advice. In the tests I examined, "none of the above" and "all of the above" answers were wildly more likely to be correct. In one college textbook with four-choice questions, "none"/"all" answers were right 65 percent of the time!

"None of the above" answers can't just be dropped in; the other answers have to be written around them. The effort apparently discourages test makers from supplying the strategic number of wrong "none" or "all" answers. In my total sample, a none/all answer was correct 52 percent of the time that there was such an answer. Assuming this is even close to being representative, it's astonishing.

Another interesting rule of thumb alleges that the longest multiple-choice answer is most likely to be correct. On this question from the Washington state driver's exam, the longest answer (c) is indeed correct:

To turn right, you should be in:
a. The left lane.
b. The center lane.
c. The lane that's closest to the direction you want to go.
d. Any one of the lanes.

Test makers have to make sure that right answers are indisputably right. Often this demands some qualifying language. They may not try so hard with wrong answers.

Still another trick is to check for what Hollywood calls continuity errors. Here's an example from the guidelines for Brigham Young University's faculty.

> A word used to describe a noun is called an:
> a. Adjective.
> b. Conjunction.
> c. Pronoun.
> d. Verb.

The hapless professor used the article *an,* hearing the correct answer, *adjective,* in his head. Then he wrote three alternatives, not stopping to think that they begin with consonants. A student could use that slip to deduce the answer.

Like true-false tests, multiple-choice tests show too much alternation. It wasn't too uncommon to find short tests in which no correct choice ever repeated twice in a row. The answer key played a game of hopscotch.

I tallied how often a correct answer's list position (A, B, C...) repeated the one before it. For the three-choice tests in my sample, the correct choice repeated its predecessor only 25 percent of the time (versus the expected 33 percent for a random sequence). For four-choice tests, it was 19 percent (versus an expected 25 percent), and for five-choice tests, it was 18 percent (versus 20 percent).

In the chart of these results, the line shows the expected chance for a truly random test. For all numbers of choices, there were too few repeats. This means that a test taker could

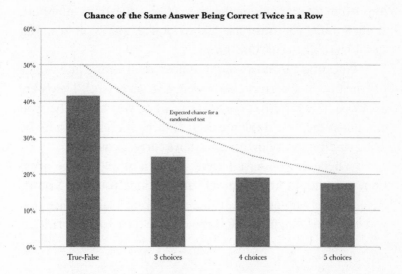

Chance of the Same Answer Being Correct Twice in a Row

Expected chance for a randomized test

True-False — 3 choices — 4 choices — 5 choices

gain an easy advantage when guessing just by avoiding the previous question's answer.

I rated that and other multiple-choice strategies by calculating how much they improved on random guessing.

Strategy	Improvement on Random Guessing
Pick the "none of the above" or "all of the above" answer	90%
Pick B on a four-choice test, E on a five-choice test	11%
Avoid the previous choice	8%

Hands down, the best strategy was picking "none of the above" or "all of the above." These choices were almost twice as likely to be true as other choices, offering a 90 percent improvement on random guessing. (A few questions offer both "none" and "all" answers. Unless you're totally at sea, you should be able to rule one out.)

Guessing the most common positional choice and avoiding the previous correct choice were also successful. They were about equally effective, particularly when you figure that you can boost the "avoid the previous choice" success rate a bit by also avoiding the following question's correct answer.

Whenever you have to guess on a multiple-choice question, you should first eliminate any options you can. Knowledge trumps outguessing! If there's a "none"/"all" choice that you can't rule out, pick it. Otherwise, use the two other rules.

```
1  ⊏A⊐  ⊏B⊐  ▬C▬  ⊏D⊐
2  ⊏A⊐  ⊏B⊐  ⊏C⊐  ⊏D⊐
3  ⊏A⊐  ⊏B⊐  ⊏C⊐  ▬D▬
```

Example. You don't know the answer to question #2, though you're sure the third one (C) is wrong. That leaves three open possibilities. There is no "all of the above" or "none of the above" answer.

The second choice is most often correct for a four-choice question, so that's one vote for B. Make an imaginary checkmark next to it.

You know that the correct answers to the neighboring questions, #1 and #3, are C and D. That's reason to favor a *different* choice here — A or B. Place checkmarks next to them.

This gives us one vote for A, two for B, none for D — and C is ruled out on factual grounds. B is the best guess.

When "voting" leads to a tie, pick any of the tied options.

*   *   *

The College Board is well aware of the failings of handcrafted tests. Its Scholastic Assessment Test is better written and harder to guess than tests created for a typical high school or college class. Where possible, the SAT's multiple-choice answers are listed in logical or numerical order. In other cases, software randomizes the order of answers. That nullifies strategies based on position in an answer list.

The College Board reveals actual SAT questions on its website—presumably not to be used again—as well as sample tests. I found that the longest-answer strategy seems to work with the SAT's practice exams. Out of twenty practice questions with phrase or sentence answers on the website, the correct answer was the longest one five times, and it was essentially tied for longest answer with another question three times. Assuming you choose one of the tied-for-longest answers, you can expect to guess correctly 6.5 times out of 20, or about 33 percent of the time. That would top the expected 20 percent guessing rate for the five-answer SAT.

Another strategy that appears to work on the SAT is to "eliminate the outlier." Here's a set of answers from an SAT question on the College Board website. I won't even give you the question—you don't need it!

(A) haphazard . . radical
(B) inherent . . controversial
(C) improvised . . startling
(D) methodical . . revolutionary
(E) derivative . . gradual

It may well be that software has shuffled the order of these answers. A human still had to write the answers. The intent is to conceal the correct answer by surrounding it with plausible-though-wrong alternatives (known in the trade as distractors). The correct answer will usually be in the middle of the pack. I don't mean it will be in the middle of the list; rather, its *meaning* will be in the middle. Outlier answers are usually *not* correct.

Here the answers' right-hand words all have similar meanings except for (E). *Gradual* is almost the opposite of *radical, revolutionary,* etc. Now think about it. Suppose that (E) was the correct answer. Why would the test designer bother to make the four wrong answers so similar? A wrong answer doesn't have to be similar to anything; it just has to be wrong. Making all the wrong answers similar thrusts the correct answer into sharp relief, and that's what a test maker doesn't want to do. It's therefore more likely that the correct answer lurks within the "radical" group.

You can narrow it down further. The answers' left-hand words do not have such an obvious pattern as the right-hand ones, but *haphazard* and *improvised* are similar in meaning. "Haphazard . . radical" and "improvised . . startling" are so close in meaning that it's hard to see how one could be unambiguously correct and the other unambiguously wrong. That probably means they can both be ruled out as candidates.

We have provisionally eliminated three of five answers *without looking at the question*. Choose one of two remaining, and you've got a fifty-fifty chance. (D) is in fact the correct answer.

There is a misconception that the SAT penalizes guessing. It's more accurate to say that the College Board's scoring system penalizes wrong answers. In scoring, the College Board takes the number of right answers and subtracts a fraction of the wrong answers. The fraction, 1/4 for a five-choice test, simply ensures that an ignoramus who guesses has no advantage over one who leaves questions blank.

This embodies the philosophy that I've been adopting here. A guessing strategy is useful to the extent that it beats random guessing. Any strategy that yields a statistical advantage works in your favor on the SAT or elsewhere.

One final rule: Always guess. It works, even without a system. Optometrists coax patients to guess on the lower line of the eye chart because they know those guesses are often right, notwithstanding the patient's insistence that she can't possibly read the print. When you're at a complete loss, ask yourself which of the answers sounds most familiar. Correct answers are more likely to ring familiar. It may be that you were exposed to the answer once and have forgotten it. All that's left is a faint sense of déjà vu. Guess the déjà vu answer.

Recap: How to Outguess Multiple-Choice Tests

- On true-false tests, "true" answers are more common.
- On multiple-choice tests with four answers, the second one (B) is most often correct.
- "None of the above" and "all of the above" answers are disproportionately likely to be correct.
- The answer that was right on the previous question ("true" or [D], say) is less likely to be right on the present question.
- A strategy for standardized tests like the SAT is to eliminate the outlier. Avoid guessing an answer that is too different from the others.

Four

How to Outguess the Lottery

State lotteries became successful only after New Jersey copied an idea from organized crime — letting bettors pick their own numbers. The Mob knew that gamblers like to feel they can control their fate. Today the two big multistate lotteries — Mega Millions and Powerball — offer bettor-chosen numbers and carve up most of the big-jackpot business.

Is it possible to beat the pick-six lotteries? That depends on what you mean by *beat*. One definition is finding a positive-expectation wager. This is a bet where the odds favor the bettor over the lottery board. Though the Mega Millions' and Powerball's profit borders on the obscene, positive-expectation wagers *are* possible for someone with a good outguessing strategy.

A more pertinent definition of *beating the lottery* is "having a good chance of making a substantial profit while I'm still alive." That may sound like it's the same thing, but sadly it's not. The strategy in this chapter is strictly for those who enjoy the lottery as entertainment and are going to play it anyway.

The outguessing approach to lottery numbers dates at least to 1981, when MIT statistician Herman Chernoff published an article in the *Mathematical Intelligencer* with the title "How to Beat the Massachusetts Number Game." His premise was that not all lottery numbers are equal.

Massachusetts' number game, introduced in 1976, used four-digit numbers. With only 10,000 possible winning numbers, and ways of betting on more than one number, ties were to be expected in every game. In case of multiple winners, the jackpot was split among them. This rule, now standard with pick-your-number lotteries, makes an immense difference in strategy. Chernoff proposed picking the lottery numbers least popular with bettors. These numbers offer greater winning potential because the jackpot is likely to be split among fewer winners.

Chernoff found clear patterns in the numbers that bettors picked (though not in the numbers that won, which were random). Bettors avoided 0s, 9s, and 8s, especially as the first number. They liked smaller digits. That was enough to create massive variation in payoffs by number.

Chernoff and his students managed to find positive-expectation wagers, or so it appeared. The expectation is how much you can expect to win, in the long run, net of costs. For a lottery jackpot, it's the minuscule chance of winning multiplied by the payoff (the actual share of the jackpot you'd get), minus the cost of the lottery ticket. Normally the expectation is negative, since lotteries exist to suck money out of bettors' wallets. Massachusetts skimmed 40 percent of everything wagered. This crushing vigorish is typical.

But Chernoff was able to engineer profitable wagers by taking advantage of the unpopular numbers and a quirky rule that favored people betting on just three numbers rather than four. Chernoff described a system that bought thirty-three tickets per game, costing $33 a day. In the first 210 days, Chernoff's numbers won ten times, leading to an average winning of $44.19 a day. That was an amazing 34 percent return on investment.

Chernoff did not take his system any further, for reasons he outlined in his article. One was the observation that "if the system were good and this became well known, the resulting popularity of the numbers constituting the system would destroy their value."

Lottery boards have gotten Chernoff's memo. Today's lotteries have plugged some of the holes he described, making them harder to beat. Pick-six lotteries have you select whole numbers in a given range (say, 1 to 49), rather than single digits. This eliminates many numbers containing the unpopular 0 and 9. Chernoff's insights have percolated down to the most naïve players. Websites and tout sheets dispensing otherwise worthless lotto folklore also counsel players to pick unpopular numbers in order to avoid ties.

Let's look at three popular games. In a standard pick-six lottery, offered by some states, you choose six numbers in the range 1 through 49. The six numbers must be all different, and the order is immaterial. In the drawing, six Ping-Pong balls imprinted with numbers are drawn from a "barrel." That's lottery jargon — it doesn't usually look like a barrel. The jackpot is divided among any players who have picked all six numbers. Smaller fixed prizes are awarded to those who match some of the numbers.

America's biggest lotteries are "two-barrel" games. In Mega Millions, one barrel has white balls numbered 1 through 75. A second barrel, for the "Mega Ball," has gold balls numbered 1 through 15. To play, you pick five different numbers to match five drawn from the first barrel, and one to match the single Mega Ball drawing. Your Mega Ball pick can be the same as one of your other picks or different. As usual, you have to pick all six numbers right to share the jackpot, and there are smaller prizes for getting some numbers right.

Powerball is similar to Mega Millions (and came first). The range is 1 to 59 for five numbers drawn from the first barrel of white balls, and 1 to 35 for the second barrel's red "Powerball."

Why two barrels? Why not? Gamblers like needless complication.

In the 1980s finance professor William Ziemba and colleagues made a study of pick-six lotteries. They found that the most popular number was "lucky" 7. It is chosen almost 50 percent more than average. That should tell you that 7 is the *un*luckiest number, jackpot-wise.

Is 13 the best pick, then? No, that's a fairly popular number. Many bettors try a little reverse psychology on Fate.

Feature stories offering lotto pointers often claim that you should avoid numbers that could be dates (like 9 and 11), on the theory that many lotto players choose significant dates. This is probably the best-known contrarian strategy. Since months fall in the range 1 to 12, days are 1 to 31, and recent years are also low numbers, that would presumably lead to (relative) neglect of the numbers 32 and higher.

Ziemba did not find overwhelming evidence for this. It's true that low numbers are generally popular, as Chernoff had found. But a date yields only two or three numbers (with year) out of the six required. Players who choose a date, resulting in some low numbers, may pick some high numbers to balance out their set of six, diminishing the effect.

The March 30, 2005, Powerball drawing had 110 second-prize winners. It turned out that they had all played numbers on a widely distributed fortune cookie fortune. In case you haven't noticed, there are six "lucky numbers" on many of those fortunes. The much-duplicated fortune read "All the preparation you've done will finally be paying off" and had the numbers 22, 28, 32, 33, 39, 40. Only the last number was wrong. Had it been the winning 42, those bettors would all have been tied for first place.

The TV show *Lost* featured the enigmatic numbers 4, 8, 15, 16, 23, and 42 throughout the series. Two episodes had hapless castaway Hurley playing them in a "Mega Lotto" game and winning a jackpot. This apparently led to thousands of viewers picking those numbers over the series' run. In the January 4, 2011, Mega Millions drawing, the numbers 4, 8, 15, and 42 came up, though the others were different. That was worth $150.

Lotto software will generate a random set of picks for any who want it. Those who opt for random picks do better than the majority of lotto players. The conscious choosers unknowingly gravitate to the same fifteen to twenty popular numbers. The random pickers usually have more unpopular numbers because most numbers are not popular. Though accepting a random pick is not the best you can do, it is simple.

Ziemba found that the overall popularity of specific lottery numbers was reasonably consistent from year to year. On a standard pick-six lottery (1 to 49) the ten least played numbers were:

40 39 20 30 41 38 42 46 29 49

At first glance, there's not much rhyme or reason. Look closer, and you'll see that —

- Most end in the unpopular digit 0, 8, or 9
- None contains a "lucky" 7
- All but one are in the higher half of the range (above 25)
- Half are in the cluster 38 to 42 inclusive

These numbers are about 15 to 30 percent less popular than average. By making sure that all six numbers are unpopular, the advantage compounds. Ziemba computed that there are thousands of six-number picks with positive expectation. It's not hard to achieve an expectation of $2 for every dollar bet.

The advantage can increase when jackpots go uncollected and roll over. The price of a lottery ticket does not go up as the jackpot does. Instead, the lottery just prints more tickets. There's a feeding frenzy to buy those tickets, diluting everyone's hypothetical share. Still, there are only so many lotto players out there, and even they can get burnt out by weeks of hype. Consequently, the number of tickets sold doesn't necessarily go up in direct proportion to the jackpot. In some cases, large jackpots boost the advantage substantially. This is more common with smaller, single-state lotteries outside the coastal media centers.

To turn picking-six-unpopular-numbers into a system, it's necessary to avoid competing with other savvy bettors who might be out there. You wouldn't want to be part of an elite group who think they're smart for picking the same six "least popular" numbers. That could be as bad as playing fortune cookie picks.

This isn't too much of a problem. For one thing, there is some ambiguity about what the "six least popular numbers" are. When a set of numbers is drawn, you learn (only) how many bettors picked that exact set. There are several ways of teasing out how many picked each individual number, all involving mathematical models. These models generally agree, but with some variation.

Ziemba's research covered 6/49 lotteries (using six numbers in the range 1 to 49). Mega Millions allows numbers up to 75, and Powerball, up to 59. Based on the popularity of second digits in Ziemba's study, it's likely that 50, 51, 52, 58, and 59 would be unpopular numbers, too.

Say you adopt a list of twenty unpopular numbers and randomly choose six of them to play. There are twenty choices for the first number, nineteen for the second (since you can't repeat numbers drawn from the first barrel), eighteen for the third, seventeen for the fourth, sixteen for the fifth, and fifteen for the sixth. Given that the order doesn't matter, there are 38,760 distinct sets of six. It's unlikely that there will be that many Ziemba-style players in a given drawing, using the exact same set of "unpopular" numbers. Provided everyone chooses from among the lucky numbers randomly, the players using this system don't have to worry too much about stepping on each other's toes.

Here is a reasonable plan for achieving favorable bets in American lotteries. You'll be using up to seventeen unpopular numbers, shown in the diagram.

1. First, select six numbers from this set *at random*. A low-tech way to do that is to write the numbers on index cards, shuffle them, and draw numbers. It should be clear by now that shuffling is preferred to a mental "random" pick.

The picks must be tailored to the specific lottery's rules. For a plain-vanilla 6/49 lottery, you'd use only the twelve numbers in the first four rows of the chart. Draw six numbers (without replacing them) from the shuffled deck of twelve.

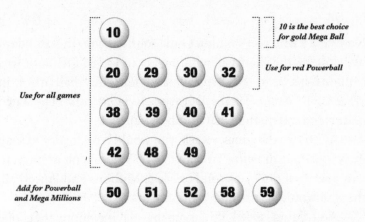

For the Mega Millions and Powerball, use all the numbers in the chart, and draw five. Then replace the drawn numbers in the deck for the second-barrel pick. For Powerball, you'll be using only the first five numbers in the chart. For Mega Millions, ten is probably the best choice for the gold Mega Ball.

2. Now you've got six legal picks of relatively unplayed numbers. Make sure they don't happen to make a geometric pattern on the physical or virtual play slip. Indecisive bettors often default to picking numbers that form a line or other pattern on the play slip. Diagonals are especially popular because they seem more random. Vertical lines are also used, and occasionally people pick a cross of five numbers (which could be horizontal-vertical or diagonal).

In the unlikely event that your picks form a pattern, you should either start over or swap one of your picks with another unpopular number, to eliminate the pattern.

3. Should it come to your attention that a popular TV show or movie or book or video game has mentioned a set of pick-six numbers, avoid them. Avoid numbers that are in the news.

*　　*　　*

Now here's why you shouldn't quit your day job. In a standard 6/49 lottery, the chance of winning is 1 in 13,983,816. For Mega Millions it's 1 in 258,890,850, and for Powerball it's 1 in 175,223,510. *Nothing in the above system changes that.* The stated odds stand, no matter what numbers you pick.

With two drawings a week, you would have to play a ticket in every single drawing for about 134,000 years, on average, to win your first 6/49 jackpot. For Mega Millions and Powerball, the wait would be a couple million years.

You could speed things up by playing more than one ticket per game — assuming you've got the spare cash. An average citizen who spent all her average income on lottery tickets might cut the wait time to, oh, a millennium or two.

The player of unpopular numbers can expect to win thousands of smaller prizes on the long, long road to the first jackpot. Won't that help tide her over?

Not really. The nonjackpot prizes are almost always fixed amounts of cash. Winners don't split these, and that nullifies the advantage of a Ziemba system.

One rare exception is California's Mega Millions lottery. It splits payouts among winners even for the small prizes. That means that there's an advantage in betting unpopular numbers, and in avoiding popular ones, for these prizes, too. (The *Lost* numbers paid only $118 in California, versus $150 elsewhere, because so many played them.)

That still doesn't help much. About 90 percent of the money returned as prizes goes to the jackpot. That makes economic sense, as the jackpot amount is the only number that sells tickets. It's comforting to know that you can win a smaller prize, but nobody pays much attention to the amounts or the odds. Though something like 100,000 smaller prizes are awarded in every drawing, they collectively return only pennies on the wagered dollar. No unpopular number strategy can surmount that. Minus the jackpot, *any* lotto ticket is a sucker bet.

Ziemba and colleagues have made the deadpan argument that a wealthy and patient "dynasty" could use an unpopular number lotto system to amass great riches over the millennia. For mere mortals, a policy of buying lottery tickets is a financial drain that almost never pays off while you're drawing breath. Fran Lebowitz had the right idea: "I figure you have the same chance of winning the lottery whether you play or not."

Recap: How to Outguess the Lottery

• These numbers are "lucky"—because relatively few players pick them, reducing the chance of a shared jackpot: 10, 20, 29, 30, 32, 38, 39, 40, 41, 42, 48, 49, 50, 51, 52, 58, 59.

Five

How to Outguess Tennis Serves

Tennis pro and coach Daryl Fisher of Ann Arbor, Michigan, came up with a secret weapon to give almost any tennis player an advantage. It's one of the few sweat-free ways to improve your game.

"There was one opponent who would serve to my backhand," Fisher explained. "When he succeeded, I would position myself for the same serve the next time." The guy *always* repeated a successful serve. When Fisher deftly returned the serve, the too-predictable player would switch to something else on his next serve. Fisher predicted that, too.

This player had a "rhythm" that Fisher could recognize and anticipate. He discovered a parallel when he happened to read about the outguessing machine in Robert Lucky's 1989 history of Bell Labs, *Silicon Dreams.* Tennis players are as predictable as the outguessing machine's players, Fisher realized. They are smart people with short strategic memories. They base decisions mainly on what worked or didn't work the last time.

To oversimplify things a bit, the server has three main

options: to hit the ball to the left of the receiver, to the right, or directly at him. Because the receiver does not know where the ball is going, he must be prepared to move quickly in order to return the serve.

A player aware of his and his opponent's strengths knows that some serves are more likely to succeed. But a player who always uses his "best" serve is predictable. "It's very easy to become one-dimensional," Venus Williams once said, "and just serve to your favorite space and the person is just waiting there." To avoid this, the strategic server will randomly pick a disfavored option some of the time.

One hurdle is getting the probabilities right. A rock, paper, scissors player knows to pick each throw with a probability of 1/3. In physical sports, it is hard to know the "correct" probabilities with any precision. A distinct challenge is generating random choices in the heat of a game. This is where Fisher's opponent failed. He fell back on a simple, easily outguessed pattern.

In recent years psychologists, economists, and game theorists have asked, how well do athletes randomize? Much of this research has made the point that athletes do not follow game theory exactly. Okay, but that's like saying their tweets aren't always grammatical and politically correct. You wouldn't expect an athlete's instinctive strategy to match the mathematical ideal. A more provocative finding is that athletes, like everyone else, are unable to generate credible random sequences. Tennis has been studied extensively because it offers so much data. A match may have hundreds of serves between the same two players.

In a 2001 article, Mark Walker and John Wooders examined videos of ten matches at Wimbledon and other pro tournaments, involving such stars as Andre Agassi, Petr Korda, John

McEnroe, and Pete Sampras. Some players served to the left and right almost equally, while others strongly favored one direction. The opponent, and whether the server had the ad or deuce side, mattered. But overall, Walker and Wooders found that the pros alternated serves too much. A sequence of tennis serves will be too close to right-left-right-left (like the heads of spectators watching tennis). However, the players were not as predictable as typical subjects in nonathletic randomness experiments. Apparently tennis pros had learned to simulate randomness better than those who didn't have a career riding on it.

These findings offer several guidelines that ought to apply (perhaps especially) to amateur tennis. When you're receiving, expect the serve to alternate. A serve to the right this time means: be prepared for left next time. A different serve is especially likely when the last serve failed, or after two or more consecutive serves in the same direction.

When you're the one serving, you need to remember that making your own random choices is like cutting your own hair. You need help. That brings us to Fisher's secret weapon: a heart-rate monitor.

Many players wear wristband monitors, and some are obsessive about checking their cardio rate midmatch—so there's nothing too suspicious about glancing at them. Because a player's heart rate is always changing in an intense match, the rightmost digit is unpredictable. Whether the last digit is odd or even is, for practical purposes, random.

Fisher advises servers to first decide their percentage strategy against a given opponent. Maybe you want to serve to the right 40 percent of the time, to the left 40 percent, and to the body 20 percent. In that case you might decide that even numbers 2, 4, 6, and 8 mean "serve right"; odd numbers 3, 5, 7, and

9 mean "serve left"; and low numbers 0 and 1 mean "serve to the body." Should the monitor read 167 when you glance at it, you'd serve to the left.

Most heart-rate monitors double as digital watches. Fisher notes that the time readout's last digit can be used to randomize spin or whether you follow a serve by remaining at the baseline or going to the net. A further advantage of the heart-rate monitor scheme is that there's no great harm, should your opponent suspect what you're doing. She can't see your heart monitor.

Those not wanting to use a heart-rate monitor can use a watch, a digital clock, or a scoreboard. The even- or oddness of the seconds figure is good for deciding two-way, equal-probability choices. When choices aren't equally favored or are more than two, you can invent a rule like Fisher's. Of course, the problem with a clock or scoreboard is that it's not private.

In my own experience, an analog watch with a second hand is easy for weekend players to use. Many choices in sports are left or right. Glance at the watch and note the second hand's position at that exact ("random") instant. If the second hand is on the right half of the dial, choose right; if it's on the left side, choose left. I find this natural because I can quickly relate the second hand's direction to a direction in space. There's no need to bring numbers into it.

Typically, you want to favor one direction but still be random. Instead of dividing the watch dial straight down the middle, do a pie slice. The sizes of the slices are in proportion to the intended probabilities. When you want to favor left, the rightward zone shrinks, and you go right only if the second hand falls in that zone. When necessary, you can add a third zone for "body" or "center."

The zones are imaginary and inexact. That's okay; the

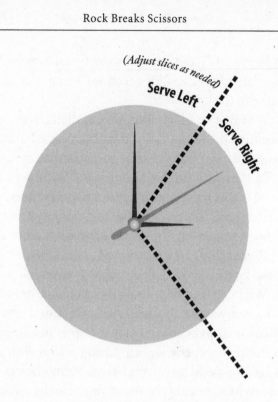

mental pie slices probably capture your intuition as well as guesstimated numbers could. They also save time. You don't have to invent a percentage number and then convert that to a percentage of a clock dial. You just go with what looks right.

Recap: How to Outguess Tennis Serves

• Expect the direction of serve to alternate, especially with novice players.

• When playing a good opponent, use a watch or heart-rate monitor to randomize your own serves.

Six

How to Outguess Baseball and Football

To "throw a curveball" is to exploit the element of surprise. In the popular imagination, baseball ranks second only to poker as the great game of American deception. A pitcher mixes up his pitches by unpredictably throwing fastballs, curveballs, sliders, and more exotic options. Though everyone appreciates that randomness is an important element of baseball, it's not easy to say how successful players are in using it. Compared to tennis serves, baseball pitches are complicated.

About 60 percent of major-league pitches are fastballs, 13 percent are sliders, 12 percent are changeups, and 9 percent are curveballs. These are averages only. The likelihood of encountering a given pitch varies greatly according to the individual player, the number of outs, how close the score is, fatigue, injuries, the wind, and who knows what else.

Economists Kevin Kovash and Steven D. Levitt examined the randomness of pitching in a 2009 study using stats on 3 million major-league pitches from the 2002 to 2006 seasons. This paper, which also examined football, is a monument of sports scholarship. Their large dataset allowed them to demonstrate convincingly that real-world baseball and football choices are unrandom and outguessable.

They parceled their mountain of data into thousands of molehills wherein all the most obvious variables were the same. There would, for instance, be a number of cases where pitcher *A* had just thrown to batter *B* while the count was *C* and there had been *D*, *E*, *F*, and *G* pitches of the various types already thrown in the at-bat. If the pitcher had thrown a fastball *this* time, what were the chances his *next* pitch would be a fastball, too? That was the sort of question Kovash and Levitt asked.

They found that major-league pitchers overalternate, like everybody else. A pitcher who throws a fastball is about 4 percentage points less likely to throw one the next time. The tendency to switch varied with the type of pitch. A slider was about 2 percentage points less likely to be repeated. Because sliders are less common (about 13 percent of all pitches), that was the biggest alternation effect in relative terms. There was no overalternation found with changeups.

Is this news that players can use? There's no doubt that it helps to *know for certain* what pitch is coming. Simply knowing that pitchers overalternate doesn't tell you what's coming next; it just shifts the probabilities around. Most of the time, the likeliest pitch will be a fastball.

Kovash and Levitt asked Major League Baseball executives to guesstimate how valuable it would be for a batter to know for certain that a fastball was coming, relative to a batter who expected otherwise and was surprised to get a fastball. (Are you still with me?) The estimated value was about .150 OPS (on-base plus slugging percentage). Among the stats-obsessed, it's generally agreed that the OPS correlates with runs scored.

Kovash and Levitt then did a back-of-envelope calculation in which they assumed that batters could make use of even incremental shifts in probability and that the effect is linear. Knowing that a fastball is about 4 percentage points less likely to follow another fastball should be worth about 0.006 OPS. Over a season, each additional .001 of OPS is estimated to be worth about 2.16 extra runs. A team whose players were able to take full advantage of the unrandomness could gain ten to fifteen extra runs a year. Any manager would love that.

The question is whether batters can use those small shifts in probability. My hunch is that alert batters have a likely pitch in mind. I would imagine that they find it difficult to think of two pitches simultaneously, though, much less to prepare their muscles for them. In that case, the excess alternation effect would be useful only when it changes the "most likely pitch." Most of the time it won't, because of the simple fact that a fastball is almost five times more common than any other pitch. Kovash and Levitt's linear estimate probably sets an upper limit on the potential advantage.

One safe bet is that the quality of randomizing in company softball games and Little League leaves something to be desired. When you are up at bat, here's a way to take advantage of it, without any math.

Before every pitch, try to decide what pitch is most likely. You're on your own there. Factor in everything you know except the psychology of randomness. When it's a toss-up which pitch is most likely, favor the one that *wasn't* just pitched.

Kovash and Levitt also examined statistics on every NFL play from 2001 through 2005. They found that NFL teams are worse randomizers than major-league pitchers. About 56 percent of football plays are passing, and 44 percent are running. A team that passed on the previous play was about 10 percentage points less likely to pass on the next play.

Teams were even more likely to switch after a play was unsuccessful. After a failed pass or run, the chance of a switch increased by 14.5 percentage points.

These huge differences ought to be exploitable. The economists compute that a team that uses this to anticipate plays could score about one extra point per game, or half a victory per sixteen-game season.

Once again, amateurs are likely to be worse randomizers. With only two common types of plays, not too different in frequency, outguessing stands a good chance of being advantageous.

Recap: How to Outguess Baseball and Football

• A pitcher who throws a fastball this time is several percentage points less likely to throw a fastball on the next pitch.

• In football, expect the opposite type of play (running or passing) next time, especially when the current play fizzled or was repeated twice in a row.

Seven

How to Outguess Soccer Penalty Kicks

Four psychologists at the University of Amsterdam were in a bar, talking about recent publications. One article was on soccer strategy. The other was on how dogs wag their tails. The dog study reported that when pets see their masters, they wag their tails to the right. The other article was about penalty kicks. The group began wondering whether goalies, in making that split-second decision as to which way to jump, might favor one direction.

Penalty kicks ought to be a near-perfect exercise in randomness. The ball is placed twelve yards from the goal. The player tries to kick it in without the goalie's intercepting it. As long as he does that, the kicker's team scores.

For the goalie the physics are unforgiving. The ball will be traveling at about 125 miles an hour and enter the goal about a fifth of a second after the kick. That's not enough time for the goalie to react. He has to guess where the ball will be and leap in the correct direction *before* the kick. (The rules used to say the goalie could not move until the kick. Had this been enforced, the goalie's task would have been a physical impossibility.)

When the goalie guesses the direction of the kick, he stands about an even chance of preventing the score. When he fails to guess correctly, the kicker scores about 90 percent of the time. The penalty goal often decides a low-scoring game.

Studies have reported that soccer penalty kicks are admirably random, *not* displaying the excess alternation that's seen in most sports. Why are soccer players good at randomizing when other athletes aren't? It probably has to do with the long interval between successive penalty kicks. The kick is awarded to the opposing team when a player is guilty of bad behavior. Bad behavior is not exactly rare in soccer, but neither does it happen all the time. For a given player, penalty kicks may be days or weeks apart. It could be years before the player faces the same goalie in a penalty kick. For that reason, the kicker is likely to frame his choice as a one-shot event rather than as part of an ongoing interaction.

This isn't to say that players don't calculate odds. Netherlands goalie Hans van Breukelen kept a card index of penalty kickers with information about how they kicked. Germany's Jens Lehmann kept a crib sheet in his sock. I imagine that players and coaches are primarily looking for habitual preferences, say that such-and-such-player kicked to the right seven of the last ten times. They don't necessarily pay much attention to the pattern of choices in time. They may figure it's irrelevant, as it seems to be.

The tail-wagging study I mentioned reported that mammals tend to move their bodies to the right when they see something they want. A friendly dog will tilt its head to the right. Humans put their head to the right when hugging and look to the right first when entering an unfamiliar room. This fact influences the design of store displays and the layout of supermarkets.

The University of Amsterdam group—Marieke Roskes, Daniel Sligte, Shaul Shalvi, and Carsten De Dreu—examined 204 penalty kicks in FIFA World Cup championships from 1982 through 2010. They found that when a goalie's team was behind, he usually dived to the right (*his* right, the kicker's left). This occurred 71 percent of the time.

When the team wasn't behind, the right-left choices were evenly split. Kickers' choices were also fairly close to even. Given that this seems to be rooted in biology, it probably applies to amateur games, too.

Recap: How to Outguess Soccer Penalty Kicks

• When your team is winning (the other team is behind), have your team's penalty kicker kick to the right (the goalie's left).

Eight

How to Outguess Card Games

Card games are exercises in keeping secrets. That's why cards have plain backs and we hold them close to the chest. Above all, players struggle to keep their next move unpredictable. Do they succeed?

Barry O'Neill tried to answer that in a 1982 experiment at Northwestern University. He invented a simple game with two players, both having the same hand of four cards: ace, 2, 3, and joker. Each player was to choose a single card and put it face-down on the table. Then the cards were compared. Player A won if both cards were jokers *or* both were number cards that didn't match (like a 2 and a 3). Player B won otherwise. The loser of each hand paid the winner five cents.

By design, this game wasn't much like any familiar game. O'Neill wanted to see how well players would strategize a completely unfamiliar game. They did pretty well. The optimal strategy would be to randomly play the joker 40 percent of the time and each of the number cards 20 percent. The players put down the joker 39.4 percent of the time. That's amazing when you consider that they were playing by gut instinct. They were not given an opportunity to calculate the best strategy and may not have known how.

There were two notable errors. One was that they over-played aces, picking them 22.3 percent of the time. The other was that the players alternated too much. A joker should be followed by a number card 60 percent of the time. But actually it was more than that. Players did not want to play the joker twice in a row, or three times in a row. They were especially likely to switch after the card they played won.

Look beneath the surface, and O'Neill's game says much about strategizing in poker, bridge, and other games. The most fundamental decision in poker is whether to bluff (to make a bet on a weak hand). When the bluffer is lucky, no one will be willing to match the bet, and he'll win the pot without a showdown.

There is a mathematical formula for bluffing. The probability of your bluffing should be *raise/pot*. Here, *raise* is how much you would raise if you bluff. This may be constrained by table rules, social norms, and how much money is in your wallet. *Pot* is the amount that would be in the pot after your raise, and after your opponent(s) sees that raise.

Example: The pot is $100 right now. You're thinking of aggressively raising a full $100. Only one other player is in the game. If you add $100 and so does the opponent, the pot will have $300. The formula says you should bluff with a probability of $100/$300, or 1 in 3. This guarantees that a player who sees your raise has a 1/3 chance of winning $300 (worth $100 on average). But since it costs $100 to see the raise, the opponent is only breaking even. He cannot expect to make a profit (a profit that would have to come from your pocket!).

Good players know all this, but even the best can be poor at inventing a suitably weighted random sequence of bluffs and folds. The usual problems of randomization are complicated by the fact that the bluff-or-fold decision arises only when a player has a weak hand. Also, the ability to outguess opponents is limited by the game's incomplete information. When opponents win without a showdown, there is no way of telling whether they were bluffing or not.

In general, card players avoid streaks of the same choice. Poker novices are embarrassed at being caught in a bluff and rarely try it twice in a row. Better players occasionally throw in two or three bluffs in a row. But after two in a row, most players feel a pressure to fold on the next weak hand, especially if it comes immediately after an exposed bluff.

A player on a winning streak—without showdowns—may have been bluffing for some of those wins. When players take a risky move (bluff) and win, they are likely to try something different the next time. They don't want to be "greedy" and "keep going back to the well." When a player on a streak raises yet again, it's more likely than usual that he's not bluffing and has a strong hand.

It's a good idea to get nonhuman help in randomizing your bluffing. I've mentioned the possibility of using a watch. Needless to say, looking at your watch only when you've got a bad hand would be a most fatal tell. You've got to glance at your watch (inconspicuously) with *every* hand.

Look to see where the second hand is, percentage-wise, on its sweep from twelve to twelve. Say you intend to bluff with 33 percent probability on this hand. If the second hand is in the first 33 percent of the cycle (between twelve and four), you bluff.

An alternative is to use the colors or values of your cards as a randomizing device. You might use the leftmost number card in your hand. This will be a value from 1 (ace) to 10. Multiply by 10 (getting a value from 10 to 100). You bluff only if the multiplied number is less than the intended bluff percentage. With a 33 percent bluff percentage, you would bluff on an ace, 2, or 3. This is less precise but much less likely to be exploited as a tell.

One classic poker tell is important to any outguesser at cards: pupil dilation. The pupil is the black, central part of the eye, within the colored iris. When a player draws a desired card, the pupils grow larger (dilate). This is no urban legend but a lab-tested effect that's reliable enough to be used in mentalism. There's a card trick where the performer shows an audience member the queen of hearts and says it represents *money* or *sex* (either works). The volunteer then draws cards from the shuffled deck one at a time. A good pupil reader can spot when the audience member draws the queen of hearts from the increase in pupil size.

Psychologist Eckhard Hess was one of the pioneers of pupil reading. Around 1960 he did an experiment with photographs, all landscapes except for one pinup picture of an attractive woman. Hess shuffled the photos and showed them, one at a time, to his male lab assistant. At the seventh photo, the assistant's pupils suddenly enlarged. It was the pinup picture.

The pupils may speak truth even when the lips lie. With the 1964 presidential campaign in full swing, Hess showed University of Chicago students and faculty photos of Democratic president Lyndon Johnson and Republican challenger Barry Goldwater. Everyone said they favored liberal Johnson over hard-right Goldwater. But Hess found that about a third of the people had a more positive pupil response to Goldwater than to Johnson. Hess proposed the "interesting possibility… that in the liberal atmosphere of the university these people found it difficult to utter any pro-Goldwater sentiment."

It's not hard to read pupils, but you have to be looking directly at the person's eyes when the change occurs. The change is fast enough to see, and you are looking for that change rather than the pupils' absolute size (which varies with room lighting and drug use). A typical positive reaction is a 10 percent increase in the diameter of both pupils (a 20 percent increase in area). A bad turn of luck may cause the pupils to shrink. It looks like this, roughly actual size:

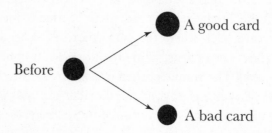

The change takes place in the half second or so after the player sees a fateful card. Not surprisingly, some serious players wear dark glasses as a countermeasure.

Recap: How to Outguess Card Games

• When card players make strategic random decisions, they avoid streaks of the same choice. A player who bluffs this time is less likely to bluff on the next weak hand.

• You might want to use a watch to randomize your bluffing, but be sure to glance at the watch with *every* hand.

• A good pupil reader can tell whether you drew the card you needed—*if* he can see your eyes.

Nine

How to Outguess Passwords

Have you ever wasted a few moments with a sketchy website that promises to reveal your Klingon name (wizard name, ghetto name, porn star name, etc.)? Some of these sites are fronts for password-harvesting operations. They'll ask you for some personal data—mixed in with Trekkie trivia—and prompt you to make up a password. Scammers know that the password you supply is likely to be similar or identical to ones you use elsewhere. They may sell collected passwords on the black market for about $20 each.

A password is like the key to your home. There are weak locks and strong locks, but neither does any good when a pickpocket swipes your key. Security is always about the weakest link.

Most identity thieves don't bother with trickery. They pick the low-hanging fruit—the passwords easiest to guess. One recent study found that nearly 1 percent of passwords can be guessed in four tries.

How is that possible? Simple—you try the four most common passwords. A typical list would run *password, 123456, 12345678,* and *qwerty.* That opens 1 percent of all sesames.

Okay, you're in the 99 percent not using an insanely bad password. You still have to consider the speed of today's hacking software. John the Ripper, a free hacking program, can test millions of passwords a second. One commercial software recovery program intended for forensic use (on seized computers of child pornographers and terrorists) claims it can check 2.8 billion passwords a second.

Initially, cracking software runs through an exhaustive, frequently updated list of thousands of the most popular passwords and then segues to a full dictionary search. It tries every single word in the dictionary, as well as all common proper names, nicknames, and pet names.

Most of us have been shamed and browbeaten into adding numbers, punctuation marks, and odd capitalization to our passwords. This is known as mangling. In theory, mangling makes it a lot harder to guess a password. In practice, not so much. Almost everyone's mind follows the same well-worn mental grooves. When a site insists on having a number, *password* becomes *password1* or *password123* with alarming regularity. A requirement to mix capitals and lowercase elicits *Password* or *PaSsWoRd*. Mandatory punctuation marks gets you *password!* and *p@ssword*. A password that might look secure, like *$pider_Man1*, isn't. Everybody is oh-so-devious in the same ways. There is reason to fear that site-enforced mangling rules cause users to pick simpler, easier-to-guess base passwords. Mangling can create a false sense of security.

News features on password security invariably cut to the cynical expert who belittles every common or realistic password practice. Many pros subscribe to the "write it down" philosophy. "Simply, people can no longer remember passwords good enough to reliably defend against dictionary attacks, and are much more secure if they choose a password too complicated to remember and then write it down," wrote consultant Bruce Schneier in 2005, eons ago in the digital world. "We're all good at securing small pieces of paper. I recommend that people write their passwords down on a small piece of paper, and keep it with their other valuable small pieces of paper: in their wallet."

Even with the paper in hand, it's a chore to peck out a long, hard-to-remember password. Good luck with a mobile device's virtual keyboard. The gulf between experts and reality is illustrated by my father's system. He writes his password on a Post-it note and sticks it to his desktop monitor. The password is nothing fancy, just a two-word phrase with no digits or funny characters. Not only do real people choose insecure passwords, they have a heck of a time remembering them.

In their digital wanderings, many users leave behind a snail trail of similar passwords. They try to use the same password for every site, damn the risk. But some sites play nanny, enforcing ad hoc rules about length and types of characters required. Users are forced to customize their usual password and then, when they try to log back in, they can't remember how they customized it.

A lot of what's known about dumb passwords comes from the December 4, 2009, security breach of RockYou.com, a publisher of Facebook games. A hacker posted the site's 32,603,388 user names and plaintext passwords. There have been many breaches before and since, but the scope of this one has made it a key dataset for the good guys and the bad guys.

The most popular RockYou password was *123456*. A reported 290,731 were using that one. There were many differences by age and gender. For men under thirty, sex and scatology supplied popular passwords: *pussy, fuck, fucking, 696969, asshole, fucker, horny, hooters, bigdick, tits, boobs,* and the like were high up on the list. Elders of both genders leaned toward dated pop-culture references. *Epsilon793* might not be such a terrible password, were it not the password of Captain Picard on *Star Trek: The Next Generation*. The seven-digit *8675309*, an inscrutably common choice, was a phone number in a pop tune way back when. Boomers, the eighties called, and they want their passwords back.

It's the easiest thing in the world to create a secure password. Use a random string of characters. You can't achieve perfect randomness mentally, but you don't have to do so. Websites and applets aplenty will give you random passwords generated from atmospheric noise. Here are some examples I just pulled from random.org:

mvAWzbvf
83cpzBgA
tn6kDB4T
2T9UPPd4
BLJbsf6r

Problem solved? Sure, for the paranoid mnemonist—or those who use a password manager app secured by a fingerprint reader. Everyone else balks at the prospect of memorizing character soup. It doesn't help that we've been told we need a different password for every account.

Most users care more about convenience and less about security than the experts do. I'm not so sure the crowd is wrong. Do you have a panic room in your home? Probably not, though the people who install panic rooms will tell you that you need one. Before you spring for the panic room, maybe it would be better to make sure you always lock your front door.

Realistic password threats fall into three categories. Call them casual, mass attack, and targeted.

- *Casual* means people you know. A snoopy coworker or family member may want to log into your accounts. He will be trying to guess your password based on personal knowledge of you (without the benefit of password-cracking software). The casual snoop might know your high school team was the Wildcats and try that. He might be completely defeated by *wildCatz1*.

- *Mass attack* is like spam, nothing personal. The pro identity thief isn't trying to break into *your* account per se, and she knows nothing about you personally. She's trying to assemble a list of cracked passwords, typically for resale. Password thieves use software and begin by trying to crack the least secure sites, those that permit many guesses. This could be a game site where the password has no financial value. When the software guesses correctly, it tries the same password and variants on more secure accounts like banking.

- *Targeted* means a private or public detective plus software. Should an informed person want to hack into your accounts, and should that someone have money and time (and the law?) on his side, he's likely to succeed. The only countermeasure is using a random password long enough to guarantee search times of your life expectancy or greater.

Don't be too sure you couldn't be a target. A small business's competitors may be willing to steal a laptop and expend the needed resources. So may a high-net-worth spouse in a divorce case. Hackers may take a disliking to someone's business or politics. Twitter, meaning the whole site, was once compromised because an administrator unwisely chose the password *happiness.* In 2009 a hacker learned the Twitter password in a dictionary attack and posted it on the Digital Gangster site, leading to hijackings of the Twitter feeds of Barack Obama, Britney Spears, Facebook, and Fox News.

Like everything else in life, passwords involve trade-offs. You can't have maximal security and maximal ease of use at the same time. One of the best of the commonly advised tactics is to convert a phrase or sentence to a password. You pick a sentence, phrase, or song lyric and use the first letter of each word as your password. *May the force be with you* would become *Mtfbwy*.

You wouldn't want to use that one, though, and that's the problem. You're going to think of a well-known phrase from a movie, a college fight song, or *South Park.* How many eight-word-or-so phrases do you know verbatim? It's not even clear that a randomly chosen phrase is harder to guess than a randomly chosen word. Few bother to mangle their pass-phrase acronym. It looks so random!

An ideal password scheme would work even if everyone used it. Should the pass-phrase scheme become popular, acronyms of all the pop-culture catch phrases would enter the lists of popular passwords, and cracking software would try these passwords first. Normally, acronyms are all letters and thus less secure than an any-character string of the same length.

Some of these drawbacks can be addressed. Never use a "famous quote." One alternative is to use private jokes. Remember the funny comment the waiter said to Brenda in Cozumel? You do, Brenda does, maybe the waiter does, and that's it. Should you pick that as your pass-phrase, the odds are high that you'll be the only one on the planet using that phrase.

It's less certain that the password itself will be unique. Different phrases can begin with the same letters, producing the same acronym. Some letters are more likely to begin words than others, and hacking software could potentially exploit this.

The best way to use the pass-phrase idea is to turn the conventional advice on its head. Instead of thinking of a phrase and converting it to a password (that won't be all that random), get a truly random password and convert it to an easy-to-remember phrase.

I used to use simple, stupid passwords. After one of my accounts was hacked, the site assigned me a temporary password. It was a random string of characters. I was going to change it until I realized that I didn't need to do so. I could remember a random password.

The mind is good at seeing patterns in random data. This is how we remember phone numbers and Social Security numbers. It also works for random-character passwords like *RPM8t4ka*. I just now got that one from random.org. Though it's authentically random, the eye and mind instantly spot patterns. In this case the first three letters happen to be all capital, and the last three are lowercase. The number 8 is twice 4.

You can easily translate a random password to a nonsense phrase. RPM8t4ka might become *revolutions per minute, 8 track for Kathy.* I don't know what that means but I do know that it's fairly easy to remember.

A password, a pass-phrase, a mnemonic — what's the big deal? The difference is that a random-character password is the gold standard of security. It's better than any human-chosen password could be. It will still be good even if everyone in the world adopts this scheme.

A random-character password of reasonable length is, for practical purposes, unguessable with today's technology. It won't appear in a list of popular passwords. A mass attacker could guess a random password only in a brute-force search. With upper- and lowercase letters and numbers, there are sixty-two possible characters. (I won't count punctuation marks, as not all sites allow them.) That means it would take 62^8 guesses to be certain of hitting an eight-character password. That's over 218 trillion guesses.

That effectively rules out an Internet mass attack and would slow down a targeted attack. Accepting the claim that some forensic software can spit out 2.8 billion guesses a second, it would take about twenty-two hours to make that many guesses. That's secure enough for most people — should you disagree, you're welcome to add a few more characters.

This doesn't mean that a random password is invincible. It can't be guessed, but it can be stolen. The Klingon name scam is one example. Careful folks fall for cons like that all the time. There is high-tech malware that records your every keystroke, and there are snoops using the low-tech method of watching over your shoulder as you type. Hackers may exploit a site's lax internal security to get its passwords, through no fault of the users and their choices of passwords.

I use the "one strong password" philosophy. In view of the importance that passwords have assumed in our lives, it's worth committing one random-character password to memory. You memorize your phone number, why not a password?

Once you've got that strong password, "protect the hell out of it," says security consultant Nick Berry. Do everything you can to keep your computer free of malware, and use the password only for sites you know to be important and trustworthy. For games and unimportant sites, I use a simpler password that is nothing like my strong password.

There are so many ways that passwords get stolen that it's

not unreasonable to want a different password for each site. One customization formula is to take the last letter of the site name and tack it onto the beginning of the standard password. For Facebook, you'd add *k* onto your standard strong password, getting kRPM8t4ka. Though this customization isn't secure in any absolute sense, it may get the job done. A snoop who sees you enter kRPM8t4ka to access your Facebook account is not going to have a clue how to generate your banking password. A mass attacker will collect thousands of passwords and find that a decent proportion of them work, unmodified, on other sites. He may not care about those that don't.

I don't have a punctuation mark or non-ASCII character in my strong password. In the rare cases where a site demands one, I add an easy-to-remember mark onto the end.

Some identity thieves skip passwords entirely. They pretend to be a user who has forgotten a password, and answer the security questions. Should they guess right, they can change the password to one of their choosing. Not only does the crook gain an identity to sell, but the legitimate user is locked out.

In 2008 someone hacked into Sarah Palin's e-mail account by guessing where she met her husband (Wasilla High). Four years later Mitt Romney's accounts were breached by someone who guessed his favorite pet. It's not just public figures who have to worry. Anyone who knows you well will be able to guess many of your answers to security questions. Hackers who don't know you from Adam or Eve can use lists of the most popular pet names, used cars, team nicknames, etc.

Lately, news features have touted the counterstrategy of giving nonsense answers. The idea is that you answer every question in pig Latin, or give the same nonsense answer to every question. Your mother's maiden name was Jimbob. Your high school mascot was Jimbob.

This probably works for the time being. That could change, should enough people adopt this strategy. Nonsense answers are probably as stereotyped as any other kind.

I always use honest answers. You don't encounter security questions much. Years after you first answer security questions, when you have to prove who you are, you definitely don't want to be in the position of not remembering your answers. Many sites let you choose security questions. I pick questions where my honest answer *isn't* a common one or easy to guess.

Personal identification numbers (PINs) are the dime-store locks on our personal money machines. Nobody knocks himself out trying to invent a secure PIN. Most automated tellers limit them to four decimal digits anyway. I'm sure you can guess the most common PIN. Would you care to guess how many people use it?

Nick Berry estimates that 11 percent of the population uses 1234. There haven't been many mass exposures of PINs. Hackers aren't that interested because PINs are useless without the physical card. So Berry took lists of exposed passwords and filtered them to include only four-digit numbers with no letters. He figured that someone who uses *1967* as a password has some special connection to that number and is likely to use it when prompted for a four-digit PIN.

The second-most-popular PIN on Berry's list is 1111 (chosen by 6 percent), and third is 0000 (picked by nearly 2 percent). Taken at face value, that means that a well-informed crook who finds your ATM card stands a 19 percent chance of guessing your PIN in the permitted three tries. After a third wrong guess the machine usually eats the card.

Here are Berry's twenty most common PINs:

1234	9999
1111	3333
0000	5555
1212	6666
7777	1122
1004	1313
2000	8888
4444	4321
2222	2001
6969	1010

All the four-identical-digit choices appear. This isn't a randomness experiment, it's an I'm-afraid-I'll-forget-this-number-and-better-pick-something-really-easy experiment.

Berry found these less obvious patterns:

- Years. All recent years and a few from history (1492, 1776) are high up on the list.
- Couplets. Many pick a two-digit number and clone it to get the needed four (1212, 8787, etc.) Digits in couplets most often differ by 1.
- 2580. Some figure they'll generate a random code by playing tic-tac-toe on the keypad. The only way to get the required four digits is to go straight down the middle: 2580. It's the twenty-second-most-popular choice in Berry's list. (For that you can thank the designer of the keypad, Alphonse Chapanis.)
- 1004. In Korean the numbers sound like the word for *angel*. This inspired a pop tune, "Be My 1004." There

are enough Koreans who figure that non-Koreans don't know this to make it a popular choice.

It's important to pick a PIN that's *not* on the popular list. The least popular PIN was 8068, but you don't necessarily want to use that, either. I would pick a number that begins with 6, 7, 8, 9, or 0 (as all of Berry's least popular choices do) and has no evident pattern. *Don't* use digits from a personal number like a MM/DD or YYYY birthday, driver's license, or credit card. Those numbers are in your wallet, and losing your wallet is the commonest way to lose an ATM card.

Recap: How to Outguess Passwords

• Be prepared to memorize one good, strong password. It's worth the effort.

• Go to a website that generates truly random passwords (like random.org). Create a list of five or ten candidate passwords.

• Pick a random password that you can convert into a memorable nonsense phrase. Use the phrase to remember the password.

Ten

How to Outguess Crowd-Sourced Ratings

We live in the golden age of crowd sourcing. Anyone with a smartphone can rate restaurants, books, movies, and songs on the go (1 to 5 stars). Focus groups rate cars, carbonara sauces, and candidates (on a scale of 1 to 10). What, if anything, do we learn from that?

It might seem that ratings ought to peak in the exact middle of the scale. They usually don't. They're more like report card grades where C is effectively *below* average. Crowd-sourced ratings have a tendency to peak at about 7 out of 10 (or around 70 percent of the maximum rating, whatever it is). On the one hand, this could indicate that we've achieved a consumer Valhalla in which the things we rate are, on the whole, pretty good. But there is reason to think it might all be an artifact. Magicians know that people tend to pick a card about 70 percent of the way through a fanned deck. Mentalists will ask the audience to think of a number between 1 and 10. The performer always guesses 7, knowing that is the most popular choice.

In 1976 Michael Kubovy and Joseph Psotka of Yale tried to find out why 7 is such a magic number. They dispatched seven(!) undergraduates to canvass the Yale campus and ask passersby to name "the first number that comes to mind between 0 and 9." Seven was by far the most popular choice, accounting for about 28 percent of responses. The least popular answer was 0.

There are many reasons why 7 might be popular. There are seven seas, seven dwarfs, seven deadly sins, seven samurai, seven brides for seven brothers, and the seven-year itch. Seven is considered lucky.

To test possible explanations for the 7 preference, Kubovy and Psotka asked a separate group of introductory psychology students for "the first number that comes to mind between 6 and 15." The results were completely different. The most popular choice was 9, by a slight margin over 8 and 7. This time only 17 percent chose 7.

Seven ought to be just as lucky, and just as mentally available, whatever the allowed range of answers. This challenges some of the popular explanations.

In a third experiment, Yale students were asked for "the first number that comes to mind between 0 and 9, avoiding fractions, and using only whole numbers like 7." Nominally this was the same as the first experiment, since everyone understood that a whole number was intended without being told it explicitly. The results were again different. The numbers 3, 5, and 7 were almost tied in popularity, with 7 now getting a bit less than 17 percent of the responses.

As we've already seen, mentioning or otherwise drawing attention to an option (7) can discourage people from picking it. That must be what happened here.

In a final experiment, one group was asked for a number between 20 and 29, and a separate group for a number between 70 and 79. For the first group, 27 was the overwhelming favorite. About 28 percent chose it, the same fraction that chose 7 in the original 0 to 9 choice.

But 77 was much less popular with the 70 to 79 group. Only 16 percent chose it. The apparent reason was that the students wanted to avoid 7 (since the range called attention to 7s), or to avoid a doubled digit, or both.

A mentalist who wants a volunteer to pick 7 will press her to answer immediately. The mentalist knows that the longer the volunteer has to think, the more likely she is to second-guess the first impulse. One way to encourage speed is for the performer to snap his fingers. "Name a number between one and ten." *Snap.*

It's unlikely that the passersby in the Yale experiment spent much time deliberating. They were asked to name the first number that came to mind — *not* a "random number." In practice, there is considerable similarity between human-invented numbers, whether described as "random" or "the first number that comes to mind" or something else. Whatever the details, 7s are common.

Kubovy and Psotka suspected that their request for a spontaneous number created a catch-22. Subjects worried that their first impulse might not be spontaneous enough and tried to second-guess themselves. "The subject is placed in a paradoxical situation — only if he does not try to comply can he comply."

In general, the subjects favored odd numbers over even numbers; numbers that were *not* at the limits of the requested range; and numbers that had not been called attention to in any way. Overall, 7 was in "the unique position of being... the 'oddest' digit."

A crowd-sourced rating is neither a randomness experiment nor a study in first impulses. The participants are asked to translate their feelings about a product into a number or a position on a scale. This is not as straightforward as it might seem. Is that gastropub a 3 or a 4? Is a candidate's attack ad a 0 (because I hate negative ads) or a 10 (because it did make me worry about the opponent)? The raters are making up numbers that correspond to complicated and mixed emotions—or no emotions at all.

You can think of the Yale experiment as a focus group in search of a product. Having no reason to rate high or low, the subjects gave whatever number came to mind. There is an element of that in any crowd-sourced rating. Some of the raters will be indifferent or have such mixed feelings that any response is defensible. They are likely to gravitate to an odd number at the higher end of the range, such as 7.

A while back the *Onion* ran a headline, "School 'Fine,' U.S. Teens Report." Giving 7 of 10 is like the sullen adolescent's "fine," a default response that can mean "I'd rather not be bothered." This is one reason why group ratings can be treacherous. An unexciting product can get a respectable score (lots of 7s), then bomb in the marketplace. If what you want to know is "Would you buy this product?" you should ask that.

In the Yale experiment, 0 was by far the least popular response, followed by 1 and 9 (the high limit, as there was no 10). That means that ratings at or near the scale limits carry the most conviction. When looking at online reviews, pay particular attention to the proportion of lowest (0-star) and highest (5-star) ratings. Assuming they're honest, these are the people who truly hate or love the product.

With many products or services, it doesn't matter how many people hate it as long as other people are passionate enough to buy it. An indie film with a high proportion of 5-star reviews ought to be a good bet for anyone who likes the film-maker or theme, and the number of 0-star reviews may be irrelevant. The film isn't intended to appeal to everyone, and there are always some online reviewers who select the "wrong" movie to see. When a business has a broader audience (such as a blockbuster movie or a family restaurant), the 0-star reviews are more informative. They help gauge the likelihood of a bad experience.

Recap: How to Outguess Crowd-Sourced Ratings

• People asked to think of a number between 1 and 10 most often pick 7. This can distort ratings of focus groups and crowd-sourced Web reviews.

• The percentage of raters giving a product a perfect 10 (or 5 out of 5 stars) may be a better measure of the product's sales potential than its average score.

Eleven

How to Outguess Fake Numbers

Mark Nigrini grew up in Cape Town, South Africa, charmed by the magic of numbers. He came to the US for a PhD in accounting. By April 1989 he was a grad student in search of a dissertation topic. One day at the University of Cincinnati he ran across a brief reference to something called Benford's law. "I went to the library that night and got Benford's paper," Nigrini recalled. Reading it changed his professional life.

Frank Benford had been a physicist working for General Electric in Schenectady, New York, in the 1920s. At that time, scientific calculations meant looking up numbers in a book of logarithms. Benford noticed that the front pages of his logarithm book were worn from long use, while the back pages looked almost new. It's this idle observation, rather than anything General Electric paid him to do, that has preserved Benford's name for posterity.

The numbers that Benford had cause to look up tended to begin with low digits, and low digits were at the front of the book. Benford found, for instance, that about 30 percent of the numbers encountered in science and engineering began with the digit 1. In contrast, only about 5 percent of the numbers started with 9. This left the back part of the book relatively pristine.

Benford mentioned this fact to GE chemist Irving Langmuir (later a Nobel laureate). Langmuir encouraged him to publish a paper on it. Methodical if nothing else, Benford pursued this obscure finding over the next decade. It was not, he found, unique to scientific numbers. He tried tallying the first digits of baseball statistics and found the same distribution. He recorded every number mentioned in an issue of *Reader's Digest*. Ditto. Tennis scores, stock quotes, lengths of rivers, atomic weights, electric bills in the Solomon Islands, and numbers mentioned on the front page of the *New York Times* produced the same pattern. It was like a conspiracy theory. Everything was connected.

Benford finally published his results in a 1938 issue of the *Proceedings of the American Philosophical Society*. There he derived a precise formula for the proportion of numbers beginning with each digit. The proportions are:

First digit	Proportion
1	30.1%
2	17.6%
3	12.5%
4	9.7%
5	7.9%
6	6.7%
7	5.8%
8	5.1%
9	4.6%

You may be wondering why 0 isn't included. Benford's observation deals with the first nonzero digit. So 7,129,600 and 0.000072002 each have a first digit of 7.

Benford's formula also predicts the proportions of second digits, third digits, and so on. In these cases 0 is a possibility. However, the preponderance of low digits is much less pronounced after the first. For that reason, Benford's observation is sometimes called the first-digit phenomenon.

Benford used another name for his paper's title, "The Law of Anomalous Numbers." Now it's almost always known as Benford's law. That's unfair, as it turns out. The same phenomenon had been discovered and published over half a century earlier by a scientist much better known than Benford, astronomer Simon Newcomb. Newcomb's paper, in an 1881 issue of the *American Journal of Mathematics,* opens with the ostensibly well-known fact, "That the ten digits do not occur with equal frequency must be evident to anyone making much use of logarithmic tables, and noticing how much faster the first pages wear out than the last ones."

I suppose this is further proof of how hard it is to be original, and how even original ideas don't always get noticed. For some reason Newcomb's article was quickly forgotten, while Benford's got traction. One possible explanation is that Benford's article piggybacked on the fame of an important physics paper by Hans Bethe that appeared after it in the *Proceedings.*

It's now known that Benford's law applies to all sorts of data that even the indefatigable Benford didn't think to test. It's also known that Benford's law *doesn't* apply to many common types of numbers: phone numbers, ages, weights, Social Security numbers, IQs, winning lottery numbers, and zip codes.

Those with mathematical intuition may find this self-evident. To everyone else, it can appear a cosmic mystery. Why does Benford's law apply to street numbers (fairly well) but not to zip codes? How does the *New York Times* "know" to mention six times more numbers starting with 1 than 9?

Benford's law applies to some numbers that express quantities or measurements, such as city populations or credit card charges. For a quick, intuitive explanation, imagine you put $1,000 in an investment account that doubles in value every ten years. The first digit of the account balance will remain 1 for the first ten years of growth. The value will increase to $1,100, $1,200, $1,300, and so on, up to $1,900, and finally hitting $2,000 at the end of the first decade.

It will take another ten years to double again. During that time the value will climb from $2,000 to $3,000 to $4,000. That means the account balance spends as much time with a 2 or 3 as the lead digit as it did with 1.

In the third decade, the account value will go from $4,000 to $8,000, spanning the leading digits 4, 5, 6, and 7. Then in the fourth decade, the value increases to $16,000, blasting through leading digits 8 and 9 and spending the rest of the decade in the 1s again.

The investment value would spend more time with a leading digit of 1 than with 2, more time with 2 than with 3, and so on. Should you choose a random moment in time to check the account's value, the chance of each possible leading digit would be precisely that of Benford's distribution.

The world is full of things that grow exponentially, from bacteria colonies to social networks. They don't usually grow as steadily as in my example, but when natural growth scatters values over several orders of magnitude, they approximate Benford's distribution. Have a chimpanzee repeatedly throw a dart at the financial pages, and the stock prices it hits will follow Benford's law quite well.

Not every set of measurements fits the Benford distribution. One example is the weight of adult American men. Obviously, 1 is the most common leading digit, to a far more lopsided degree than the 30 percent predicted by Benford's law. A leading digit of 6 is much less common than in the Benford distribution: not many men weigh 60 to 69 or 600 to 699 pounds.

Nor does Benford's law apply to assigned numbers like phone or Social Security numbers. There the assigners use all or almost all of the possibilities. Those beginning with 1 are about as common as those beginning with any other digit.

Benford's law is a reminder that numbers are an artificial way of talking about the quantities we find in the world around us. As Benford himself wrote, his law "is really the theory of phenomena and events, and the numbers but play the poor part of lifeless symbols for living things."

"I thought, if there are indeed predictable patterns to numbers, then maybe auditors can use this to tell whether data was authentic or made up," said Mark Nigrini.

Accountants and tax agencies would love to have a formula for determining which numbers are honest and which aren't. Nigrini quickly resolved to do his dissertation on using Benford's law to detect financial fraud.

He found that little had been written on this subject since Benford's paper. The only one to see practical value in Benford's law was economist Hal Varian (now head economist for Google). In 1972 Varian proposed using the law as a baloney detector. Public policy decisions are based on elaborate projections of costs and benefits. The numbers in these projections ought to fit the Benford distribution, Varian argued. Otherwise, it could indicate that the forecaster was pulling numbers out of the air or tweaking the figures for political ends.

Varian had not followed up his idea, nor had anyone else. This stoked Nigrini's enthusiasm, though not that of his advisor. "They prefer you to be the eightieth person to write about a topic," Nigrini explained. He went ahead with his dissertation anyway. Not until he had written two-thirds of the research was he able to get it approved. He finished it four months later.

The idea that struck Varian and Nigrini lends itself to a picture. When you have a lot of numbers, you can make a bar chart (histogram) showing how many times each digit occurs as the first digit. Just count how many of the numbers start with the digit 1, how many start with 2, 3, and so on. For honest data that follows Benford's law, the chart will look like this:

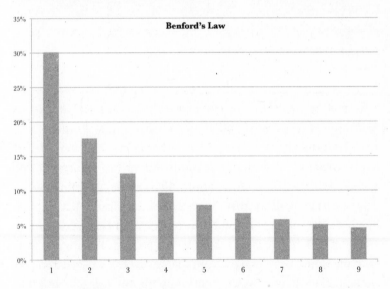

This smooth curve is Benford's law in visual form.

Varian and Nigrini's brainstorm was that people who make up numbers won't know about Benford's law. An embezzler or tax cheat will have no reason to think that any digit should be more common than any other. Therefore, a set of made-up numbers might be expected to show an even distribution of leading digits, without the curve.

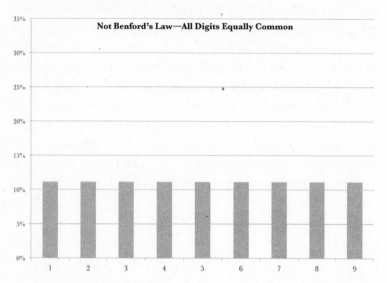

That was the back-of-the-envelope concept, anyway. Randomness experiments (which were not widely known) had already shown that fabricated numbers almost never use all digits equally. Alphonse Chapanis made bar charts of his results, and they didn't look anything like a flat distribution.

Another issue is that honest financial data often fits the Benford curve to a T—and then sometimes it doesn't. It can be tough to tell beforehand which case you're dealing with. One example would be sales data from the 99 cents store. The amounts would include a lot of 9s. As Nigrini points out, this tells you that prices *are* made-up numbers, invented by humans as part of a marketing strategy. But if you're managing a 99 cents store, that's your reality, and it doesn't indicate fraud. There are many other situations where the nature of a business might produce an un-Benford-like distribution of first digits, for perfectly innocent reasons.

Nigrini's basic idea was right, though: Invented numbers *are* different from honest ones. He began to haunt the Cincinnati courthouse, looking for criminal cases involving numbers.

One of the early fraud cases he studied was from Arizona. Wayne James Nelson, a forty-three-year-old manager in the office of the Arizona state treasurer, launched a short embezzling career with a check for $1,927.48 from the State of Arizona to a fictitious vendor. Over the next few days he made twenty-two more fake checks, for a total of almost $1.9 million.

When caught, Nelson claimed that he had written the checks in a noble effort to demonstrate vulnerabilities in Arizona's accounts payable system. He had "neglected" to enlighten anyone in the treasurer's office about these vulnerabilities, and the funds had been directed to Nelson's own accounts.

At a glance, you can see some patterns in Nelson's check amounts.

$1,927.48	$96,879.27
$27,902.31	$91,806.47
$86,241.90	$84,991.67
$72,117.46	$90,831.83
$81,321.75	$93,766.67
$97,473.96	$88,338.72
$93,249.11	$94,639.49
$89,658.17	$83,709.28
$87,776.89	$96,412.21
$92,105.83	$88,432.86
$79,949.16	$71,552.16
$87,602.93	

Nelson "was the anti-Benford," said Nigrini. All but the first two check amounts start with high digits 7, 8, and 9. Nelson kept the amounts under $100,000, probably because six-figure sums would have attracted unwelcome attention.

Here's a histogram of the leading digits of Nelson's check amounts.

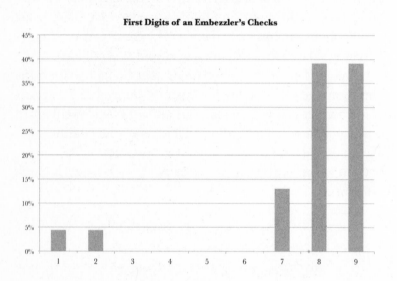

First Digits of an Embezzler's Checks

Dodgy numbers are usually mixed in with legitimate ones. An auditor would not just be looking at the fake check amounts (how would he know which were fake?). He would look at all of Nelson's check amounts, or all of his department's amounts. Even so, Nelson's lopsided preference for 8s and 9s in the fake amounts would augment the 8s and 9s in the aggregate amounts. This might be detectable.

Nigrini found that Nelson's check amounts showed other idiosyncrasies typical of invented numbers. Suppose we tally the very last (rightmost) digits of the check amounts. These represent pennies, and surely Nelson had no financial interest in that. There is a pattern nonetheless. Nelson favored amounts ending in 6 and 7. He didn't use 4 at all.

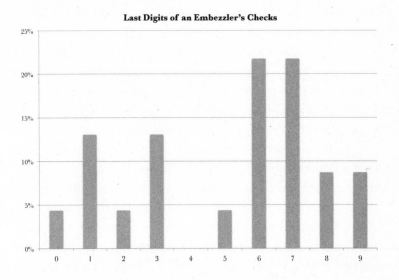

Last Digits of an Embezzler's Checks

This looks much like the charts that Chapanis made. Just like Chapanis's volunteers, Nelson unconsciously repeated himself. In twenty-three check amounts, he managed to repeat 87, 88, 93, and 96 as the first two digits. He likewise repeated the cents figures 16, 67, and 83.

The IRS sells tax form data, with identifying information stripped out, to researchers. Nigrini bought a package of 100,000 returns for tax years 1985 and 1988 and began analyzing them on the university's VAX minicomputer. He wanted to see whether he could tell which entries had the most cheating.

Many entries on a tax form are calculated totals, differences, or products of other entries. It would make no sense to manipulate them, as IRS computers check the math. Other entries are backed by third-party documentation, such as W-2s for wages or 1099-INTs for interest income. That provided useful comparison. Nigrini found that reports of interest income fit Benford's law to high precision. Interest *paid* did not fit the curve, however. At the time, mortgage lenders did not report interest amounts to the IRS. Consumer credit interest was deductible (and was not backed by documentation, either). This meant that taxpayers were tempted to exaggerate their interest paid and hope they didn't get audited. Nigrini's analysis suggested that many were doing just that.

At the time of his run for president, Bill Clinton released his tax returns from 1977 onward. Nigrini was able to cull 380 income numbers and 511 deduction numbers, all honor-system entries, from the Clinton returns. He found nothing suspicious except a preponderance of round numbers—a common finding in tax returns. There was, for instance, a used men's suit donated to charity and valued at $100. The suit's value is obviously an estimate. One of the ways we indicate estimation is through round numbers. Claiming a hundred dollars is more honest than inventing an implausibly precise amount like $107.03.

One of Nigrini's first believers was Robert Burton, chief financial investigator with the Brooklyn district attorney's office. In 1995 Burton used Nigrini's software to analyze checks at seven companies suspected of criminal ties. Burton found evidence of invented numbers and, upon further investigation, charged bookkeepers and payroll clerks with fraud. This resulted in a favorable write-up in the *Wall Street Journal*. Benford's law was called "a tool worthy of Sherlock Holmes." Burton was quoted: "Bingo, that means fraud."

The *Wall Street Journal* piece helped publicize Benford's

law, while also contributing to the myth that it was some kind of magic lie detector. Since then, use of Nigrini's techniques has greatly expanded in law and tax enforcement and in the private sector. Today's routine analysis of consumer data makes it easy to flag suspicious numbers for further scrutiny. Yet digit analysis remains a new field, incompletely tested. It is important to understand what it can do, and what it can't.

"I get very upset, regularly, when I read about people using Benford's law badly," Nigrini told me. Doubtless some hear about Benford's law, skim the Wikipedia article, and take it to mean that any numbers whose first digits don't fit the curve are fraudulent. That is definitely *not* a proper conclusion. There are so many reasons why legitimate first digits may fail to fit the Benford distribution that first-digit tests are rarely of much use. Nigrini finds a test of the first two digits much more useful. This produces a column chart with 100 bars. When there is enough data (thousands of numbers), Benford-compliant data produces a smooth curve.

Another useful test charts the last two digits of big numbers. This isn't even properly a "Benford's law" test. What you're looking for is Chapanis-style idiosyncrasies of invented numbers. Note that the last-two-digit test works even for data that ought not to obey Benford's law.

In the hands of a professional, digit analysis entails many distinct tests and calculations of the tests' statistical significance. The ultimate standard of comparison should be the history of that particular set of data. *This* quarter's expense invoices should be compared to previous quarters'. Nigrini calls this principle My Law. The name refers to the generic file names that some software proposes for new files (My File, My Worksheet, etc.). The My Law approach avoids the most common error of half-cocked numerology, which is to assume that all numerical datasets fit Benford's law closely. They don't. Nor are Chapanis's features of invented numbers 100 percent foolproof. These paradigms may or may not apply in a given instance, for inscrutable reasons. It's easier and more relevant to adopt past digit distributions as the baseline.

After all, every fraud has to start at some point in time. Should Stan in accounting start embezzling next Tuesday, that will shift his digit patterns—and will do so regardless of how closely the original numbers may have been "random" or fit the Benford curve.

As an illustration of the My Law approach, Nigrini cites a 2011 experiment devised by seventeen-year-old student Kha Bui for his math class in Koblenz, Germany. The class was divided into five groups of four students each. Some of the groups were given newspapers and instructed to make a list of 500 numbers that they found in the news. The other groups were told to invent 500 numbers. The point was to see whether it was possible to distinguish the news numbers from the invented ones by digit patterns alone.

To make the challenge as difficult as possible, the fakers were told to invent numbers such as would be found in a newspaper (as opposed to random numbers). This made the task more like a real-world fraud, where the faker is playing chameleon.

None of the five sets of numbers, real or faked, had an especially good fit to the Benford curve. But anyone could see that they fell into two groups. One group had "big spikes"—a few first-two-digit pairs that occurred far more commonly than expected. The other group had smaller spikes and conformed better to the Benford curve. As we've seen, repeated digit pairs can betray the unconscious repetition of a faker. You might think that the "smaller spikes" group was the honest newspaper numbers. You'd be wrong.

Remember, the fake numbers were invented by teams of four. Because the digits that people unconsciously favor vary from person to person, each faker's quirks were diluted by a factor of four. This would have made it much harder to detect fraud.

The real tip-off was this. The newspapers had many mentions of the then-current year (2011) and recent years. The digit charts therefore had a spike for 20 as the first two digits. The fakers invented some recent year numbers, too, but not nearly enough.

Someone using either Benford or Chapanis as their standards would have guessed that the shorter-spikes sets were the honest ones. A wiser approach would have been to first examine the digit patterns of other newspapers. This would have revealed the profusion of recent-year mentions and led to the correct identification.

When the digits of important numbers *don't* fit the expected distribution, a good forensic investigator will be able to find out why. There are nonetheless a couple of easy, do-it-yourself tests that anyone can use to get a quick read on whether numbers appear honest. In the following pages I will show some ways to identify the likelihood of invented or manipulated numbers. These tests are intended mainly to distinguish real data from that which is 100 percent fake, made up by a single individual. You won't always have that stark a contrast. Nevertheless, there have been plenty of cases where a lone bad guy presented his victims with numbers that were completely bogus. Used as a preliminary screen, these tests are quick and independent of all the other due diligence you're likely to do.

Every Sunday, the owner of a fast-food restaurant began the week by making up the dollar sales for the previous week. Every number was fake! She needed something to report on her taxes.

The restaurant's bookkeeper happened to be one of Nigrini's students. Nigrini took a look at the invented numbers. "It wasn't the first digits that caught her," he explained. A fast-food outlet with steady business might have, say, about $5,000 of business each weekday without too much variation. The first digits didn't follow the Benford distribution, nor would they be expected to. It was the last two digits that betrayed the fabrication. None of the numbers ended in 00. That's a common tip-off, as fakers often think a round number doesn't look random enough. Also, about 6.5 percent of the numbers ended in 40 (you'd expect it to account for just 1 percent). Using 40 for the last two digits was an unconscious tic of this particular business owner.

Someday that fast-food place will be sold, and the buyers will scrutinize the books. Perhaps the owner will invent a new, inflated set of numbers to show. Will the buyers suspect that the numbers were pulled out of the air?

Daily sales figures for a small business are the sum of a great many register totals. The last two digits of these sums tend to be random, with each digit pair from 00 to 99 occurring about 1 percent of the time.

You don't always have cents figures. Some reports are rounded to even dollars, and others may be truncated to thousands of dollars. In these cases you can use the two rightmost reported digits.

To run a last-digit test, tally how many times each possible pair of last digits occurs in the reported numbers. There are 100 possible pairs, so make a histogram chart with 100 bars.

The chart will give you some idea of what honest numbers look like. It records 500 random numbers (generated by an Excel spreadsheet). Five hundred is a reasonable amount of data for a small business—about seventeen months of daily

Last Two Digits: 500 Random Numbers

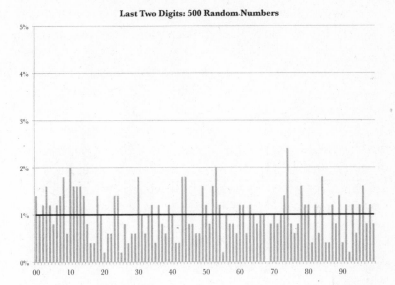

sales or ten years of weekly figures. Even with 500 numbers, the chart is noisy, with a great deal of variation. In this case, there's a pair (68) that doesn't occur at all in the data, and three pairs (10, 53, 74) that occur twice as much as the expected 1 percent. This is the normal variation you should expect for random data.

Now let's look at fabricated data.

The chart on the next page shows the last two digits of 500 human-invented numbers. Even at a glance you can see there's a lot more variation. Two pairs (93 and 94) occur more than 4 percent of the time, something very unlikely with honest numbers. Twelve pairs don't occur at all, and that's also highly improbable.

Ask the following three questions. A "yes" answer to any of the three should raise the suspicion level.

Last Two Digits: 500 Invented Numbers

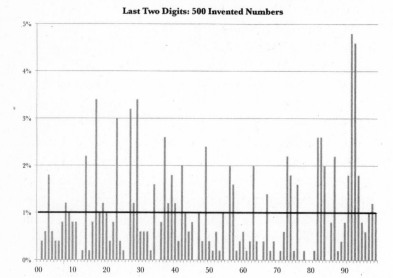

(a) Is there a pair (or pairs) that is unaccountably more common than the others?

(b) Are doubled digits (especially 00 and 55) consistently less common than average?

(c) Are descending pairs (10, 21, 32, 43, 54, 65, 76, 87, 98) consistently more common?

In the example here, the answer to (a) is a resounding yes. The data also avoids doubled digits (b). You would expect that 10 percent of all numbers would end in a pair of doubled digits. Here are 20 occurrences out of 500, only 4 percent. The pairs 00, 55, and 77 do not occur at all.

There are 44 descending pairs out of 500. That's almost exactly the expected 9 percent (as there are nine descending pairs out of 100 possibilities). By criterion (c) the data is unsuspicious.

This data fails two of the three tests. Were this a small business's sales, it would be wise to ask for more figures, or more detailed figures—and to see how the seller reacts to that request.

You don't have to worry about counting all those digits. In practice, it's just a matter of cut and paste. Request the data as an Excel file or something compatible and copy it into a Benford's law test template. Examples can be found on the Web for free, including one by Nigrini (NigriniCycle.xlsx). After you paste in your numbers, follow the instructions to fill down some columns with preexisting formulas. Tabs then give already-formatted charts for the two last digits and other common tests. They also give mathematical measures of statistical significance, which are of course a lot more reliable than eyeballing the data.

Recap: How to Outguess Fake Numbers

- When the digits of recent data depart from the company's customary distributions, it can be a tip-off to fraud.
- Embezzlers and fraud artists making up numbers unconsciously overuse descending pairs of digits (like 10, 21, 32, etc.)
- Fakers underuse doubled digits (like 00 or 55), thinking they don't look "random" enough.

Twelve

How to Outguess Manipulated Numbers

A New York–based insurance salesman had a generous expense account and the perfect swindle. In the interest of going paperless, his company instituted a policy of requiring scans of submitted receipts rather than the receipts themselves. The salesman discovered that he could change a printed 1 to a 7 or 9 with a black pen, and the modification would be undetectable in a low-resolution scan.

He thereafter went to great lengths to make sure his receipt amounts started with 1. He might order an $18 breakfast, or stay in a hotel where the room cost $178. Then he'd doctor the amounts, getting reimbursements for a $98 breakfast or a $778 hotel bill.

In a stroke of the pen, he was netting $70 to $800 per expense. By a stroke of bad luck, the insurance company's audit department was an early adopter of Benford's law analysis. In this case the first digits were enough to tip off the auditors. They found an excess of 7s and 9s and a deficit of 1s. An investigation confirmed the deception, and the company sued the salesman for full restitution.

Manipulated numbers may be a bigger problem than completely invented ones. Here *manipulation* refers to cases where someone adjusts an honest number upward or downward for personal gain. The adjustment need not be so bold as changing a 1 to a 7. It's often just enough to meet a limit, goal, or threshold. Expense accounts usually have a limit beyond which expenses will not be reimbursed, or will require preapproval and/or documentation. You can expect to find that expense claims will cluster just below that limit.

"This is usual for government," Mark Nigrini said. He investigated one agency where employees were given purchasing cards good for purchases of up to $2,500. The result: "globs of purchases at $2,500, $2,499, $2,496...Obviously these are genius people who said, 'Don't go for the $2,501, go for $2,496. I'm the only one, out of the entire 35,000 employees of this government agency, who knows how arithmetic works!' However, we tend to think alike as people so we *each* think we're the only one."

One check for manipulated numbers is the *second-digit test*. Count the occurrences of the ten digits in each number's second position, immediately to the right of the leading digit. For $749.91 the second digit is 4, and you would add one to the tally for 4. Chart the results.

With honest numbers, not much variation is expected in the frequency of second digits. Benford's law predicts that 0 will be the most common second digit, occurring about 12 percent of the time, and 9 will be the least common, occurring 8.5 percent of the time. But often you'll see something like the chart on the next page. The line is the ideal Benford curve for second digits, and the bars are the actual tallies. It may not look like there's too much difference, but the differences are telling. The bars show an excess of 8s and 9s and a shortage of every other digit. This can happen when there is a round-number limit like $1,000. People tend to submit expenses that are a little under the threshold.

Threshold effects are common, so don't rush to judgment

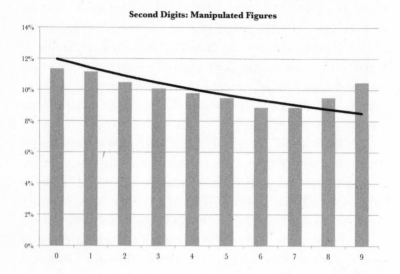

Second Digits: Manipulated Figures

the first time you see something like this. An employee who knows that the company will reimburse meals up to $50 may try to run tabs of $49 and change. She's not doing the company any favors, but she's playing by the rules that the company set up.

On the other hand, an employee who overreports meal expenses — or makes them up — has reason to lurk under the threshold, too. With a result like this, you might want to check on whether the employee submitted receipts for the just-below-threshold amounts, whether they match, and whether there is any sign of tampering.

Occasionally thresholds end in 5, such as $25. In that case manipulation will produce an excess of 3s and 4s as second digits.

Kevin L. Lawrence came to investors with a can't-lose business plan. His company, Health Maintenance Centers (HMC), was developing electronics and software to allow health clubs to monitor their members' performance on exercise equipment. It would make every workout a stress test, allowing the club or physicians to tailor personal exercise and health regimes. Lawrence sold $74 million worth of HMC and a related security to 5,000 investors nationwide.

On January 17, 2002, the Securities and Exchange Commission filed suit against Lawrence and HMC, charging investment fraud. A promised IPO had never happened. Instead, at least $16.3 million of investors' money had apparently been funneled to Lawrence and associates. The SEC charged that Lawrence had spent $2.1 million on twenty-three luxury cars, $1 million on boats, and $1.7 million on real estate and jewelry, including a $330,000 engagement ring for Stacy Gray, another defendant.

Lawrence probably didn't set out to be a con artist. He was an entrepreneur who was better at raising money than deploying it into a successful business—less Bernie Madoff than Max Bialystock. The numbers in HMC's books were real transactions. But some digit tests were highly suspicious. Those tests, unfortunately, were done only after HMC's problems had become public (by Financial Forensics of Lake Oswego, Oregon, and separately by Mark Nigrini). Had HMC's investors examined the digit patterns beforehand, they might have saved money and aggravation.

In a chart of the second digits of HMC's payments data (next page), 0 and 5 occur far more commonly than in the Benford curve. The digit 9 was shunned, occurring considerably less often than 8. This is evidence of someone's using round numbers like $10 (which occurred 459 times) or $15,000 (122 times) or $1,000,000 (four times). HMC often dealt in round figures.

So do Colombian drug cartels and grandmas writing birthday checks. There is nothing necessarily wrong with round numbers. You go to the ATM and withdraw a round number of dollars, like $300. You don't know what all you'll spend it on, so you just pick a number from the touch-screen

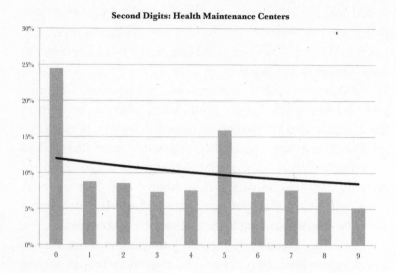

Second Digits: Health Maintenance Centers

menu of round amounts. When we make up dollar amounts, and aren't trying to deceive anyone by making them look random, we almost always pick round numbers.

The only thing wrong with round numbers is that, in some contexts, they aren't businesslike. Companies have a responsibility to negotiate the best deals and to buy no more than is needed. Even when a price happens to be a round number, a Brownian motion of discounts, allowances, transportation charges, and taxes tends to move the net amount away from the round number. The discipline of running an honest business exerts a gravitational pull, bringing the associated dollar values into line with Benford's law. When the money handling is more lax or evasive, the dollar values diverge.

HMC's principals had been using its funds like a personal checking account. Or an ATM machine, literally. A total of 111 of HMC's payments turned out to be for $301.50. Employees had been given ATM cards to draw on HMC's accounts. The maximum withdrawal permitted was $300, and the bank tacked on a $1.50 fee.

An excess of $10, $15, $20, and $25 charges was due to bank fees for cashier's checks and wire transfers. These services are intended for individuals. Companies have cheaper ways to move funds. At the very least, this shows that HMC's employees weren't interested in saving the investors' money. It also raises the question, why weren't HMC's own checks good enough?

The answer was also to be found in the numbers. Another bump came from a fee for bounced checks.

The investigation concluded that HMC was using checks and transfers to shift large round-number amounts from one dubious entity to another, most of it eventually landing in the pockets of HMC's principals. The financial shell game was probably intended to make it hard to follow what was going on.

In the five years leading up to its collapse, Enron, the notoriously fraudulent energy company, reported these revenue figures:

1996	$13.289 billion
1997	$20.273 billion
1998	$31.260 billion
1999	$40.112 billion
2000	$100.789 billion

In hindsight, we know that these numbers were a fiction woven by chief financial officer Andrew Fastow. Enron's managers had become mesmerized by the Pavlovian connection between revenue and stock price. The stock price was posted in the company's elevator. Fastow found ways to report the revenues to justify the stock prices that everyone at the company desired.

Enron president Jeffrey Skilling spent much of his work-day rebutting doubting Thomases. In a now-famous conference call, Highfields Capital analyst Richard Grubman remarked that Enron was the only company he knew that did not produce a balance sheet or cash flow statement with its earnings. "Well, thank you very much," Skilling replied. "We appreciate it...*asshole!*"

The few figures that Enron did release were suspicious enough. When a company is on track to sell a million widgets, 998,300 will be a disappointment. Three of the five revenue figures just top a psychologically potent round number—of $20, $40, and $100 billion.

Each of Enron's threshold-beating numbers has a second digit of 0. Benford's law predicts that the chance of a number's second digit being 0 is 11.97 percent. When you get several narrowly threshold-beating numbers in proximity, the odds grow longer. The chance of three out of five numbers having a second digit of 0 is about 1 in 75.

Revenue is a headline number, one likely to be featured in the financial media. There aren't many headline numbers, but they're the ones that drive stock prices. Another widely reported number is earnings per share. Here are Enron's:

1996	$1.08
1997	$0.16
1998	$1.01
1999	$1.10
2000	$1.12

Earnings were a lot less impressive than revenue. Enron was straining to make a dollar a share, and there's scant indication of growth over five years. The outlier year was 1997. "Operating results" were said to be $.87 a share, but "items impacting comparability" whittled that down to $.16. Creative accounting allowed Enron to sweep expenses and markdowns into one big pile—the annus horribilis of 1997—and keep the other years' earnings above $1 a share.

Enron's pitch was that revenues mattered, not earnings. Revenues are easier to manipulate. In early 2001 Enron folk spoke of doubling revenue again, to the nice round figure of $200 billion. That fine plan was preempted by the management team's prison terms.

It's not just Enron. There have been studies looking at the second digits of reported earnings or revenues for all large American corporations. Because there are so many companies of so many sizes in such different lines of business, the reported numbers ought to follow Benford's law closely. They do, with the striking exception that there are more second digits of 0, and fewer of 9, than would be expected.

Call that the Enron bump. Instead of reporting earnings of 99 cents a share, companies find a way to top $1. Studies of aggregate data can't say *which* corporations are misreporting, but the fraction must be sizeable.

There's a smaller bump for second digits of 5. Instead of reporting 24 cents a share, it's creatively massaged to 25 cents.

Nigrini notes that you see the opposite type of fudging with losses. Here is the biggest loss ever reported by an American corporation:

$99,280 million

That was from American International Group (AIG)'s 10-K filing for 2008.

Now here is the second-biggest loss reported by an American corporation:

$98,696 million

That was AOL TimeWarner's filing for 2002. Do you see something similar? The worst corporate losses look like the prices at the 99 cents store.

Given that big and allegedly reputable companies connive to land on the better side of psychologically important round numbers, think how much worse it is with start-ups and wannabes. Banks, venture capitalists, and investors often have to form an opinion of a new company's credibility from limited data. The relevant numbers may not be income or even revenue but units sold, downloads, or clicks. These may be reported on a quarterly, monthly, weekly, or daily basis. Whatever the metric is, there is a temptation to top important thresholds.

A good reality check is to examine the second digits of numbers you're given for an excess of 0s. How many barely threshold-beating figures qualify as suspicious? First count how many headline numbers you're given. Call that N for *numbers*. Then count how many of those numbers have 0 for the second digit. Call that Z for *zeros*.

Open a spreadsheet. You'll need to use something called the binomial distribution function. You don't need to know what that is. It's been built into Excel and every comparable financial program. Type this into an Excel cell:

=1-BINOM.DIST($Z-1,N$,0.1197,TRUE)

Substitute the actual numbers (or links to cells containing them) for Z and N. The formula will return the probability of at least Z second-digit 0s in a list of N numbers.

Example. Say you were thinking of buying out Enron in early 2001, and the management gave you the ten numbers above, revenues and earnings per share for five years. N would be 10 and Z would be 5.

Subtract 1 from Z to get 4 and plug that in as the function's first argument. The second argument is 10, and the third is the Benford's law probability for 0 to be the second digit, 0.1197. Don't worry about the "TRUE," just type it in.

The result is 0.368 percent, or 1 in 272. That tells you that it was a serious long shot for Enron to just top *all* those milestone numbers, by the normal operation of chance.

What probability should cause you to walk away? No statistician can tell you that. Coincidences do happen. For a venture capitalist, the goal is not to prove that financial numbers are accurate but to target due diligence and establish a comfort level.

Here's one comparative. When testing a new drug, a 1 in 20 (5 percent) confidence level is generally required for publication in a medical journal. The researcher needs to show that the probability that the drug's observed effects are merely due to chance is less than 5 percent.

This 5 percent criterion is arbitrary. It need not have any relevance to the business world. Still, you might adopt it as the starting point for your conversation. Should the chance be less than 5 percent, consider it a red flag. You should then ask for more figures.

Repeat the process with the new figures and compute with the updated N and Z. Now is the chance less than 5 percent? This is something like checking out a new restaurant. Go there once and get a lousy meal, and it might be the chef's bad day. Go there a few more times, and you'll get a better sense of the ground truth.

Should the proportion of second-digit zeros remain high, that makes a case that the company is puffing up its figures. Is the business any good? Your call. The odds are it's not entirely honest.

In the 1980s and 1990s the Internal Revenue Service's most dreaded audits were those conducted under the National Research Program (NRP). A random-number generator spat out a nine-digit number. Whoever had that Social Security number won the booby prize, namely an audit from hell in which the taxpayer had to supply documentation for every single entry on the tax return. By auditing random taxpayers and checking everything, the IRS was able to learn which entries produced the most fraud. Scientifically it was perfect; politically not so much. Enough taxpayers griped that Congress pressured the IRS to discontinue the NRP audits in the mid-1990s.

With the NRP shut down, the IRS focused on analytics. Few doubt that these analytics involve Benford's law, though the ever-secretive IRS will not confirm it. (They did not reply to my inquiries on the topic.) As far back as 1998, however, the *New York Times* reported, "The income tax agencies of several nations and several states, including California, are using detection software based on Benford's law, as are a score of large companies and accounting businesses."

Mark Nigrini was doing this long before tax collectors were. In his early work with US tax returns, he examined entries such as interest and mortgage expense, gifts to charity, capital gains, and the Schedule C expenses of small businesses. These departed from the Benford distribution in consistent ways. Small-business rent and office expenses reported on Schedule Cs were especially problematic.

Nigrini found that undocumented entries of low-income taxpayers were more suspicious than those of high-income filers. This could mean that poorer filers know their risk of audit is small and are more reckless in inventing figures. Alternatively, it might mean that the wealthy are more likely to have competent professional preparers who talk them out of doing anything too stupid.

The paradox was that Nigrini couldn't tell which returns were misreporting. Most small businesses report a single number for rent. Some of these rent numbers are honest, and some are inflated. It was the aggregate of thousands of rent numbers that implied fraud.

This sort of finding could be immensely useful to tax collectors, not only in determining which entries and types of returns to audit but in writing regulations and influencing legislation. The IRS now requires mortgage lenders to report interest with a Form 1098, and consumer interest is no longer deductible at all. Stockbrokers began reporting the original (basis) price of securities to the IRS in 2011, and mutual funds followed in 2012. In 2011, the IRS resumed some random audits, focusing on self-employed business owners with high cash flow.

A few years ago, Inland Revenue ran digit tests on British tax returns and found that small-business owners were unusually likely to report sales starting with the two digits 14. The evident reason was that at that time Britain allowed small businesses to file a short-form return provided sales were less than £15,000. The threshold has since been raised several times. Each time the manipulations crept upward in lockstep.

Middle-income American taxpayers use a tax table to compute their federal income tax. These tables divide incomes into $50 ranges. In 2011 a single person making $71,049 in taxable income owed $13,894 in taxes. If that person made a dollar more ($71,050), she'd be bumped onto the next line of the table and owe another $12 in taxes ($13,906).

You might think that no one would bother to cheat on her taxes for $12. Nigrini charted the last two digits of taxable income and found evidence that filers were adjusting their incomes to fall just before a step. There were excesses of reported incomes ending in 48 or 49; 98 or 99. There were also fewer-than-expected incomes falling at or just above the step (ending with 50 or 51; 00 or 01).

To prove that this was conscious evasion, Nigrini compared tax-table returns to those of higher-income filers, who are instead required to multiply their taxable income by a marginal rate. Their digits showed no sign of this manipulation.

Taxable income is calculated from other entries and can't be changed on its own without creating a math error. A filer who's just over the tax threshold would have to go back and find a way to add a couple of dollars to a deduction, or shave a few dollars off income. To put the best possible complexion on that, it could indicate a taxpayer with a sharp pencil who racked her mind and remembered a deduction she'd forgotten about. Less optimistically, it might mean that a taxpayer is willing to cheat a little when the chance of detection is small.

The IRS's audit formula is generated by predictive analytics. Statistical correlations allow it to predict which returns are most likely to be dishonest and to yield the most additional tax on audit. The IRS computers have *all* back returns to draw on, and surely they do make use of that information. It may be coincidence that your taxable income is a dollar below the threshold this year. If it's been just below…00 or…50 every year for the past ten, it's no coincidence.

Threshold effects offer a simple honesty test. It's entirely conceivable that the test figures in the audit formula. It's not that tax agencies care so much about a few dollars. But should a taxpayer consistently game the tax thresholds *and* show other red flags, like a Schedule C business or large charitable deductions, that would raise the suspicion level.

The best advice is to be scrupulously honest in small things. The outguessing machine is watching, and it knows more than you think.

The political blogosphere has latched onto Benford's law in a big way. It has acquired a reputation as a magic black box that needs only precinct level vote counts — available to any blogger working in his mother's basement — to uncover electoral fraud. The result is a growing number of claims of rigged elections. A charge of a stolen election, dressed up with statistical jargon that few understand, will be picked up by the next tier of supposedly more responsible journalists. On the Internet, errors can be refuted but never retracted. The next thing you know, there's a new, partisan conspiracy theory.

Too many of these claims are based on first-digit tests only. The first-digit test is never definitive and can be utterly meaningless. One ought to compare this election's digit patterns to those of previous elections. That is rarely done.

Partisan bloggers can also succumb to data mining. There are thousands of precincts in a state or national election. Comb through enough of them and you are sure to find some in which the statistics look suspicious. They're *not* suspicious when you look at the big picture, but the big picture is precisely what's missing in the mind of a zealot.

The idea of checking election results through digit analytics is credited to Alexandar Sobyanin. He studied Russia's notoriously corrupt 1993 parliamentary elections. Sobyanin proposed several statistical tests, one based on Benford's law and all founded on the idea that invented numbers would be different from authentic numbers. Sobyanin claimed that his tests of the 1993 election showed fraud. The conclusion, at least, was incontestable. Many such claims have followed. After Iran's 2009 election, reelecting Mahmoud Ahmadinejad, Nigrini looked at the precinct totals and found evidence of fabrication.

A recent article by Joseph Deckert, Mikhail Myagkov, and Peter C. Ordeshook has the title "The Irrelevance of Benford's Law for Detecting Fraud in Elections." The authors caution that there hasn't been much research on how well honest election results fit Benford's law. One unknown is how much precinct sizes vary. One would like to think that election boards split up districts more or less evenly and avoid huge disparities in precinct size. Unless there's a partisan reason for gerrymandering... who knows?

Imagine a stretch of Iowa farm country in which the precincts are laid out as regularly as the cornfields, with 5,000 voters in each. This is a uniformly conservative region favoring Mitt Romney over Barack Obama, 70 to 30 percent. Romney averaged 3,500 votes per precinct, and Obama averaged 1,500, without too much variation for either. The first digits of Romney's totals would be 3s and Obama's first digits would be 1s. The magic black box lights up red! But nothing's wrong. It just means that we're looking at a region where the precincts and the politics are pancake-flat.

In this scenario, both candidates' results would generate false alarms. More troubling are cases where only one candidate's results would look falsely suspicious. It's common for one candidate to do better in cities and another to do better in rural areas. Precinct size might vary more in urban areas than rural communities (or vice versa). Either could cause one candidate's results to fit Benford's law better than the other's.

In order to use digit patterns to detect fraud, it's vital to have some theory of how election fraud happens. In some parts of the world, corrupt apparatchiks sit down and invent a list of numbers to be passed off as precinct counts. In Russian elections, many precinct counts are shamelessly rounded, ending in 0(s), with no attempt to cover up the inexactitude. "There has been fraud of course," admitted Vladimir Shevchuk of Russia's 2000 presidential election, "but some of it may be due to the inefficient mechanism used to count ballots.... To do it the right way they would have needed more than one night. They were already dead tired so they did it in an expedient way." Shevchuk sat on Tatarstan's electoral commission.

In the annals of American corruption, cheats may register names from the local cemetery and use them to stuff ballot boxes with forged votes for their candidate, or they may "lose" ballots for the opposition candidate. The net effect of much ballot fraud is to multiply a candidate's count by an approximate factor: however much the cheats think they need to win. This would be difficult to detect by Benford's law. One of the law's properties is that you can multiply a set of numbers by any factor and the numbers will still conform to the Benford distribution.

Tests of last digits are better for detecting invented totals. It probably wouldn't be one person inventing the numbers, though. Should an army of corrupt poll workers invent a single number each, the group effort would eliminate any personal signatures. You would have to rely on relatively universal features of invented numbers.

In a 2012 analysis of Nigerian elections, Bernd Berber and Alexandra Scacco suggested looking at doubled last digits (00, 11, 22, through 99). As we've seen, these are usually less common in invented numbers and can be useful in raising a red flag for further investigation.

The troubling thing about digit analysis of elections is that partisans often aren't interested in a search for truth. They want any anomaly to be taken as instant proof of fraud. Should investigation in the field fail to substantiate wrongdoing, partisans may want to claim fraud anyway, based on the digits alone. Such claims need to be taken with a grain of salt.

All of the applications of digit analytics are based on the assumption that the bad guys don't know about it. So far this has largely been true, but someday it won't be.

There was a time when only a few criminologists knew about fingerprints. Now the dumbest burglars know to use rubber gloves. There are ways to defeat digit analysis, and they're not that difficult.

Nigrini has made the optimistic case that wider knowledge of Benford's law would be a deterrent, just as knowledge of fingerprints and DNA analysis is. Those who decide to commit fraud would first have to plan the misrepresentation and then adjust the figures to conform to the Benford distribution. That's more work; the adjustment would tend to diminish the amount of fraud, or require additional actions that could lead to detection, or both.

The problem is that criminals are not easily deterred — that's what makes them criminals in the first place. They are people who have trouble understanding the long-term consequences of their actions. That cuts both ways. Everyone's seen CSI shows, yet forensic technology remains useful because most crimes are done on the spur of the moment, with little planning. That's true of many financial and electoral crimes, too. An embezzler starts because he lost the rent in Las Vegas. A would-be entrepreneur "enhances" a balance sheet for a meeting with an investor. A ruling party cheats at the last minute because it looks like it's losing.

In any application, it's worth asking yourself: How likely is it that the person reporting the figures is aware of Benford's law, expects that the figures might be subjected to forensic analysis, and has the mathematical skills to pull off a countermeasure?

Recap: How to Outguess Manipulated Numbers

• The second digits of financial numbers can help uncover manipulation. When there is an incentive to top a round number, manipulators will produce relatively more second digits of 0 and relatively fewer of 9.

• When there is an incentive to fall under a round number, manipulators produce more second digits of 9 and fewer of 0. This is common with expense accounts.

• Digit analysis cannot "prove" anything by itself. Its value is in flagging data meriting investigation by a good auditor. Be skeptical of claims (of election fraud, say) based on first-digit Benford tests.

Thirteen

How to Outguess Ponzi Schemes

From the 1970s through 2008, three longtime employees of Bernard L. Madoff Investment Securities—David Kugel, Annette Bongiorno, and Joann Crupi—did the paperwork. "I worked together with them to create the false trades and make them appear on investment advisor client statements and confirmations," Kugel told a federal judge. The trades were invented to correspond to a return on investment that Madoff himself decreed for each of his clients. It was the Bizarro World version of money management. Instead of calculating the return from the trades, Kugel and company made up trades to match the return.

This isn't the way Bernie Madoff started, assuming he can be believed. "I...was successful at the start but lost my way after a while and refused to admit that I failed." Soon afterward Madoff began inventing numbers.

The money management business is founded on trust. How does an investor know whether the numbers on the statements are for real? The standard advice is to be a judge of character and deal only with those managers you're sure you can trust. That's exactly what Madoff's clients did. A line on the company's website once ran, "Clients know that Bernard Madoff has a personal interest in maintaining the unblemished record of value, fair-dealing, and high ethical standards that has always been the firm's hallmark."

Another rule of thumb is *never invest in anything you don't understand*. Though the sentiment is laudable, it's unrealistic in today's complex financial universe. Some people don't truly "understand" money market accounts or index funds. Should they keep their money in a mattress? In any case, someone investing with a miracle-working manager should not expect a complete explanation of how he makes the money. That's the secret sauce.

Madoff's investors believed he had achieved annual returns of something like 10 percent a year with low volatility, and had done so over an otherwise volatile decade. Despite what you may have heard, this wasn't too good to be true. Other money managers have racked up better records.

Jim Simons started his Medallion Fund a couple of years before Madoff did. Since 1988, Medallion's return has averaged 45 percent a year. Simons is a mathematician who hires only mathematicians and scientists and sequesters them in a compound on the north shore of Long Island, where they invent top secret trading algorithms. The fund has done especially well when the general market plummets. Medallion's best year was 2000, with a return of 99 percent. In 2008 Medallion was up 80 percent. "When everyone is running around like a chicken with its head cut off," said Simons, "that's pretty good for us."

Simons doesn't offer details, and neither will anyone else who aims for comparable returns. Successful hedge funds must constantly invent new strategies as old ones are reverse engineered by competitors and become played out. Were the methods disclosed to investors, the secrets would leak faster.

The black-box nature of the business is well illustrated by a mortifying incident. Stony Brook University asked Simons, formerly of its math faculty, to recommend a good manager for its endowment fund. Simons introduced them to...Bernie Madoff. The university invested with Madoff and lost $5.4 million. Some might have looked at Madoff's returns and figured they were too good to be true. Simons knew they weren't.

The rule should perhaps be reworded: *Never invest more than you can afford to lose in something no outsider understands.* Many of Madoff's victims violated that rule, putting practically all their assets with him. One of the more suspicious things about Madoff was how *transparent* he was. He claimed to use a split-strike conversion strategy. That jargon is meaningful to professionals (though no one could figure out how Madoff made it pay the way he claimed). At least some clients got statements that ostensibly listed every trade. That should have made it possible to figure out Madoff's system, assuming he had one.

At least one person tried. In 1991 hedge fund manager Ed Thorp—also known as the inventor of blackjack card counting—was asked for his opinion on a company's investments. Thorp saw that the returns for the account with Madoff were fantastic. Curious, Thorp asked Madoff for more detail on his trades. He got it and quickly determined that something was fishy. On April 16, 1991, Madoff had supposedly bought 123 call options for Procter & Gamble on behalf of the client. Thorp found that a mere twenty Procter & Gamble calls had been traded that day. In other cases, too, Madoff claimed to have bought or sold more of a security on a given day than was traded in total. Thorp advised his client to pull its money out.

Retaining a trusted expert is the best way to check out a

money manager. Thorp's reputation must have helped him get the trade-by-trade information he needed.

Mark Nigrini argues that the numbers themselves could have pointed to Madoff's fraud or similar ones. Madoff had at least two sets of made-up numbers, the monthly returns (evidently set by Madoff himself) and the fake trades (invented by his minions). There were three people making up trades, and they made the prices fit the historic record. Given that the fictitious sale prices were constrained by the day's trading range and the prescribed returns, it's hard to say what their digit distributions should look like. The monthly returns, however, apparently came straight from the mind of Bernie Madoff. Returns are the one thing that any manager, no matter how secretive, must disclose to investors.

At least one set of Madoff returns has been disclosed, those for the feeder fund Fairfield Sentry. Founded in 1990 by Walter Noel and Jeffrey Tucker, Fairfield Sentry gave Madoff a global reach, pitching Madoff's "algorithmic technology" to wealthy institutions worldwide (minimum investment $100,000). The Abu Dhabi Investment Authority, JPMorgan Chase, Banco Bilbao Vizcaya Argentaria (Spain), Nomura Holdings (Japan), and numerous Swiss banks were among those that bought a piece of Madoff's wizardry via Fairfield Sentry.

In its first month, December 1990, Fairfield Sentry claimed a return of 2.77 percent. It reported monthly returns through October 2008, when it had a small loss of 0.06 percent. By that point its reported assets were over $7 billion, accounting for more than a tenth of the assets under Madoff's management. A dollar invested in Fairfield Sentry in December 1990 would have turned into $6.04 by October 2008—had you only been able to collect it. That averages out to a 10.6 percent annual return.

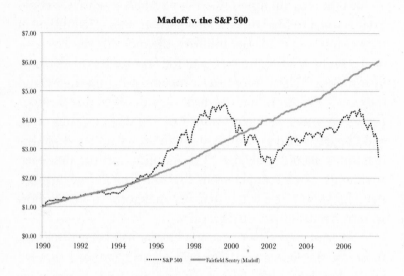

Madoff v. the S&P 500

More eyebrow-raising was how steady the claimed returns were. The chart shows the value of a dollar invested in Fairfield Sentry against a dollar invested in the S&P 500 index. Fairfield Sentry was not only steadier than a stock index but steadier than US Treasury bonds.

Madoff knew all about volatility. But when he came to invent fake numbers, he fell back on the not-so-rational instincts we all share. He apparently felt a need to keep monthly returns close to the average he was pitching. Only once (January and February 2003) did he deliver two negative returns in a row.

You might look at the chart and say that returns *can't* be that consistent. Then you wouldn't have put your money with Madoff, and that would have been the right call. Fairfield Sentry's investors, some of them the world's most astute bankers, were hardly naïve. They understood that everyone who runs a hedge fund is claiming to walk on water, one way or another. They assumed that Madoff's preternaturally low volatility was a feature of his winning algorithm—whatever it was.

Things started to go sour in August 2008. JPMorgan Chase redeemed a quarter of a billion dollars from Fairfield Sentry. The official story was that they'd become "concerned about lack of transparency." Meanwhile Madoff and Fairfield Sentry were working on a new fund. It would use more leverage to achieve returns of 16 percent. Fairfield Sentry reportedly warned its investors that anyone who dared to withdraw money, and anyone so foolish as to *not* invest in the new fund, would be punished in the severest way possible, by being blacklisted from investing in any future Madoff funds.

Madoff was arrested on December 11, 2008.

Fairfield Sentry's monthly returns were given to the hundredth of a percentage point. That means there are only two or three significant digits. Rounding discards information (or in this case, it means Madoff didn't bother to invent the information in the first place). Despite that, it's easy to see that Madoff's monthly return numbers were unusual.

Let's start with first digits, the test in which Benford's law comes most into play. Nigrini recommends omitting negative values (or analyzing them separately), as the incentive is to minimize a loss. I've also omitted a few cases where there were fewer than two significant digits. That leaves 190 values, all two- or three-digit positive numbers. The bars show the actual first-digit tallies, and the line shows the ideal Benford distribution.

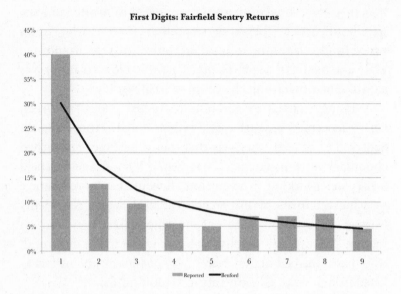

First Digits: Fairfield Sentry Returns

Forty percent of the returns start with 1. That's well beyond the 30 percent predicted by Benford's law. The digits 2 through 5 are underrepresented, and there's an excess of 7s and 8s. These differences are statistically meaningful.

Madoff was claiming returns of about 11 percent a year. That means the monthly returns would tend to be close to 1 percent. These returns were rock steady, never straying too far from the mean. Take all that at face value, and you'd expect a disproportionate number of months with returns in the range of 0.70 to 1.99 percent. That would create an excess of first digits of 7, 8, 9, and 1, and a deficit of the other digits.

That's what we do see, with one exception. The first digit 9 occurs in just about the Benford proportion. This contrasts with the greater-than-Benford occurrence of the digits around it.

A likely explanation is manipulation. Like everybody else, Madoff knew that a return of 1.00+ percent feels a lot bigger than one of, say, 0.99 percent. So he avoided 9s. Monthly returns that otherwise might have started with 9 were bumped up to 1.00+ percent. It's difficult to think of an alternative explanation *even if you buy Madoff's claim of fantastically low volatility.* Why else would steady returns skip over values starting with 9?

Now let's look at the last two digits of the monthly returns. The chart of last two digits, from 00 to 99, shows a ragged picket fence with some slats missing. Several digit pairs are far more common than the others. The chart's most remarkable feature is the spike for 86. Those are the last two digits for eight of Fairfield Sentry's monthly returns. There are also three pairs that occur 6 times: 14, 26, and 36.

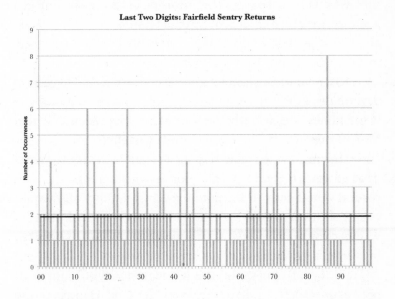

Last Two Digits: Fairfield Sentry Returns

This is consistent with the unconscious repetition of invented numbers. This idea becomes more compelling when you look at which digit pairs were repeated: 86, 14, 26, and 36. All but one end in 6.

In fact, there are nine last pairs ending in 6, and they occur 33 times total. That is twice what you'd expect.

The Fairfield Sentry returns are routine by tests of doubled last digits and descending pairs. With 190 numbers, you'd expect about 19 to end in doubled last digits. In fact, there are 24, more than expected. (Remember, fabricators usually shy away from doubled pairs.) The only thing slightly suspicious is that 55, which many fabricators avoid, does not occur.

There are nine descending pairs (10, 21, 32...) and they occur 17 times, almost exactly what would be expected.

In short, the Fairfield Sentry returns seem to have been manipulated to yield more months topping 1 percent. The figures are also suspicious for the profusion of returns ending in 6 and 86. Two other criteria of invented numbers were not present. Overall, these findings don't prove that the returns were made up, but they are far from reassuring.

As a potential investor your first concern would have been deciding whether you were comfortable enough to hand over your money—that, rather than proving beyond doubt that Madoff was a fraud. Were you to find yourself in a similar situation, the most reasonable response would be to ask for more detailed return figures, with more significant figures. This request would pose no threat to the confidentiality of the trading algorithms. Should the manager say no, you'd ask yourself whether you want to invest with someone who won't even tell investors exact returns.

In the aftermath of the scandal, a CNBC journalist obtained Madoff's golf scores from the Golf Handicap and Information Network. Madoff self-reported twenty games played between 1998 and 2000 at Palm Beach Country Club, Atlantic Golf Club, and Fresh Meadow Country Club. The scores were as weirdly consistent as his investment returns, and three of the twenty scores were 86.

Recap: How to Outguess Ponzi Schemes

• Financial schemers may fabricate and manipulate data. Be suspicious when too many numbers just top a psychologically significant threshold.

• A last-two-digits test can help detect fraudulent managers who unconsciously favor certain digit pairs.

Part Two

The Hot Hand Theory

Fourteen

In the Zone

Basketball was an obsession of 5'9" Israeli-American psychologist Amos Tversky. He watched the game as a fan, and he played it with friends, aggressively. "He was a rough player," Tversky's wife, Barbara, told me. "He came home from a basketball game *wounded*. I said, 'Basketball is not a contact sport!'"

As a fan, Tversky was aware of the *hot hand theory*. This is a belief in winning streaks, widespread among hoops players, coaches, sportscasters, and fans. But not just any winning streaks: *predictive* winning streaks. A player who's made several shots in a row has the "hot hand" or is "in the zone." He is judged more likely to make the next shot than he would be otherwise.

There is nothing illogical about the idea. It stands to reason that making baskets boosts a player's confidence, and confidence is good. Success breeds success. The hot hand theory is ingrained in sportscaster commentary, and it influences court strategy. Players try to pass the ball to a teammate with the hot hand, reasoning that he will have a better chance of scoring. The opposing team's counterstrategy is to intercept passes to the player with the hot hand and to block his shots.

Many fans regard the hot hand theory as so self-evident that it doesn't need any proof. Just watch the game awhile and you'll *see* the hot hand. Players who've experienced it have no doubts. Purvis Short of the Golden State Warriors once said of it:

> You're in a world all your own. It's hard to describe. But the basket seems to be so wide. No matter what you do, you know the ball is going to go in.

Pressed for evidence, more wonkish fans can rattle off accounts of legendary winning streaks. On December 8, 1992, the Atlanta Hawks' Dominique Wilkins made twenty-three consecutive field goals. On January 22, 2006, Kobe Bryant scored 81 points for Los Angeles against Toronto. Both are considered to be prime examples of the hot hand.

Tversky gave a seminar at Stanford in which he discussed randomness experiments. One of his students, Thomas Gilovich, suggested doing a research project about the hot hand. He felt there was a connection. Given that people are unable to produce random series, they may also have trouble understanding events that are close to random, like basketball shots. Gilovich supposed that fans exaggerated the importance of the hot hand.

"I went to talk to Amos about it," said Gilovich, "and was surprised to find that he had an interest in it." But Tversky insisted there was no such thing as a hot hand. It was a myth! The game was more random than fans believed.

"He said you couldn't really test it because you couldn't get enough data," Gilovich recalled. "He'd gotten some small sample of data when he was spending a year at Harvard. And I said, 'Look, I bet I can get enough data to test this idea.' "

To do that, Gilovich needed a complete record of hits and misses in sequence. At the time, only one NBA team had that kind of data—the Philadelphia 76ers. Their meticulous statistician Harvey Pollack supplied his records, and Gilovich's idea evolved into a paper. Another student, Robert Vallone, was brought on to help with the statistics. Gilovich, Vallone, and Tversky published their research in a 1985 paper in *Cognitive Psychology*, "The Hot Hand in Basketball: On the Misperception of Random Sequences." It ignited a controversy that's still blazing white-hot.

This article isn't just about basketball. It uses the sport to speak of how the mind perceives the world's blend of predictability and randomness. The three authors analyzed the hot hand belief from many angles. They interviewed NBA players and college fans, asking whether a player who'd just scored was more likely than usual to make the next shot. Overwhelmingly, those polled said yes. The researchers examined shooting records of the 76ers and the Boston Celtics (who had free-throw data), subjecting them to extensive statistical analysis. They ran free-throw experiments with the men's and women's teams of Cornell University, and they let volunteers wager money on the hot hand in an economic experiment.

In all cases, evidence for the hot hand was lacking. Everyone believed (and/or bet) that he or she could predict something that was in fact unpredictable.

The article drew a crucial distinction between a hot hand and a lucky streak. It goes without saying that there are cases where a player makes an unusually large number of consecutive shots through, for lack of a better word, luck. There are likewise lucky streaks in roulette, dice, and the lottery. Reasonable people agree that roulette streaks are *not* predictive because roulette is pure luck.

The psychologists drew an equally important distinction between a hot hand and talent. Obviously, some players are better at making baskets than others. A good shooter is more likely to have a string of baskets than a weak one. Julius Erving, a star player at the time of the study, made about 52 percent of his shots in the 1980–81 season. You might then compare his record to the result of tossing a biased coin that has a 52 percent chance of heads. Did Dr. J have more or longer winning streaks than such a coin would have, with sequences of heads? If so, that would support the hot hand theory. Otherwise, it would suggest that Erving's winning streaks were only those to be expected from the usual operation of chance.

The research found the latter. A player's talent determined the overall probability of making baskets, but otherwise, winning streaks were no longer than to be expected by chance.

It's conceivable that an opposing team's players put more effort into blocking a winning player because they believe in the hot hand. This could erase the evidence for a hot hand—which might nonetheless be real. To test that possibility, Gilovich's group arranged free-throw tests with Cornell's basketball teams. There was no opposing team and no strategizing to confuse matters. It was the cleanest test of the hot hand theory, and the results were the same. The hot hand was an illusion.

Celtics coach Red Auerbach was famous for predicting victories midgame. When he felt the Celtics were on an unbeatable hot streak, he would light up a cigar. Told of the hot hand paper, Auerbach asked, "Who is this guy? So he makes a study. I couldn't care less."

"There are so many variables involved in shooting the basketball," said Indiana Hoosiers coach Bobby Knight, "that a paper like this really doesn't mean anything."

NCAA broadcaster Billy Packer suggested, "Please tell the stat man to get a life."

The hot hand theory has since been poked and prodded in the psychological and statistical literature; in basketball blogs, sports bars, and occasionally the general media. Scores of studies have supported and built upon GVT (the inevitable abbreviation for Gilovich, Vallone, and Tversky). A 2011 article by Tal Neiman and Yonatan Loewenstein, both of the Hebrew University of Jerusalem, looked at field goal attempts in the NBA and WNBA. The player attempting a field goal can try for an easier shot worth two points or a harder one worth three points. The decision is one measure of the player's confidence. The study showed that pro ballers who made a successful three-point field goal were more likely to attempt a three-point goal the next time around. This would indicate a hot hand belief. Kobe Bryant, in his 2007–08 season as Most Valuable Player, was almost four times more likely to choose a three-point field goal immediately after a successful one.

But Bryant, and most everyone else, was making an error, going by the outcomes of those decisions. Neiman and Loewenstein showed that players were slightly *less* likely to make the shot after a successful three-point shot. The chances were 36 percent after a success versus 38 percent after a failure.

The researchers also found that players have short memories. The decision whether to attempt a three-point goal was based primarily on the outcome of the player's last field goal (going by the observed statistics). The field goal before that had less influence, and everything still earlier was virtually forgotten as far as the present decision was concerned. NBA players' field goal choices were about as easy to predict as those of people playing the outguessing machine.

Hot hand perceptions (and refutations) exist in many

other sports. Since not all sports achievements involve a hand, the term *streakiness* is used. There are perceptions of greater-than-chance winning and losing streaks in baseball, football, tennis, and golf; seemingly in any sport where stats are kept. Streaks apply to teams as well as players, and to winning games and seasons, and are not limited to humans—there are streaks in horse racing and dog racing, too.

It's now clear that the hot hand is not *always* a myth. An authentic hot hand seems to exist in bowling. The bowler who makes a strike gets ten points *plus* the value of the next two rolls. This motivates players to try extra hard after a strike, and it works. There is solid data showing that bowlers who score a strike are a bit more likely to follow it up with another strike or spare.

There is also evidence of streakiness in certain tournaments. Winning a tennis match requires winning two out of three sets. A player who wins the first set can do a full-court press (so to speak) to clinch the prize on the second. The same goes for pro golfers who are a game or two away from qualifying for a lucrative championship tour. These authentic hot hand effects exist in individual sports where the scoring system rewards consecutive wins. Team sports are usually more random, as there are so many variables beyond an individual's control.

That doesn't change the fact that fans are hardwired to see streakiness where none exists. Thanks to its viral propagation on the Internet, belief in the hot hand is probably stronger than ever. Impassioned bloggers still rage against Gilovich, Vallone, and Tversky's decades-old paper. "When your whole life is telling you one thing and you directly experience it, and then you're told the opposite, you're going to resist it," said Gilovich. "I don't mean to suggest that people who believe in the hot hand are flat-earthers, but when people first said the earth *isn't* flat, that seemed crazy."

The hot hand is a consequence of the misunderstanding of chance revealed in randomness experiments. In fact, Gilovich's group did a novel type of randomness experiment. They showed people strings of *X*s and *O*s and asked them to say whether they looked random or not. The cover story was that these *X*s and *O*s represented successful shots and misses in basketball. This encouraged the participants to treat the sequences as real-world data.

To give you the flavor of it, I'll show you a string of black and white squares (easier to take in at a glance than letters). Imagine that the black squares represent a player's successful shots and the white ones his misses, arrayed on a horizontal time line.

In the 1985 study, most people agreed that sequences like this are random.

No surprise there — except that they were wrong. Here's what a random sequence really looks like:

It has fewer alternations of black and white, and longer sequences of the same color, than the first diagram.

The essence of randomness is unpredictability. If you can't guess what comes next, and neither can anyone else, it's random. The paradigm of randomness is a coin toss. You can think of the second diagram above as the result of tossing a fair coin fifty times, with the results displayed as black squares for heads and white for tails. The chance of a white square being followed by a black square (or vice versa) is 50 percent.

But when Gilovich's team showed people this random sequence, only 32 percent classified it as due to chance. Most believed that the same-symbol streaks were too long to be just coincidence. This implies that the hot hand is not just a sports myth but a universal illusion.

The psychologists tested sequences in which the chance of alternation was 40, 50, 60, 70, 80, and 90 percent. The perception of randomness was greatest when the alternation rate was 70 or 80 percent. In the first such diagram above, it's 75 percent, meaning that that's the chance that a white square will be followed by a black square, or vice versa.

Only when the alternation probability was increased to 90 percent did most people recognize that the back-and-forth was too consistent to be random. Here's an example of a sequence with a 90 percent alternation rate:

This is an almost-perfect black-white-black-white sequence. There are just two same-color strings, and they're only two squares in length.

Once again, magicians were using these ideas before psychologists wrote about them. Illusionists have long known that an honestly shuffled deck of cards runs the risk of *not* appearing random to the audience. There will usually be "suspicious" clusters of similar cards, like four face cards in a row. A statistician would expect that, but average folks don't.

Certain illusions use a stacked deck that looks more shuffled than a shuffled deck does. This is a counterpart, in cards, to the overalternating sequences that were perceived as random. In the so-called Si Stebbins arrangement, the cards alternate black-red-black-red-black-red in perfect lockstep. The suits run clubs-hearts-spades-diamonds throughout the deck. The values run A-4-7-10-K-3-6-9-Q-2-5-8-J. These patterns may sound like they would stick out like a sore thumb. They don't. The deck just looks random.

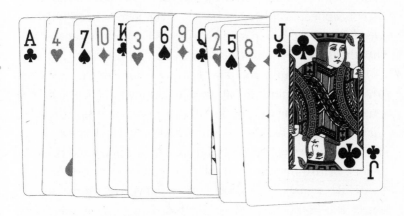

The Stebbins arrangement is easily memorized, and that's the point. A performer who glimpses the bottom card of a cut can instantly deduce the card below it…which becomes the *top* card of the restored and squared-up deck. He can, if desired, name that card and every other card in the deck.

For the most part we are more than capable of fooling ourselves. Once you understand the hot hand illusion, you see examples of it everywhere. Many iPod users complain that the shuffle play feature isn't random, *can't* be random. It just played four Lil Wayne songs in a row! Streaks like that are to be expected. The bug isn't in the software but in our heads.

The Manhattan bus schedule means little on busy corners, where traffic and lights cause buses to arrive in an approximation of randomness. Yet it doesn't seem random at all. It seems like you wait twenty minutes for a bus, then two or three arrive in tandem.

Cognitive scientist Steven Pinker tells of an experiment in which volunteers had to press a button whenever they heard a beep. The subjects knew the beeps were supposed to occur randomly in time. They complained that the machine was broken: "The beeps are coming in bursts. They sound like this: 'beepbeepbeepbeepbeep...beep...beepbeep...beepitybeepitybeepbeepbeep." Explained Pinker, "They didn't appreciate that that's what randomness sounds like."

When the hot hand plays out in two or three dimensions of space rather than one of time, it is known as the illusion of clustering. During the London Blitz, rumor had it that the German bombs spared the neighborhoods of Nazi spies. Maps showed clusters of hits in certain neighborhoods and none in others. British intelligence took these rumors seriously enough to divide a map of London into squares and painstakingly count the bomb hits. They concluded that the bombs were indeed striking at random. Statistician William Feller remarked, "To the untrained eye, randomness appears as regularity or tendency to cluster." Many refused to believe it. As Chico Marx asked, "Who are you going to believe, me or your own eyes?"

Belief in the hot hand might seem to conflict with the better-known "gambler's fallacy." In the casino of Monte Carlo on August 18, 1913, "black" came up twenty-six times in a row. After about fifteen spins of black, word spread through the casino. Gamblers threw down cards and dice to mob the enchanted roulette table. Most wanted to bet on red. They believed that after so many blacks, red was due and stood a greater-than-usual chance. When this belief was proven wrong—as another, and another spin came up black—many doubled down, convinced that red was all the more likely on the *next* spin. The casino raked in millions of francs from the unusual run.

The gambler's fallacy is the belief that chance outcomes that haven't occurred in the recent past are more likely to occur in the near future. It's called a fallacy for a reason. ("I'm overdue for a win!" thinks every loser.) The gambler's fallacy incentivizes losers to keep on playing and to *not* learn from experience. Were gamblers endowed only with the survival instinct of rats in mazes, they would catch on that *nothing good happens when I play this game*. Instead, they keep on playing and may up the ante in reaction to losses. Unfortunately, roulette wheels have no way of knowing that they're due for a win. The odds remain the same, stacked against the player.

By this point you may be confused. It sounds like I'm saying that people believe that random winning streaks will continue… except when they believe the complete opposite. The gambler's fallacy and the hot hand theory are really two sides of the same coin. Both are consequences of the "law of small numbers."

That is a semifacetious rule proposed in 1971 by Amos Tversky and Daniel Kahneman. It runs,

> People's intuitions about random sampling appear to satisfy the law of small numbers, which asserts that the law of large numbers applies to small numbers as well.

To understand the point, and the verbal wit, you need to know what the "law of large numbers" is. It's one of the most fundamental rules of probability. When I toss a fair coin a few times, I don't necessarily get an even split of heads and tails. That would be asking too much of a random process. When I toss the coin a very large number of times, however, the proportion of heads will approach the expected value (50 percent) ever more closely.

The law of large numbers acknowledges that very small samples can't be expected to be representative of the process or the whole. We all know this, minus the fancy language, and sometimes we joke about it. The average American household has about 2.6 people. Not many have exactly that.

Tversky and Kahneman's law of *small* numbers is a rule of psychology. It says that we unreasonably expect small samples to reflect the underlying odds. Should you toss a fair coin ten times, the math says it's common to get a lopsided result like seven tails and three heads. Public opinion thinks otherwise. Show most people a coin that has just come up heads seven times out of ten, and they'll tell you there's something wrong with the coin.

No one is saying there *couldn't* be something wrong with the coin. A coin that came up heads 700 times of 1,000 *would* be biased, to near certainty. There's nothing suspicious about seven of ten, though, not if that's all the data you have.

To put it another way, we expect small samples to be like reality show casts: one jock, one dumb blonde, one gay, one black, one Asian, etc. They're supposed to "look like America." But those so-called reality shows have to be cast that way. A random sample of the population would be demographically lopsided one way or another.

The hot hand paper presents a unified theory embracing the hot hand and the gambler's fallacy. Gilovich, Vallone, and Tversky wrote,

> A conception of chance based on representativeness, therefore, produces two related biases. First, it induces a belief

that the probability of heads is greater after a long sequence of tails than after a long sequence of heads—this is the notorious gambler's fallacy....Second, it leads people to reject the randomness of sequences that contain the expected number of runs because even the occurrence of, say, four heads in a row—which is quite likely in a sequence of 20 tosses—makes the sequence appear nonrepresentative.

What causes people to switch between the gambler's fallacy and the hot hand theory? When confronted with something that is understood to be mechanical and outside human control, we default to the gambler's fallacy. When human will and agency are involved, we favor a hot hand belief.

The gambler accepts the unpredictability of the little ball skittering over the roulette wheel. He also believes in the law of small numbers. The only way to reconcile these two convictions is to imagine a Lady Luck who will put her thumb on the wheel, favoring red after a run of blacks—just to even things out. This is the gambler's fallacy.

In contrast, the basketball fan has no reason to believe that the game is random. It's about skill, strategy, and sports medicine (as well as luck). When a player has a long winning streak, unrepresentative of that player's long-term average, it's easy to believe that a mysterious hot hand is at work.

Hot hand thinking is probably more important than the gambler's fallacy in human affairs. The gambler's fallacy is a belief of the naïve that applies mainly to gambling equipment. More educated readers may scoff at the notion of a Lady Luck who micromanages cards and dice. The hot hand theory applies to human actions. It's *not* so obvious that hot hand beliefs are wrong, in basketball or anywhere else. Gilovich didn't know it was a misconception until he did the research. Smart people fall for the hot hand belief and base important decisions on it.

Did you hear the one about the optimist who fell off the Empire State Building? After falling fifty floors, he said, "So far, so good!"

This joke is a good introduction to the *representativeness heuristic.* Kahneman and Tversky coined that term to describe the tendency to believe that limited experience is representative of the big picture. (A *heuristic* is a mental shortcut.) The joke's optimist does not have much experience in falling off tall buildings, yet he's confident that his brief plunge—falling fifty stories without a scratch!—is representative of the fate that awaits him.

One day Kahneman and Tversky found themselves predicting the future careers of tots in their social circle. A fast-talking three-year-old would grow up to be an attorney, they joked. They knew they were making flippant forecasts from inadequate evidence. Despite that, they found considerable agreement on each child's future. In analyzing this, they realized that they were simply matching stereotypes. A motor-mouthed kid is representative of the lawyerly stereotype, and this prompted the prediction.

What's wrong with that? Nothing, as long as you take the prediction for what it is—a guess that is unlikely to pan out, given the huge number of possible adult occupations and the relatively small proportion of lawyers.

In an influential 1972 paper, Kahneman and Tversky argued that many of our informal estimates of probability are based on representativeness. Their method was to survey people, describing hypothetical situations and asking them to estimate probabilities. They found that people were wrong in consistent ways.

One scenario ran like this. In a certain city, every family with exactly six children was interviewed. It was found that seventy-two families had exactly six children with the birth order girl-boy-girl-boy-boy-girl (GBGBBG). Estimate how many six-children families had the birth order BGBBBB.

This may remind you of the Zenith radio experiments (a parallel that Kahneman and Tversky mention). Were girls and boys equally likely, all sixty-four possible combinations, from GGGGGG to BBBBBB, would be equally probable. A reasonable estimate for the number of BGBBBB families would therefore be the same as the given number of GBGBBG families, seventy-two. But the median guess offered was thirty. People felt that BGBBBB had to be less common than the "better-shuffled" GBGBBG. That, of course, is the intuition that guided the Zenith experiment guessing.

When presented with a difficult question, we sometimes ignore it and answer an easier one. (Watch the politicians on Sunday-morning TV shows for examples.) This tactic is most common when the answerer feels the "wrong" question has been asked and there is a greater truth to be spoken. That's probably what was going on here. The estimators knew that birth order was random and wanted to emphasize that in their answers. They favored the well-shuffled option, as it better fit their stereotype of randomness.

The *least* important conclusion to draw from this is that average people are bad at math. The real message is that we all make intuitive judgments of probability. The most important are judgments involving human actions. These generally can't be reduced to math or outsourced to an expert. Instead, we make these probability judgments largely by matching stereotypes. An athlete or a CEO with several successes in a row fits the "winner" stereotype, not the "random" or "loser" stereotypes.

We feel that successes *have* to be significant; that a winning streak will continue.

The question remains, why are we so predictable, and so bad at predicting? It is easier to demonstrate *how* the mind works than to say *why*. One guess is that people are reproducing their faulty conception of randomness—much as the domestic dog's bark is said to be an unsuccessful attempt to mimic human speech.

An embezzler cooking the books could avoid same-digit streaks in the mistaken belief that they wouldn't be random. A basketball coach may believe that five baskets in a row are more statistically meaningful than they are. Doubtless people do have such thoughts.

This kind of thinking can't be the whole story. Perceptions and intuitions, not just conscious beliefs, are wrong. Some have asked why evolution would shape our minds to make inaccurate predictions.

It's been proposed that the representativeness heuristic has survival value after all. A splash of water, followed by a rustle in the bushes, could mean a crocodile is about to snatch the baby… or it could mean nothing at all. In this and many similar scenarios, it's better to foresee and take action (sometimes needlessly) than to shrug off the unpredictability of life and do nothing.

One thing is certain: The human problem with randomness is deep-seated. Psychologist Lola Lopes compared it to the parable of the blind men and the elephant—with the crucial difference that "unlike the situation with elephants, *no one at all* has ever seen what randomness is like."

The first half of this book dealt with the direct consequences of our inability to act randomly. Much of the time we deal with others who are playing the outguessing game themselves. We make *predictions about the group's predictions*. This second-order outguessing is the basis of the markets that assign values to sports bets, real estate, stocks, and much else.

As early as 1989, behavioral economist Colin F. Camerer asked, "Does belief in the hot hand matter for economics?" He proposed that it might in inefficient markets such as labor and housing. Companies could pay too much for a "winning" CEO's services; home buyers could overpay in the belief that a string of recent price increases will continue. Few would doubt either proposition today. In the years since, hundreds of studies have established the real-world impact of hot hand thinking. You can often beat the markets simply by betting against the hot hand. The following chapters will show you how.

Fifteen

How to Outguess Basketball Bracket Pools

Buttons won $10,000 in a 2010 Yahoo! Sports NCAA bracket contest. Buttons is a guinea pig.

The rodent's owner, University of Tennessee MBA student Jake Johnson, was peeved at how often his sister won the family bracket contest. The sister didn't watch basketball. Johnson figured that Buttons was more ignorant than his sister and therefore ought to do better. He read the team names to Buttons and picked the one that made the creature purr the most loudly. It worked. Johnson donated part of his winnings to a local guinea pig rescue shelter.

Buttons's victory demonstrates that sports outcomes are more random than we think and that our ability to outguess the game is often an illusion. Another conclusion is that—with all that misplaced confidence—sports bettors are leaving a lot of money on the table, for someone else to scoop up. In dollars wagered, National Collegiate Athletic Association (NCAA) bracket betting rivals the Super Bowl.

Ever since Gilovich, Vallone, and Tversky's 1985 paper,

gamblers have been trying to mint a sports betting system out of the hot hand. In its literal meaning, the *hot hand* pertains to the sequence of baskets or misses by an individual player. You can't normally bet on that. There are analogous beliefs about a team's sequence of winning and losing games, in basketball or any other sport. These beliefs must drive many bracket picks.

To win the NCAA championship, a team must win six games in a row. By normal standards, that's a hot streak. Of course, the tournament guarantees that exactly one team will achieve just that. Thinking about the needed streak of six wins prompts bettors to pick teams that they believe to be on a hot streak already. The sports media supplies an echo chamber for such thinking. Anytime a team wins a few games in a row, ESPN pundits dissect it and take it as a portent. "Will Duke go all the way? Only time will tell." Most of these streaks are meaningless, with little or no predictive value going forward. The result is that bracket bettors are much too inclined to favor a few "hot" teams.

In an office contest, bettors pay a fixed entry fee and fill out a tournament diagram (bracket) predicting the winners of all sixty-seven games of the NCAA Men's Division Basketball Championship. It's a single-elimination tournament where the first loss disqualifies a team from further play. Winners are matched against fellow winners, funneling down to the one undefeated team that becomes the tournament champion.

Each bettor must submit a complete bracket before the tournament begins. The picks have to be logically consistent. You can't predict that a team will be eliminated in one round and then have it reappear later on. Bettors score points for every winner they predict, and the bettor with the most points either wins the pot or gets the largest share of it. Note that predictions about losers are irrelevant. You might, for instance, predict that Ohio State will beat West Virginia in a second-round game. As long as Ohio State wins that game (against whomever), that counts as a correct prediction.

Many pools offer decreasing shares of the pot for runners-up. Ties are uncommon with most scoring systems. Perfect brackets—picking all the winners correctly—never happens. That's because the number of possible game outcomes is 2^{67}, an utterly astronomical number exceeding a hundred million trillion. If everyone on earth picked a bracket randomly, the chance of *anyone* coming up with a perfect bracket would be something like 1 in 20 billion.

Most picks are far from random. Since 2011 the tournament begins with the "First Four" games between eight evenly matched teams. These games are hard to call. After that, the first round pits sixty-four teams in thirty-two games. In each of four divisions, the teams are ranked from best ("#1 seed") to worst ("#16 seed"), based on their record. The #1 seed team always plays the #16 team. That's an extremely lopsided contest, so much so that in twenty-five years, no #1 team has ever lost to a #16.

The #2 team plays the #15 team, the #3 team plays the #14, and so on, down to a near-even matchup between the #8 and #9 teams.

The bracket form almost always gives the seeding rank, so this is public information that the most casual player can use. Serious bettors have many other sources of information. There are prediction markets that handicap teams, and scores of experts post their picks on the Web. You're free to copy them. There are clever apps that will pick your bracket for you. You can use them, and your coworkers may be using them against you. With all that allegedly good advice out there, is there a way to outguess an office pool in the digital age?

*   *   *

The first thing to realize is that there are three distinct goals in filling out a bracket:

- to predict as many winning teams as possible.
- to score as many points as possible.
- to win the pool.

Most bracketeers imagine these goals to be interchangeable. It's true that a bracket genius who can predict all the winners will max out points and win the pool. But you're not going to predict all the winners. Points are a fake currency that has value only insofar as it helps you win the pool. How many points you need depends on the competition. It's like the joke about the hunter who puts on running shoes in bear country. "You think you can outrun a bear?" asks his friend.

"I don't have to," the hunter answers, "I just have to outrun you."

The good news is that you can expect to pick about 58 percent of the winning teams in your bracket (around thirty-nine out of the sixty-seven games, on average). The bad news is, everyone else has about the same advantage.

Some think they can predict more accurately by listening to sports shows or copying brackets of the smartest experts. Good luck with that. That's one message of a 2001 paper in *Management Science* by Edward H. Kaplan and Stanley J. Garstka of Yale. They wrote,

> The authors of this paper have unsuccessfully participated in NCAA pools for more than a decade. Simply put, we decided that we would like to win once in a while.... Surely there must be better and worse strategies

for garnering points in an office pool, but our experience suggested that we had only mastered the latter.

They compared several readily available sources of information: the seeding, the pre-March performance of the teams (converted into a "strength rating" to allow comparisons), the Las Vegas point spread, and such expert rating systems as Sagarin, Massey, and the Ratings Percentage Index. Their finding was that all the sources performed much better than random picking, and none was much better than any other. "Going with the seeds"—always picking the higher-ranked team—called games correctly 56 percent of the time (in four NCAA and NIT tournaments, 1998–1999). Sagarin was right 57 percent of the time, and picks based on the Vegas line or pre-March performance were each right 59 percent of the time. These differences were not statistically significant.

You may have discovered already that picking the seeds, or piggybacking on expert picks, is not the lazy man's road to riches. There are several reasons for that. One is that the other players have similar sources of information. Another is the scoring formula. Almost all pools award successively more points to correct picks in later rounds. Typically, the points double with each round. A big bucket of points goes to anyone who picks the tournament winner. It's rare to win unless you pick the tournament winner.

Some pools award extra points for calling an upset game, one where a lower-seeded team beats a higher-seeded team. The rationale is that upsets are harder to predict and therefore ought to be worth more points. This has consequences, some of them unintended. It can be best to pick an underdog *because* it's an underdog and will be worth more points, should it beat the favorite.

A lot of math, computer science, and psychology professors are basketball fans. They have studied point-maximizing strategies extensively. One takeaway is that there is no one-size-fits-all strategy. The optimal point strategy depends on the granular details of the pool's scoring and on how strongly the other bettors favor "hot" teams.

In their 2001 paper, Kaplan and Garstka looked at how four point-maximizing algorithms would have performed in an upset-bonus pool run by mathematician Erik Packard in 1998 and 1999. In both years a point-maximizing app would have won Packard's tournament, had one been entered.

Computer scientist Tom Adams followed this up with an ambitious digital simulation. In effect, he simulated 100,000 Mad Marches in 100,000 parallel universes, using the estimated win probabilities that existed in this world, in 2001. Every possible match-up of Team A versus Team B was modeled as a biased coin. The estimated chance of A beating B equaled the chance of the coin coming up heads. The simulation essentially flipped that coin 100,000 times. The software tallied how well specific bracket entries would have fared in both of Packard's pools.

The computer-generated picks all did very well. The top three brackets, all algorithm based, together won 21 percent of simulated tournaments. Someone betting the top-performing bracket could have expected to more than triple his money on average.

Adams also did a simulation of another pool that *didn't* have upset bonuses. In this pool the humans beat the apps. The top six brackets were all by living, breathing fans.

Why the difference? All the computer entries picked Duke to win the tournament. Duke was the favorite, and Duke won. Common sense says you can't go wrong by picking the winner. But this is a case where common sense is wrong.

Though Duke *did* win, any reasonable model would allow that this was not preordained. A freak loss, anywhere in the tournament, would have nixed Duke's shot at the championship. All the expert models granted a substantial probability to Duke's *not* winning. Adams's simulation took that into account. Duke won in some of the simulated games and not in others.

The problem was that Duke was overbet. In general, pool players are too inclined to pick favorites. Harvard economist Andrew Metrick, who looked at twenty-four pools in cities from Boston to San Francisco, found that 78 percent of brackets picked one of the four #1 seed teams to win the tournament. But the record books show that these four teams win only about half the time.

This is partly a hot hand belief. A single-elimination tournament is like a pinball game, subject to a good deal of randomness. The teams that win tournaments are usually good *and* lucky. Fans underestimate the luck part. They suppose that the team's recent performance is representative of its underlying talent, and that a regular-season hot streak will persist into March.

The preference for favorites also demonstrates a failure to understand bracket strategy. Look at what happened in Adams's simulation. In the virtual games where Duke won, those who called it were competing with many others who had also picked Duke. That decreased the chance of any individual Duke-favoring bracket happening to be the one to score the most points. This is the same principle discussed earlier that applies to picks of popular lottery numbers.

The most successful brackets in Adams's simulation were contrarian. They picked Stanford or Michigan State to win. Though the chance of this happening was less, when it *did* happen there was less competition. Contrarian brackets stood a greater chance of winning the pool.

Adams's simulation also confirmed that the best strategy depends on the precise scoring formula. When a pool rewards players who pick upsets, that can override everything else. Though upset bonuses were intended to make the game more interesting, the average person is unable to factor them into a set of picks. Software prevails over humans, *not* because the software is better at predicting winners but because it's able to optimize for the scoring system.

Pools with upset bonuses have therefore opened a gap between merely human and computer-aided players. Should your office pool have that kind of scoring, you'll need to use an app. There are a number of good, free ones online. Make sure you pick one that lets you enter the details of the scoring formula (like Tom Adams's Poologic.com).

Why doesn't everyone use an app? When Poologic first came out, efficient-market types insisted it would be useful only for a couple of Marches. Then everybody would start using it. This hasn't happened. "In spite of the publicity, Poologic gets only a few thousand hits per year," Adams told me. The fact is that many players enjoy betting on teams they like. With a small office pool, there's a fairly good chance you'll be the only one using a point-maximizing app.

Let's follow the money. A typical pool costs $10 to enter. Most pools have no commission (sometimes the pool manager reserves the right to submit a bracket without paying). You need to have an expectation of winning back your $10 to break even.

It's impractical to figure your return from experience. March comes but once a year. In a big office, a bracket entry is like a lottery ticket. You may *never* win, as long as you work at the company. So Jarad B. Niemi, Bradley P. Carlin, and Jonathan M. Alexander estimated bettor returns from three years of a Chicago office pool they entered. They found that

60 percent of the submitted brackets were net money losers. But about 15 percent were good enough to double the player's money. Even richer opportunities are out there. Metrick estimated that a bracket picking Arizona in 1993—an underbet team that did in fact lose—offered expected returns as high as 423 percent. A $10 bet would get you $52.30 on average, in a pool of 200. It's hard to top those odds.

This and other profitable brackets were both probable (Arizona had a decent chance of winning the tournament) and contrarian (not too many were betting on Arizona). When the outcome deviates from the favorites, the winning bracket will be one that has predicted some upsets. This is true even when the scoring system doesn't give extra points for upsets. As a result, the winning bracket will almost always be quirky. This is behind the folk wisdom that you need to challenge the experts; that people who don't follow basketball beat fans; that guinea pigs beat humans, sometimes. The question is when to go rogue and by how much.

"People tend to pick upsets early and go conservative in the Final Four," explained Bryan Clair, a Saint Louis University mathematician and avid player. "If you're in a big pool, you need to flip-flop that: Go boring in early rounds, and slightly strange in the Final Four."

I'll describe a practical way to fill out a bracket for a small office pool.

1. Listen to the other bettors. You'll probably hear plenty of hot hand magical thinking. Such-and-such a player or team is on a streak that is sure to continue. You should pay attention to this talk. You won't learn who's going to win but you will learn how your coworkers are going to bet.

With many pools, you can review the last year's entries. This is informative, too, for most bettors don't change their strategy or favorite teams much from year to year. If, for any reason, you're not able to learn your coworkers' picks, there are other sources of information. Yahoo!, ESPN, and other websites supply pick frequencies for the current year. While a website's national data needs to be tailored to your office's geographical loyalties, they give a first approximation of how your coworkers are filling out their brackets.

2. Get a printout or link to the exact scoring formula.

3. Go to Poologic or another good app. Enter your pool's scoring formula. It will generate a point-maximizing bracket. You won't be using it as is, but you will use it as a template to be customized.

4. Change the bracket's tournament winner. The most favored team rarely has much of an advantage over other highly favored teams. The people who insist on picking the top team are overpaying for a small advantage.

The research suggests that the sweet spot for a tournament winner pick is the team ranked second to sixth overall. That would be the four #1 seed teams *minus* the favorite and the two best #2 seed teams.

Many bettors pick a team that's close over one that's far away. "I live in a Big Ten town, so as a rule, the Big Ten is overbet," said Bradley Carlin, a biostatistician at the University of Minnesota. "Because everyone has seen a lot of Gopher games, they've seen Purdue, Indiana, Illinois. They're thinking, 'I saw them play the Gophers, and they were pretty good that day.'"

This is another example of how people think their limited experience is representative of an uncertain reality. Find the high-rated team that is most underbet in your office. You replace the app's tournament winner with the moderately contrarian one applicable to your office. Then work backward, changing any app picks to be consistent with that champion.

5. An optional step is to switch a few other picks for close games—in each case going for the slight underdog. This will help to distinguish your bracket from someone who might have used the same app.

In most bracket pools there is no taboo against submitting more than one entry. You might want to play several brackets that differ only in the pick of the tournament winner. Apps can provide guidance here, too. Poologic has an ROI (Return on Investment) calculator that estimates the profitability of the various choices for tournament winner. You enter as much information as you know or can guess: how many people in your office are picking each team as champ, and the total number of brackets in the pool. The calculator guesstimates the likely return, in dollars and cents, for betting on each possible champ.

A team with a return of $1 would be a break-even bet. A wild bet on a low-seeded team might return a billionth of a cent. In general, only about four teams are judged to be profitable bets. Those betting just one bracket should pick the most profitable one. When submitting more than one, stick with the profitable bets.

It won't come as a big surprise that some NCAA pools are hostile to app picks. Adams has many tales of harassment. In Chicago, Bradley Carlin won three out of five years. "The pool was disbanded and then reorganized, and he was uninvited to play."

Another algorithmic player, *New York Times* editor Victor Mather, won a first, a third, and a fifth place over a six-year period, in a 250-player pool. He wrote Adams,

> ...Last year the pool organizer sent me an e-mail saying I was cheating by picking so many long shots!

Then this year's pool contains the following note:
"The Board has discovered that some entrants in previous years have used a formula for trying to pick upsets. This runs counter to the spirit of the pool and the awarding of bonus points. The purpose of the pool is to pick winners of games and be rewarded by identifying unlikely victors. It is not to capitalize on a formula and gain an edge on entrants who are playing by the spirit of the rules. Therefore any entry deemed by the Board to be a 'formula play' will be rejected."

Pool managers aren't always quick to see the ramifications of the rules they make. Adams tells of one manager who decided—just for fun—to offer a substantial prize to the bracket that did the *worst*. Naturally, the worst-bracket winner was a guy who just bet all the worst seeds. The pool manager never saw that coming. He disqualified the worst-bracket winner for violating the spirit of the game.

I'll leave it to you to decide whether you care to subject your coworkers to your superior bracket outguessing. Victor Mather offers these observations: "No matter how successful you are, few people will copy you. And you're not likely to develop a reputation as a basketball oracle, either. Instead, if my experience is any guide, you'll be viewed as a nut, or at best an absentminded professor, who seems to get awfully lucky in the pool every year."

Recap: How to Outguess Basketball Bracket Pools

• Try to learn how other pool players are betting, or check last year's brackets.

• Enter your pool's scoring formula in a bracket app like Poologic.com. The app tells you the bracket most likely to win, but that is not necessarily the most profitable bet.

• Pick an underdog for tournament winner—a team ranked second to sixth overall that is *not* favored by other pool members. Make any necessary changes to the app's bracket. In large pools you may want to pick another close underdog in the Final Four.

Sixteen

How to Outguess Office Football Pools

For many sports bettors, the most serious impediment to monetizing the hot hand is the bookie commission. As you may have gathered, sports books are not charities. They take a cut of each bet placed. For a standard point-spread bet, you need to be right 52.38 percent of the time just to break even.

Spread betting was invented by math-teacher-turned-bookie Charles K. McNeil in the 1940s. McNeil's intention was to manage risk. Though bookies are in the business of selling risk, they don't much care for it themselves. The point spread is designed to eliminate unhappy surprises—for the bookie, not his customers.

Most gamblers like to bet on a favorite. To attract bets to the underdog, bookies have to offer long odds. This inducement is often inadequate. Bettors *still* want to wager on the team that's more likely to win, requiring the bookie to offer longer odds yet on the underdog. That worries bookies, for an upset win could be bankrupting.

McNeil's solution was to convert every bet into a fifty-fifty proposition. For a wager on the favorite to win, the favorite has to beat the underdog by a specified number of points. Say that Cincinnati is favored over Baltimore with a spread of 4.5 points. (The spread is often quoted in half points to avoid "ties.") Cincinnati wins the game narrowly, 22 to 20. But since it didn't "cover the spread"—win by at least 4.5 points—those who wager on Cincinnati lose, and those who bet on Baltimore win.

In McNeil's conception, the point spread is chosen so that half the money wagered will be on the favorite and the other half on the underdog. The result is a bulletproof business plan. When the bets are balanced, the bookie can skim his vigorish off the top and use the losers' wagers to pay off the winners. No matter who wins, the bookie never has to dip into his own pocket.

The media often refers to point-spread betting as a prediction market, a term that has lately taken on an aura of infallibility. A spread of five points supposedly means that the median bettor believes the favorite will beat the underdog by five points. It's the crowd's prediction.

This is *not* quite true, and it's important to understand why. In 2004 economist Steven Levitt (the coauthor of *Freakonomics*) advanced the theory that bookies set the point spread to maximize their profits—not to run a fancy-schmancy prediction market. They don't always balance bets exactly, and the point spread might not reflect the crowd's average opinion. This theory is now called the Levitt model.

I'll give an extreme example to illustrate Levitt's point. A crooked bookie knows that the big fight is fixed and the crowd's favorite is sure to take a dive. The bookie would prefer that as many people as possible bet on the favorite. He would have no interest in balancing bets. The bookie might even want to move the point spread in the "wrong" direction to encourage more bets on the favorite. He knows that every bet on the favorite will lose and be money in his pocket.

Bookies usually aren't that certain, but the same principle applies whenever they know more than the bettors do. Bookmakers are presumably aware of all the common bettor biases (including hot hand beliefs) and bake them into their point spreads. Levitt showed that there are limits to how far bookies can press their advantage. They have to make sure that a bettor who's just as smart as the bookies cannot profit from these intentionally misplaced point spreads.

Consider the *bet-the-underdog strategy*. From 2001 to 2008, NFL underdogs—the teams expected to lose, according to the point spread—won 51.1 percent of resolved bets. (This excludes "tie" cases where no money changed hands because the teams just made the point spread.) A bettor who knows zilch about football and simply wagers on every underdog will win more often than not. He just won't make any money. The win rate isn't good enough to beat the bookie commission—and the bookies make sure it's not.

Studies of real-world betting have confirmed that Levitt was right. Bookies do not stand in awe of the wisdom of bettor crowds. They believe they're smarter than the crowd, set point spreads accordingly, and make more profit than would be possible with balanced bets. To find out what the betting crowd thinks, then, you can't just look at the point spread. You've also got to look at how much money was bet on each side. Many researchers have done that, and some have examined the hot hand specifically.

One 2011 paper found that betting on an NFL home team increased 3.15 percent when the team had won the past two games. There was no evidence that such hot streaks budged the likelihood of winning the next game. They just increased the willingness to bet hard-earned money.

There is some reason to believe that bet-the-underdog can

be made profitable by choosing wagers selectively. Levitt examined bets from a Las Vegas sports book's promotional tournament. He found that point-spread bets on an NFL underdog playing at home won an amazing 57.7 percent of the time. That's well over the 52.38 percent needed for a profit net of commission.

To make that absolutely clear: Find an NFL game where the point-spread underdog is playing in its home stadium. Bet $110 on that underdog. When you win, you gain $100 and also get your $110 wager back. If Levitt's 57.7 percent win rate is typical, you'll be looking at a 10 percent average profit on every bet.

Why should it be good to bet on a team playing at home? Most likely, bettors forget to factor in the not-entirely-mythic home court advantage. The home team sleeps in their own beds, knows the stadium, and has the hometown media's support. The visiting team is battling jet lag and the temptation to party in an exciting new city; they aren't so motivated to perform for a crowd that's jeering them. This isn't news to any real gambler, but someone who's sure the Giants are superior to the Cowboys may not always check the travel schedule before placing a bet.

It's tough to say whether the casino tournament that Levitt studied was typical. Research on regular betting points in the same direction but is usually less optimistic. A wager on home underdogs would have won 53.3 percent of the time in the NFL (over twenty-one seasons, from 1980 to 2001); 53.2 percent of the time in NCAA college football games (2002 season); 53.0 percent in the National Basketball Association (2002 season). All would have narrowly beaten the bookie commission.

In a 2010 article, Sean Wever and David Aadland, two economists at the University of Wyoming, looked at all the

NFL games from 1985 through 2008, some 5,976 matches in all. They found that the higher the spread, the more profitable the underdog strategy was. One likely reason is that teams that are way ahead don't bother to run up the score in the game's final minutes. Coaches hate to risk injuries for points the team doesn't need. This would yield more games where the favorite won but not by enough to beat the spread. That would work to the advantage of those betting on the underdog.

Wever and Aadland describe one strategy that they project to have about a 53 percent chance of winning. You bet on an underdog home team when the spread is at least 6.5 points, or an underdog visiting team when the spread is at least 10.5 points.

For example, the Indianapolis Colts began the 2006 season by winning their first nine games and ended it by winning the Super Bowl. Throughout the season, the media fawned over them. In six games the Colts were a seven-point-or-more home favorite or a ten-point-or-more visiting favorite. Despite that, they covered the spread in only one of these six games. In three games Indianapolis won, but not by the needed margin. Had you been betting on Indianapolis in these high-spread games, you would have lost five games out of the six. Had you been betting against the Colts, you would have won five out of six.

One problem with sports betting systems is that anyone who looks hard enough for a pattern tends to find one. It might be that the Denver Broncos always won on odd-numbered days in February when playing teams named after animals. Analytics is good at finding such patterns. It's not so good at saying whether you should believe in them.

Wever and Aadland derived their strategy from the period 1985 to 1999 and then tested it on the years 2000 to 2008. In six of those eight seasons, their strategy would have had a profit over the bookie commission. Another season would have been virtually break-even, with a 52.0 win percentage. That bolsters the case that the system's success is not just a fluke.

On average, about two NFL games a week meet the criteria for the Wever-Aadland strategy. Had it been applied over the entire twenty-three-year time frame, it would have won 53 percent of bets, enough to secure a 1 percent profit net of commission. It's possible to do better yet by being more selective. By focusing on underdogs with even larger point spreads (and making fewer bets), Wever and Aadland believe it's practical to achieve a win rate as high as 60 percent.

Publicizing a winning strategy may cause too many people to adopt it, thereby making it useless. That's worth considering. Ironically, one point in favor of the Wever-Aadland system is that it isn't all that new. The home and underdog advantages have been known for decades, and analyses of them turn up with some regularly in the *Journal of Sports Economics*. Most sports bettors aren't influenced by that discourse. They already "know" how to pick a winning team, from gut instincts and what they see on TV.

Bookies, of all people, must be aware of the home underdog advantage. They seem to have a hard time policing a handful of contrarians while profiting from the great mass of think-alike bettors. Levitt found that three-quarters of bettors pick favorites more than underdogs.

For those who like to gamble for recreation, betting the underdog—especially the long-shot home underdog—can shrink the bookie advantage to the vanishing point. Don't expect to get rich. Think of it as a way to gamble for free.

The title of this chapter promises advice on outguessing an office football pool. As with a March Madness pool, beating coworkers is a lot easier than beating bookies.

A typical football pool has a weekly list of about ten games. Each bettor must guess the point-spread winner for every match. The point spreads are lifted from the websites of the big Las Vegas sports books, offering the Las Vegas line without the bookie's cut. The player who predicts the most games correctly wins the pot. The pot is split equally in case of a tie, and some pools give lesser prizes to runners-up.

One drawback is that you can't cherry-pick the games where you believe you have an advantage. You have to guess the winners of all the games on the list.

In the early 1990s, Emmy's, a Dartmouth tavern frequented by the math faculty, was running a football pool. Grad student Joseph DeStefano noticed that many players were betting randomly. Some literally tossed a coin to decide which teams to pick. Why not? The point spread is supposed to offer fifty-fifty odds, and it comes close to that. It might seem there's no way to wring a profit from fair bets. DeStefano realized that there is.

He called his scheme the Evil Twin. It repurposes an idea from the self-correcting codes that cell phones use to communicate with the tower. Signals often get garbled, but the code allows software to guess the original data with amazing accuracy. DeStefano applied that principle to guessing which teams would win.

You don't have to know the theory to use DeStefano's system. With the Evil Twin strategy, you make two bets, each the mirror image of the other. If the first bet is for Green Bay to win, the second, "Evil Twin" wager would be for Green Bay to lose—and so on, for every other game in the pool's list.

It sounds crazy. Normally there is no advantage in placing competing wagers. You may bet on two horses in a race, or on every horse running, and it won't do you a bit of good. It'll just draw your bankroll down all the more quickly.

Football pools are different because the objective is to come *closest* to a hard-to-attain goal. The goal in this case is to guess every game right. With ten games, there are 2^{10} or 1,024 possible outcomes. In a midsize office pool, it's unusual for anyone to get all the predictions right. Ties are common. When three bettors each guess seven games correctly out of ten, and no one else does better, they split the pot three ways. The advantage of the Evil Twin strategy comes from minimizing ties.

Look at the simplest possible case. There is just one game on the list (Bengals versus Ravens), and just two bettors. Call them Joe and Jane. Each wager costs $1. Joe places two bets (one for himself and one for his imaginary twin) and Jane places one, so the pot comes to $3.

Joe bets on the Bengals and, separately, on the Ravens. Jane picks whichever team she wants. Assuming the point spread is right, Jane has a 50 percent chance of winning. If Jane wins, she will share the $3 pot with Joe. That's because one or the other of Joe's two bets has to win. Jane's share would be $1.50. Jane can expect to win only half the time. Her average winning is half of $1.50, or $0.75.

That's not so good, considering that she wagered $1. In the long run, Jane can expect to lose $.25 every time she wagers.

That money is vacuumed up by Joe. It can't go anywhere else. Joe guarantees himself a win by betting both sides. Should Jane pick incorrectly, Joe gets the $3 pot to himself. Otherwise, Joe shares the pot with Jane and gets $1.50. Both scenarios are equally likely. Joe's expectation is half of $3 plus half of $1.50, or $2.25. Deduct the $2 Joe wagered, and he's got a $0.25 profit—which of course comes from Jane.

DeStefano used math to show that the Evil Twin scheme always delivers an expectation of profit, no matter how many players are in the pool or how many games they're betting on. The strategy's profit peaks when there are four players (five bets, counting the Evil Twin one) predicting an odd number of games. Then the strategy player can expect a 17.2 percent profit on every dollar wagered.

As the number of players in the pool increases, the profit slowly decreases. The expected gain is close to one divided by the number of players in the pool. An easy-to-remember rule: With ten players betting on ten games, the system's profit is about 10 percent.

These profits are possible because of clustering. When bettors pick winning teams randomly, their choices tend to cluster (like the random bomb hits in the London Blitz). Many bettors will pick the same teams purely by coincidence. By making a bet *and* its complete opposite, you increase the chance that one will be a contrarian pick, with less competition and less likelihood of a shared jackpot.

On top of the random clustering is a psychological clustering. In general, bettors think alike. They pick favorites, local teams, and teams on winning streaks. None of these have much or any predictive power in a point-spread game, but they do nudge bettors into making similar picks. Office pools are further subject to groupthink. Water-cooler theorizing will enforce shared beliefs about which teams are likely to win. This makes it all the more profitable to challenge the crowd. The Evil Twin works when bettors pick randomly, and it works even better when they don't.

The Evil Twin strategy applies only to pools where the goal is to pick the most winners in point-spread games (or games where the chances are fifty-fifty). In practice, that limits it mainly to football pools. At Dartmouth, DeStefano's strategy raised ethical questions as well as mathematical ones. Is it cheating? Most football pools don't have complicated rules about what's legal and what's not. Normally, each player places one bet only. It's easy to get around that by teaming with another player. You and your partner coordinate bets and agree to split winnings. It would be difficult to prohibit that. Of course, it's also difficult to prevent coworkers from stealing staplers.

While mulling that over, consider this: The Evil Twin strategy is counterintuitive because, deep down, most serious bettors think they *can* predict winners. Why stake half your money on a bet that's the exact opposite of what you believe will happen?

You *shouldn't* do that, provided your predictions are sufficiently accurate. Were you 100 percent certain your picks were right, you should stick with them and forget the Evil Twin. But no one should be that confident in football, least of all with point-spread bets.

There is a threshold probability beyond which you don't need the Evil Twin. This threshold isn't a very high bar, about 52 percent. Anyone who can pick the winners of games in the pool with much greater than 52 percent accuracy is better off simply placing his own bets and forgetting about the Evil Twin.

That may sound tempting, but remember, you can't select the games to bet on. Also, the 52-percent threshold is a theoretical value for bettors picking winners randomly from among all the possible permutations. When you factor in psychology, the Evil Twin system probably performs better than the math says.

Recap: How to Outguess Office Football Pools

• Bet-the-underdog strategies appear to offer profits net of bookie commission. One system is to wager only on underdogs playing at home when the spread is 6.5 points or more, or on underdog visitors when the spread is at least 10.5 points.

• The Evil Twin strategy can offer a substantial edge in small-to-medium office pools. Place two bets: one your usual set of picks, and the other an Evil Twin wager picking each of the "losing" teams of the first wager. To avoid suspicion, you might partner with another player and split winnings.

Seventeen

How to Outguess Oscar Pools

I recently won a small Academy Awards pool. To my competitors I appeared not just well informed but clairvoyant. I of course knew that *Argo* would win Best Picture, and I also correctly predicted Christoph Waltz's upset win for Best Supporting Actor. I even had a bit of an idiot savant mystique, for I had not seen some of the nominated films, and I beat players who had seen them all. How did I do it? I simply did some real-life mentalism using the strategic elements of Oscar pools.

A typical office pool lets you place your bet as late as Friday before Oscars Sunday—sometimes right up until the telecast. By then the writers', directors', screen actors', and producers' guilds have announced their own awards. There are strong statistical correlations between these other awards and the Academy's, for one thing because the memberships overlap. From 2005 to 2013 the Screen Actors Guild "best actor" won the Oscar, too.

More to the point, there are accurate prediction markets for Oscars. In sports, prediction markets are hampered by the games' built-in randomness. Look at the shape of a football.

The way it bounces can be as capricious as a coin toss. Sometimes that bounce decides a close game. The crowd can't anticipate that, no matter how wise they may be about the teams' overall strengths.

Prediction markets are good at aggregating what the crowd already knows. That describes the Oscars, where the votes reflect opinions that Academy members have held for weeks or months. Oscar prediction markets are not forecasting the future but deducing a poorly kept secret.

The first step to winning an Oscar pool, then, is to consult a prediction market like Betfair or the Hollywood Stock Exchange. I am not suggesting that you place a bet. The sites that offer real-money wagers charge a fee, and you would have to have a substantial information edge to make a profit that way. I am saying you can use the free information on prediction markets to gain an edge in office pools.

On Friday, two days before the 2013 awards, the now-defunct site Intrade was quoting these chances for the favorites:

Best Picture: *Argo* (83.0%)
Best Actor: Daniel Day-Lewis (95.9%)
Best Actress: Jennifer Lawrence (60.0%)
Best Director: Steven Spielberg (69.9%)
Best Supporting Actor: Tommy Lee Jones (40.7%)
Best Supporting Actress: Anne Hathaway (89.9%)

There was a clear favorite in each of these categories except Supporting Actor.

Based on the above odds, you would expect about two upsets. That's exactly what happened. Ang Lee won Best Director instead of Spielberg, and Christoph Waltz won Best Supporting

Actor instead of Jones. Intrade had given Lee a 22.0 percent chance of winning and Waltz a 39.0 percent chance.

You shouldn't automatically pick the prediction market favorites. The best way to cast your ballot depends on your fellow entrants.

They can be categorized into three groups. One is the low-information bettor who is only playing because everyone else is. This person will favor the most recognizable name in each category.

Another is the hipster-cinefile who sees every nominated movie and votes on the basis of what she and her social circle like. These players fall victim to the law of small numbers. They imagine that their friends' tastes are representative of the Academy voters'. That's highly unlikely. A 2012 *Los Angeles Times* investigation found a nun, a bookstore owner, and a retired Peace Corps recruiter who were voting members. Academy membership is for life, but Hollywood careers aren't, so many voters haven't worked on a film for years. The *Times* reported that the Academy voters were 77 percent male, 94 percent white, with a median age of 62. That's right—half are retirement age or older. Compare that to your office pool's demographics.

A third category of player is the hard-core strategist who consults the prediction markets. This is the type you have to worry about.

Should you believe that all the other players are Oscar buzz–deficient, you'd do best by going with the straight prediction market picks. These choices have the best chance of being right. The strategy needs to be adjusted when there are other well-informed players in the pool. In that case, you may want to choose a contrarian pick. That will usually be a second-place choice, going by the prediction market odds. Should you luck out and be correct, you would leap ahead of the pack of informed voters.

That's what I did. In 2013 Tommy Lee Jones's Intrade chances for Best Supporting Actor (40.7 percent) were only marginally greater than Christoph Waltz's (39.0 percent). I wasn't giving up much by going with Waltz. I did so because I believed that a disproportionate number of players were backing the front-runner, Jones, and/or a sweep for his film *Lincoln*. That made Waltz a smart choice. It turned out to be the right pick — but really, I didn't know anything beyond the odds and some strategy.

I didn't predict Ang Lee's upset win. Neither did any other well-informed player, so my loss there didn't hurt.

I use this formula to evaluate contrarian picks:

$$N_F P_U / N_U P_F$$

It's the estimated number of pool players betting the favorite nominee (N_F) in a category times the prediction-market probability that the underdog nominee (P_U) wins, divided by the number of pool players betting the underdog (N_U), times the probability that the favorite wins (P_F). Here *underdog* means the nominee rated second most likely to win. The prediction markets will give you exact numbers for the probabilities. The number of people betting will be your guesstimates.

This ratio is a measure of how advantageous it is to bet the underdog. It equals 1 when the percentage of people betting on the favorite and on the underdog is in proportion to the chances of those nominees winning. When it's more than 1, you can increase your expected win rate by betting on the underdog. When it's less than 1, you're better off with the favorite.

In a large pool, like a national contest on the Web, it would make sense to bet on every underdog with a favorable ratio. In a small pool, a player who makes a single contrarian pick is unlikely to be sharing a jackpot. There's no point in diminishing the chance of winning further by additional underdog picks. You're better off choosing one underdog with a favorable ratio *and* a decent chance of winning. In this case Lee was too much of a long shot (22 percent chance of winning), and so was Emmanuelle Riva, a contender for Best Actress (31 percent). I chose Waltz as my underdog pick and stuck with the favorite in the other categories.

Recap: How to Outguess Oscar Pools

• Check the prediction markets at the last possible moment before casting your ballot. In most categories, you'll bet on the favored nominee.

• Pick an underdog or two to minimize the chance of ties. This should be a second-place nominee (going by the prediction market probabilities) that few in the pool are betting on.

Eighteen

How to Outguess Big Data

Predictive analytics is the technology of wringing predictions and profits from the seemingly irrelevant. It silently churns data to guess locations of meth labs and carjackings; to put a price tag on the value of customers, employees, and managers; and, above all, to predict who will buy what and pay how much. Big Data makes the most of its ninja invisibility. The consumer rarely suspects how many of his actions have been tracked and outguessed. The predictions are not perfect (yet). And just as Claude Shannon could outguess his own prediction machine, you can outguess Big Data. This chapter will describe a few of the more widely applicable tricks.

You've probably gotten weird calls from your cell phone carrier, cable company, or health club. The caller will ask if there's anything she can do to serve you better. She's not being neighborly. The call means that an algorithm has predicted that you're likely to "churn" (cancel your service).

Customers are hard to dissuade once they've made up their mind to cancel. So predictive analytics is used to guess which customers will cancel before they know it themselves.

Every time you go to the gym, you swipe your card. The algorithm knows whether your gym visits have been trailing off of late. It also knows how often people in your demographic group, with similar declines in attendance, have canceled.

Or maybe it's your cell phone company and they know, based on your data usage, that you'd get a much better deal with a competitor's plan. They also know that the competitor is launching a big ad campaign.

Since the predictions are not a sure thing, the conversation starts out chatty. The caller, following a script, is stalling to see whether you volunteer any complaints. Should the caller determine that the prediction was wrong and you're a satisfied customer, the call ends there.

Otherwise, you'll be presented with the so-called primary offer — a discount or freebie to accept a new contract. *Never accept a primary offer.* Once you reject it, the caller will bring up the secondary offer. It's all in the script. Sometimes the secondary offer is better; other times it's just different. You might as well hear both offers. You can always reverse yourself and ask for the first after hearing the second.

A still better strategy is to reject all offers. Wait a few days, then call to cancel the service. (Do this even if you intend to keep it.) You'll find that scripts sometimes offer sweeter deals for customers who initiate the call to cancel. Once again, you want to reject the first offer and listen to the second. Accept the best deal — assuming you want to continue the service.

Here's a grim thought for the next time you're waiting to speak to a customer service representative. Whether you're put on hold is sometimes determined by a prediction of how profitable a customer you are. The jargon is ARPU, for "average revenue per user." To Big Data, we're all slabs of consumer meat.

The call center's software uses caller ID, just as some psychic hotlines do. In case you've never tried it, Googling a phone number usually returns a name and address. Another search or two, and you've got plenty. Boiler-room psychics play out this information to convince the gullible of their powers. Big Data has other methods.

Neustar Information Services, a data firm based in suburban Virginia, specializes in "real-time consumer insights." When people call Jenny Craig, one of Neustar's clients, an algorithm "pinpoints a caller's location within feet." It knows whether the person is calling from a cell phone or landline and has the mailing address of the account. Neustar is able to rate customer profitability instantly. Its software can predict the odds that a credit card applicant will qualify. When the chance is high, the customer gets to speak to a human being immediately. Presumed deadbeats are shunted to an overflow call center far, far away.

The next time you have trouble getting through to a business, you might want to hang up and call back using an Internet phone service like Google Voice. This time the software will see your Internet phone number, not your regular one. That won't always work in your favor, but sometimes it will. Phone numbers are more useful in weeding out "unprofitable" customers than in identifying good ones. "Knowing the bottom is more important than knowing the top," explained Gordy Meyer, founder of the consumer analytics firm eBureau. "If we can find twenty-five percent who have zero chance of [buying], we can say 'don't waste your money on them.'" Your Internet phone number is likely to have less data attached to it than your main number. Companies want new customers, so they are unlikely to lump blank slate numbers in with the bad apples.

Why not just dial *67 on your regular phone to block caller ID? It's a little-known fact that *67 doesn't work with toll-free numbers. Not only can the company read your phone number, but they also know you blocked caller ID for that call. That *does* look suspicious.

Go into Starbucks and you'll find three sizes of coffee with confusing names: Tall, Grande, and Venti. A Starbucks newbie might imagine that Tall is the large size... until she notices that it's cheapest and is actually the smallest. Since new customers don't know quite what they're getting, they tend to order the middle choice, Grande. Guess what? The three sizes are twelve, sixteen, and twenty ounces. The Grande is sixteen ounces, and you've just ordered *two* full cups of expensive coffee.

Analytics of sales data reveals just how contingent our choices are. The customer does not necessarily walk in the door knowing exactly how much caffeinated beverage she wants. That is a detail invented on the spur of the moment while checking e-mail or checking out the barista. When you give a customer three choices — say, small, medium, and large — and when that customer has no overriding reason to choose one over another, there is a tendency for the customer to go with the middle choice. In the marketing literature, this is known as extremeness aversion. It's comparable to the way a magician's volunteer picks a card or cup in the middle, not too close to either end.

In this case it's the retailer who is the magician. The retailer engineers choices in such a way as to maximize profits. That typically means making the middle choice a little bigger or more expensive than what the median customer would otherwise choose.

This devious tactic works best with customers who aren't

that price sensitive—as at Starbucks or the Apple Store. Apple's iPads currently come with 16, 32, 64, and 128 gigabytes of storage. The second choice, 32 GB, has been the most popular. Is it because the customer knows he needs exactly 32 GB? No, most couldn't tell you how many gigabytes they've got on their laptop. They pick a choice in the middle precisely because they *don't* know what they need.

Whenever you're not sure which of several options is right for you, take that as a cue to think seriously about picking the smallest or cheapest one.

The most ambitious goal of Big Data may be differential pricing. This means tailoring prices to the individual, based on predictions of how much that consumer is willing to pay. It sounds unfair and un-American and *Blade Runner*–ish. Well, that ship has sailed. We've long had differential pricing in certain markets. Vacationers who plan ahead get lower airfares than businesspeople who can't. Coupons, rebates, and loyalty cards are other examples. The shoppers who bother with them save pennies over those who can't be bothered.

There is industry talk of a not-too-distant day when posted prices will be obsolete. Each consumer will, by technology to be determined, see a price customized to him or her alone. We're already starting to see the outlines of that. The cashier at my supermarket recently invited me to apply online for a new program offering personalized discounts. There are no coupons to bother with; you just download an app to your smartphone. It gives you a list of discounts based on your shopping history.

What history? *Everything.* You've been using a loyalty card, right? The algorithm knows everything you've ever bought, as long as you swiped that card. The program is called Just for U and the supermarket's FAQ page has a pertinent question.

Why don't you just give me these prices in the store?
If every shopper were exactly like you, we could! But the reality is every Vons customer is different. This program is personalized just for U!

Uh-huh. A more complete answer is that they're trying to learn how much of a discount it takes to make you switch brands. Personal discount apps engage in price spoofing, offering consumers discounts on brands or products they don't normally buy, to see whether they react. Maybe your family likes Rice Krispies. You might get a good price on a store-brand rice cereal, or Cocoa Krispies, or Kashi granola. If the algorithm learns that many customers of a particular product are brand loyal, the company may be more inclined to raise prices (or to offer discounts only to those who would otherwise switch to a cheaper brand).

A Colorado blogger, Emily Vanek, discovered that she could milk her Safeway store's discounts by switching between Starbucks and Dunkin' Donuts ground coffee. Starbucks is more expensive. When Vanek switched to Dunkin' Donuts, she looked like a price-sensitive shopper. This got Vanek a discount on Starbucks. Next time she bought Starbucks, and that ultimately triggered a special deal on Dunkin' Donuts. This can apparently be continued indefinitely. Just as political campaigns lavish attention on those few voters who are on the fence, digital discounts flow to likely buyers who switch brands a lot.

Browser cookies customize your Web experience: Sometimes they customize your price. Navigate to the page of a product you intend to buy and note the price and shipping charges. Then clear your browser's cookies and check the price again. You may find it's lower (or there's free shipping or a coupon for your next purchase).

As a general rule, repeat buyers care less about price. The first time you sent your aunt chocolates on her birthday, you researched the many online chocolatiers and their prices. The second time, you probably skipped the comparison shopping and reordered from the same company. It had the best value before, so why reinvent the wheel? This is the sort of pattern that analytics zeros in on. Some sites offer a better deal to new customers.

It's not hard to clear cookies. Go into your browser's settings, choose "Privacy" or some such heading, and click "Remove all website data." The drawback is that you'll be starting from zero with all websites. It's much easier to use two browsers. I use Safari for everyday use (with cookies enabled) and Firefox (with cookies turned off). When I use Firefox, I'm a new customer to every site.

Then there's the abandoned shopping cart ploy. Put whatever you want to buy in a retail site's shopping cart. Click "check out." Begin filling out the form. Make sure you enter your e-mail address but don't enter any payment information. Leave the purchase in limbo and wait for the discounts to roll in.

Within a few days, you may get an e-mail reminding you about your abandoned shopping cart. Much of the time it will offer a discount, free shipping, or other inducements. A 2012 Reuters article noted that a litany of Web businesses, from Best Buy and Home Depot to Lands' End and Zappos, were doing this.

According to one study, about 65 percent of online shopping carts are abandoned. Some buyers are interrupted by the boss walking in, while others experience sticker shock at seeing the grand total with shipping and tax. A follow-up e-mail gives retailers a second chance to close the deal. Analytics shows that follow-up e-mails are more likely to be opened, and that discounts do indeed work. Some companies are willing to discount their profit to gain a new customer, knowing that repeat customers might not care so much about price (see above).

From the consumer's perspective, abandoning your shopping cart is like walking away from the car salesman. It may be necessary to get the best deal on the table.

Recap: How to Outguess Big Data

• When a company that bills you regularly calls to ask how they can serve you better, it's usually because their software has predicted that you're about to discontinue service. Seize the moment to negotiate a better deal.

• Retailers offer a confusing range of options to sell customers up — to persuade them to buy coffee or megabytes they don't need. When in doubt, consider the cheapest option.

• Supermarket discount apps and cards offer special deals to consumers who switch back and forth between two competing brands.

• Abandon your online shopping cart for a better deal. Select an item you intend to buy, start to check out, and enter your contact information but not payment. Then leave the site. In a few days you may get an e-mail reminder, often with a discount or free shipping.

Nineteen

How to Outguess Retail Prices

Is now a good time to buy a plasma TV, an airline ticket, or an apartment? Those with the knack of outguessing sales can live larger for less. That knack is becoming more and more important. Few people realize how often Amazon, Walmart, Target, and other big retailers change their prices. Most consumer prices are set by software that fluidly adjusts to competitor prices, consumer demand, and the calendar. Buyers who pat themselves on the back for Googling the "best" price often fail to consider the time element. Those who pay the best price at the wrong time can shell out double what someone else did a few days before or afterward.

On the next page is a price chart for a Microsoft Xbox 360 (Limited Edition Gears of War 3 bundle) as reported by the price-tracking app Decide.com. These are the *lowest* prices you could have obtained on the Web at any given moment in 2012. Though erratic, the price is clearly not a random walk. That means it's predictable to a degree.

The average rock-bottom Web price for this Xbox bundle was $379. The price hovered close to that average for most of the year. You could have paid as little as $280 or as much as $600. The

Xbox 360 Gears of War 3 Bundle
Lowest Web Prices

chart's main feature is the sharp increase on September 1, followed by a decline to Black Friday. This is a not-uncommon pattern for holiday gift items. Retailers raise the price so that it can be lowered for holiday "sales." The Xbox price sank to a favorable level for Black Friday and Cyber Monday, and then went abruptly up to $462. It would have been unwise to buy at that price. Bargain hunters shop on Black Friday and a few days afterward. Those shopping just after that are usually less price sensitive. But prices tend to revisit the Black Friday lows before Christmas, assuming the item remains in stock. Buyers and retailers are playing a game of chicken. Some buyers will blink and pay a high price to be sure of having an Xbox under the tree. Others will be willing to gamble and wait for the prices to come down. On December 1, Decide.com's outguessing machine was predicting that the Xbox bundle's price would "hold steady or drop ($133 on avg.)" over the following two weeks with 93 percent confidence. In fact, by December 4 it had dropped to $349.99.

Retail prices have become an emergent phenomenon. The retailers themselves don't know exactly what's going to happen next. The upward and downward jags in the chart are the result of individual sellers undercutting the competition or raising prices. These short-term price jitters are nearly impossible to predict. The scale of the biggest price changes is reasonably predictable.

For the most part, prices are confined to an envelope. Retailers prefer to sell at a markup to the wholesale cost. Even when they *don't* do that—when they get into a price war or intentionally sell at a loss to build traffic—they aren't going to allow themselves to lose too much money. This limits how far the price of a popular product can drop.

There is also a limit to how high prices can go. Should retailers get greedy and build too much profit into their pricing, somebody will undercut them and win most of the business.

Hence the envelope. When the price is at the low end of a range, you can be pretty sure you're getting a good deal. When it's at the high end, you should wait for prices to fall. It's that simple—but most buyers have no clue what the envelope is.

That's why price-checking apps are valuable. A good rule of thumb for many products is to never pay more than the average of the lowest Web prices over the past year.

There are exceptions, one being smartphones, tablets, high-end TVs, and other tech gadgets that become quickly obsolete with the introduction of a new model. For these purchases you need to be aware of the new product cycle, and the apps help there, too.

Recap: How to Outguess Retail Prices

• Use a price-tracking app or site (like Decide.com) for big-ticket purchases. Never pay more than the past year's average-lowest Web price.

• Buy anytime you find a 20+ percent discount from the average best price over the past year. It probably won't last long.

Twenty

How to Outguess Home Prices

In the 1980s the Boston housing market had gotten ridiculously expensive. Or so many believed, including Wellesley economist Karl Case. Case wondered whether there was an objective way to establish that homes were expensive. After all, a free market had set Boston's home prices. Buyers were paying them, and sellers were getting them. Case got the idea of comparing sales prices of the same homes over time. This would track the home market better than the usual practice of taking an average of recent sale prices. The problem with a simple average is that there are times when cheaper homes sell in greater numbers than more expensive ones, and vice versa. That distorts the average price. Case's approach compared apples to apples.

He collaborated with Robert Shiller and Allan Weiss in developing the idea. The Standard & Poor's Case-Shiller Home Price Indices, as they're now called, cover the entire US and twenty metropolitan areas. They express home prices relative to the first quarter of 2000, a reasonably average time for valuations. The index for the first quarter of 2000 is defined to be 100, and it's *not* adjusted for inflation.

I'll make that reasonable adjustment for you. I took the Case-Shiller national index and scaled it to the changing value of the dollar, using the Bureau of Labor Statistics' Consumer Price Index. This was done so as to leave the 2000 value at 100. Here is the chart of US home values.

US Home Prices

The first thing you'll notice is that there was a big peak in 2006, followed by a sharp correction. This is the bubble that many homeowners (and former homeowners) are still reeling from.

The second thing you'll observe is that the long-term return of the home market is approximately…zilch. Had you bought an average house in an average American community in 1987, held it for twenty-five years, and sold it in 2012, you'd be selling at just about the same price you paid, after allowing for the shrinking dollar. With broker commission and taxes, you'd *lose* money.

Sure, some property has appreciated in real terms. You could have bought some desert land in Nevada and found that, decades later, it's in middle of the Las Vegas Strip. That would post an impressive return, but only because the land was virtually worthless to begin with.

Residential real estate is different. In order to afford mortgage payments, homebuyers usually have to buy into a mature community with jobs (and schools, shopping, transportation, etc.). The land has already appreciated from zero to hero. The most the buyer can realistically hope for is that the property will maintain its value and be a hedge against inflation. A home isn't a growth stock. It's more like a car, and you don't want to get ripped off by paying too much.

A third observation from the chart is that the home market strayed up from the mean more than down from it. The highest valuation was a 61 percent premium on the benchmark. The lowest was a 13 percent discount. People need places to live, even when times are hard. That tends to prevent homes from becoming too undervalued. In the Case-Shiller time frame, there were a few very bad years to buy a home—2004 to 2008—but no not-to-be-missed buying opportunities when homes were absurdly cheap. Homebuyers should forget about making a good investment. The goal should be to not make an incredibly bad one.

Why do people think real estate is a good investment? I'll give you three reasons. One is that we've been told it's a good investment by construction and real estate interests that spend lavishly on ads. Another is that most people forget about inflation. A third is the hot hand. In the early 2000s everyone watched home prices spurt upward. They told themselves that the hot streak would continue a few more years. Many feared being locked out of the home market forever unless they took the plunge.

Memories are short. In early 2013 the Case-Shiller Index posted double-digit year-to-year gains for battered markets like Phoenix and Las Vegas. Case himself worried that reports of those gains might start a new frenzy.

Immense misery could be avoided, were there a way to tell when prices are too high to justify buying a home. The Case-Shiller Index supplies that, for those willing to pay attention. Clearly, you should buy a first home when prices are average, not high. One approach is to set an arbitrary limit, as in "never buy when the inflation-adjusted Case-Shiller Index is over 140." That's not the worst idea in the world. But a one-size-fits-all number won't work for every buyer. Everyone has different motivations for buying a home. Some are willing to make a bad "investment" to buy at a convenient time in their lives or to get a unique home they love.

A more flexible system is to figure how much you stand to lose should the market revert to the mean, and ask yourself whether the home is worth that to you.

In other words, figure the home's baseline value, defined as what it would be worth in a "normal" market with an inflation-adjusted Case-Shiller Index of 100. You should use the index for your metropolitan area when possible. Subtract that baseline value from the price you're thinking of paying. The difference is an estimate of how much equity you stand to lose if and when the market returns to normal levels.

Though hypothetical, this loss demands to be taken seriously. Real estate bubbles don't last long, and homes spend most of the time at close-to-normal valuations. Those who buy high and stay in a home a long time will find that inflation masks their loss. But the penalty is real and ought to figure in your decision making.

Example #1. You're thinking of buying a house, and the Case-Shiller Index for your city is 123. The Consumer Price Index (CPI) is 228. In the first quarter of 2000, it was 169.8. Therefore, consumer prices are 228/169.8, or 1.34, times higher than they were in 2000.

Divide the Case-Shiller Index (123) by 1.34 to get 91.6. That is the inflation-adjusted Case-Shiller. Because it's less than 100, it's telling you that homes are cheaper, in real terms, than they were in the average year of 2000. You needn't worry that the general market is overpriced. It's a good time to buy.

Example #2. The Case-Shiller Index is 177, and the CPI is the same as above. The inflation-adjusted Case-Shiller would be 131.8. Prices are about 32 percent higher than they would be in a normal market.

You're thinking of paying $800,000 for a home. Should prices revert to the mean, your home will be worth about 100/131.8 of what you paid, or $607,000. That's almost a $200,000 drop. Are you willing to forfeit $200,000 to buy that specific home at this moment? If so, go for it. Otherwise, you should think about delaying a purchase until the market cools down.

Here's a streamlined version of the math. *CS* is the Case-Shiller Index for your area, and *CPI* is the Consumer Price Index. This tells how much you stand to lose.

$$\text{Home Price} \times \left(1 - \frac{CPI}{CS \times 1.698}\right)$$

The above advice is most relevant for those buying their first home. Most homebuyers will own several houses or apartments in their lifetime. They sell one to buy another. There is much less risk when you're both buying and selling real estate at the same time. Trade-up buyers should plug just the *difference* in price between their new and old homes into the above formula (in place of "Home Price"). Those downsizing have little to worry about.

Analytics has uncovered a number of surprises in the real estate market. Consider the day of the week that a home is listed (goes online). It's an arbitrary choice, and many sellers never give it a thought. Others try to choose strategically. Some agents believe it's best to list just before a weekend. That way the home gets maximum attention its first weekend, when it is freshest to the market. Buyers like to think they're getting the first crack at a property, and a home listed on Monday may already be a little "stale" by the next weekend.

In 2012 the brokerage firm Redfin reported that Friday was indeed the best day to list. Friday listings sold for an average of 99.1 percent of the original asking price. In comparison, homes listed on the "worst" day, Sunday, sold for 98.4 percent. As it's hard to believe that Sunday listers have more unrealistic asking prices, this suggests that a seller could net as much as 0.7 percent more just by listing on a Friday. On a $600,000 home, that would come to over $4,000. That's far more than a few extra days' mortgage and holding costs. In fact, Redfin also found that Friday listings sold the fastest.

Trade-up buyers might consider listing their homes on Friday and prioritizing looking at homes listed on Sunday, which may have less buyer competition.

Recap: How to Outguess Home Prices

• There are times when homes are seriously overpriced. The would-be homebuyer should avoid buying then.

• Look up the current Case-Shiller Index (CS) for your metropolitan area and the Consumer Price Index (CPI). Calculate this:

$$\text{Home Price} \times \left(1 - \frac{CPI}{CS \times 1.698}\right)$$

If the result is positive, the market is overvalued. The formula tells how much a first-time homebuyer could lose if (when) home prices revert to the mean.

Twenty One

How to Outguess the Future

Predicting the future is big business. It was estimated that companies worldwide spent close to $400 billion in 2012 on forecasters of all kinds. Most of that involves old-fashioned human expertise, though increasingly the prediction business is touting data analytics. Either way, some skepticism is in order.

"Each year the prediction industry showers us with $200 billion in (mostly erroneous) information," complained William A. Sherden back in 1998. "The forecasting track records for all types of experts are universally poor, whether we consider scientifically oriented professionals such as economists, demographers, meteorologists and seismologists, or psychic and astrological forecasters whose names are household words." Sherden was himself a business consultant.

In a now-notorious study, psychologist Philip Tetlock followed some 284 political and economic experts over two decades, ending in 2003, to see how accurate they were. He found that the experts did no better than nonexperts.

We reach the point of diminishing marginal predictive returns for knowledge disconcertingly quickly. In this age of academic hyperspecialization, there is no reason for supposing that contributors to top journals—distinguished political scientists, area study specialists, economists, and so on—are any better than journalists or attentive readers of the *New York Times* in "reading" emerging situations....Experts in demand were more overconfident than their colleagues who eked out existences far from the limelight.

In 2011 Tetlock initiated a tournament, sponsored by the Intelligence Advanced Research Projects Agency, in which thousands of experts compete to make accurate predictions in their fields of expertise. It's hoped that the tournament will reveal something about how intuitive predictions succeed—when they do succeed.

We are often asked to evaluate predictions about future events that may not be predictable at all. To avoid being suckered, it's worth knowing a little about the art of making poor predictions look better than they are.

Faith Popcorn, futurist and CEO of the consulting firm BrainReserve, is famous for issuing annual lists of predictions (not unlike the psychics in the *National Enquirer*). A few examples:

- People will become so starved for human contact that "mechanized 'hugging booths'" will take the place of payphones.
- There may be "a surge in popularity of 1950s slang."
- Reality shows will stage *American Idol*–style auditions for "risky but life-saving organ transplants, skin grafts, and limb replacements."

• Robots will walk dogs, drive buses, and serve fast food. Technology "will turn battlefield decisions over to robot troops."

• "As the cost of genetic modification plummets, engineering services will...create pets from scratch and pepper your future companion's DNA with your own....These animals will be such an accurate reflection of your temperament that therapists will begin seeing pets as proxies for their patients."

You may think this is funny, but the Fortune 500 isn't laughing. BMW, McDonald's, Procter & Gamble, American Airlines, and Target are among Popcorn's clients. Like other successful forecasters, Popcorn understands that she's partly in the entertainment business. Her wilder predictions keep her name in the news, the better to build a client list. Like psychics, business forecasters pretend to have a magical ability that is inexplicably channeled to the prediction of amusing trivia. It's hard to see who would profit from advance word of the hugging booth meme (least of all any poor soul who tried to invest in them). The magic is in thinking that the prolific forecaster can predict anything—and will, if the client keeps her on retainer. Asks Popcorn's website, "If you knew everything about tomorrow, what would you do differently today?"

The core expertise of business forecasters is in convincing clients that their circumscribed powers constitute miracles. That's what mentalists do, and it's not as easy as they make it look.

I recently saw a prediction effect by magician Dave Cox. An attractive young woman from the audience was brought onstage. Cox gave her some large prop cards that he said were an aid to focusing her thoughts. He showed one card to the audience. It had the word *ROMANCE* printed on it.

Cox had a small whiteboard. He wrote a prediction on it, out of audience view. He then asked the volunteer to imagine herself in a restaurant. What kind of restaurant would it be?

"Italian," she answered. Cox turned the whiteboard around to show that he had written *Italian*.

I happened to be seated at the far left end of one of the closest rows to the stage. I was able to see Cox's board quite plainly while he wrote—as most of the audience could not. There was no funny business. What I saw him write was what he showed to the audience.

Cox wiped off the answer, wrote another prediction, and asked the volunteer to imagine that she was in the Italian restaurant with a celebrity dream date. Who would that be?

"Brad Pitt," she said. Cox showed that he had written *Brad Pitt*.

Cox asked what she and Brad would order for dinner. "Pasta." Cox asked what kind of pasta. "Spaghetti." Cox showed the board: He had written *chicken* and was wrong this time.

The woman was asked to describe the pattern of the table-cloth in the restaurant and the type of beverage she would be drinking. Her answers were a red-and-white-checked table-cloth and red wine, both matching Cox's written predictions.

Cox asked her to imagine what the bill would be. She said around $30. Cox's prediction was $5.99. He flashed it to the audience and comically erased it by rubbing the whiteboard against his vest. He then displayed the erased board to the subject, saying the meal was free because Brad had picked up the check.

To the right of the stage was an easel announcing the performer. At the end of the act, Cox lifted up the show's announcement to reveal a Photoshopped picture of Cox and Brad Pitt having dinner in an Italian restaurant with red-and-white-checked tablecloths. They were having chicken, and the bill was $5.99. The easel had been in plain view through the show, and I was almost close enough to touch it.

Cox does what successful business forecasters do, exploiting an illusion of representativeness and carefully managing memories. The volunteer was neither a plant nor a random audience member. At the outset Cox announced that he wanted "a young woman," and that's what he got. Few women (or men) who don't meet that description will volunteer. Sexism and ageism that wouldn't pass in the workplace are alive on the variety act stage.

The volunteer, in her early twenties, came onstage and was shown some cards. The audience assumed that the card that Cox showed (saying *ROMANCE*) was typical of the cards they didn't see. Wrong. Some of the other cards were different, offering a multiple choice of answers.

```
 _____

   FRENCH                          ITALIAN


          PICK A FAVORITE TYPE OF
                 RESTAURANT


   JAPANESE                        CHINESE
 _____
```

These cards cued the volunteer with possible answers for the choices she would be given. Most people are a little tongue-tied when onstage and the center of attention. They will gladly choose one of the four canned responses. But the audience, unaware of the cards, will leave the theater wondering "What if she'd said 'Korean barbecue food truck'?"

Another card cues the celebrity. The audience supposed the woman was choosing from the whole starry universe of celebrities. But prompted with the right four choices, most "young women" will choose Brad Pitt.

```
ANGELINA                     BRAD PITT
  JOLIE

        PICK A CELEBRITY DREAM
                  DATE

  GEORGE                      LADY GAGA
  CLOONEY
```

Not all the answers were cued. After the volunteer chose an Italian restaurant, Cox asked about the tablecloth and type of beverage, predicting the most likely answers (red-and-white-checked, red wine). The questions might have been different had other restaurants been chosen. Two of Cox's answers were wrong. This was probably the result of the volunteer's testing Cox's powers or forgetting a cue. Cox was prepared to get comic mileage out of his mistakes, and the goofs "proved" that he was not just making safe guesses.

The easel had multiple versions of the picture, one for each cued restaurant choice. They were gimmicked so that Cox could lift up his title card to reveal just the picture he needed.

All the pictures had Brad Pitt. They differed in the type of restaurant and details like the tablecloth and beverage.

The techniques of business forecasters are founded on similar psychology. Faith Popcorn makes it her business to learn about new pop-culture trends before her clients do. She is able to point out various instances of hot new things — and then argue that they are poised to be much bigger. Both the strength and the weakness of most forecasts is that they predict the continuance of recent trends. Valid or not, such projections are easy for the client to buy into because they appeal to our shared belief in hot hands. What just was, will be.

The skillful forecaster is an expert in managing memories. Cox's mind-reading act is absolutely dependent on those mysterious cards shown the volunteer. The cards are also the first thing the audience forgets. When an audience member recounts the act to someone two weeks later, the cards will be long forgotten. They don't fit the mental narrative, as they don't serve a purpose that the audience member understands.

Business forecasters know that it's the recollection of what happened in a meeting that counts. That's why they like to end on a PowerPoint slide summarizing their successes. (Cox did almost the same thing.) A slide show for a 2011 talk lists some of Popcorn's correct predictions, including

> 1987: Told Kodak to prepare for a "Filmless Future."
> 1989: Told Coke to Bottle Water.
> 2006: Told Pepsi to stop bottling water.
> 2012: Predicting the "SHE-change," a decade of feminine energy fueled by money, power, and compassion.

The Kodak bit was good advice—though at this remove, you may be left wondering exactly how ahead of the curve it was for 1987. Mainly, what people remember is the slide's unverifiable heading—"95% accuracy predicting the future"—and Popcorn's unforgettable name. She was born Faith Plotkin.

Recap: How to Outguess the Future

- Research argues that business and political forecasters are not much more accurate than educated nonexperts. Successful forecasters use mentalism-like techniques to enhance their credibility.
- Most forecasting invokes hot hand beliefs: Current trends will continue in the near future. This isn't necessarily true, but forecasters know that their clients will believe it.
- Whatever happens last in a slideshow or meeting is most likely to be remembered. Successful forecasters are good at creating strong last impressions.

Twenty Two

How to Outguess the Stock Market

Some have made fortunes out of gyrating markets, and others have lost them. One who's done both is Victor Niederhoffer. Son of a policeman, Niederhoffer took an economics PhD at the University of Chicago, the bastion of the random walk theory, which holds that short-term changes in stock prices are completely unpredictable. "I criticized all those who had concluded that markets were random, including most of the professors in the room," Niederhoffer said. "Further, I cautioned them that their failure to disprove a hypothesis...was methodologically inadequate to support a conclusion that prices were random. When I put it in the vernacular, 'You can't prove a negative,' pandemonium broke loose."

Niederhoffer collaborated with M.F.M. Osborne on a paper that could be called the Magna Carta of high-frequency trading. Osborne was another outsider to the economics profession, an astrophysicist who worked for a navy think tank. He had done important work on the random walk hypothesis. But in "Market Making and Reversal on the Stock Exchange," published in the *Journal of the American Statistical Association*

(1966), Niederhoffer and Osborne argued that stock price movements are not random at all. They described a way to outguess the market.

Here is a chart redrawn from one in their paper. It shows a few minutes of trading in the stock of Allied Chemical. At that time, stock prices were quoted in eighths of a dollar (12½ cents).

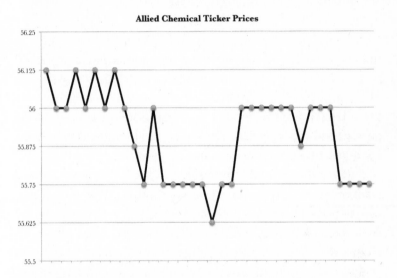

Allied Chemical Ticker Prices

The line in this chart doesn't look too random, and it's not. At upper left, the Allied Chemical price zigzags between two price points like a Ping-Pong ball. Elsewhere, it seems that traders liked the prices of $56 and $55¾, for there were streaks of trades executed at these values. Niederhoffer and Osborne proposed that a floor trader could predict these price movements with enough accuracy to turn a profit.

Average investors imagine that a stock has a single price fluctuating in time, like the "market price" lobster on a summer resort's menu. The reality is that there are always two prices, a bid and an ask. The bid price is the highest amount that buyers are willing to pay. The ask price is the least that sellers are willing to accept. In a well-regulated market, the difference is minimal.

Some investors place market orders to buy at the current price, whatever it is. In the 1960s humans executed these orders, much as operators routed phone calls. Someone wanting to buy at the market price would get the ask price, and someone wanting to sell at market would get the bid price.

When market orders come in haphazardly, with as many to buy as to sell, you'd have a Ping-Pong pattern as at upper left in the chart. The execution price fluctuates between the bid and ask price ($56 and $56⅛ in this case). This goes on until there are no more limit orders—commitments to trade at the current bid or ask price. Then the price crashes through the ceiling or floor and moves to another level.

Niederhoffer and Osborne discovered that traders setting limit orders greatly preferred round numbers. They would give instructions to buy or sell at $56, say. To a lesser degree they liked half-dollar amounts like $55.50; to a still lesser degree they favored quarter-dollar amounts like $55.75. Least popular were odd fractions like $55⅝. This has important consequences.

A trader who wants to make a quick profit would do well to place a buy order a little above a round number. Price movements are constrained by whole-dollar values and simple fractions. Should a trader buy at $38.01 (today prices are quoted in cents), and should the market sag, the backlog of buy orders at $38 would be a firewall delaying movement below that. That might give the trader time to sell at $38, for a penny's loss.

It's equally likely that prices would move upward. In that case, the trader would be in great shape. The price might go up to $38.10 or $38.50 or $39. The alert trader would have ample opportunity to make a profit. Because the likely profit would be much larger than the penny at risk, the odds are in the trader's favor.

Niederhoffer and Osborne were not the first to realize this fact. In their paper they admitted that "professional traders will recognize these rules or their equivalent as quite familiar." That was one of the most interesting things about their system. It allowed them to pick the brains of the pros. When a stock was frequently traded a little above or below a round number, it meant that the smart money was interested in that stock. These may have been people who had some kind of inside information, and that information was more often than not correct.

In effect, Niederhoffer and Osborne described an early high-frequency trading algorithm. It was purely mechanical, involving no traditional stock-picking skill. It profited from the market's short-term jitters and flows of information rather than from the long-term growth of businesses.

Osborne, a scientist at heart, did not commercialize his insights. Niederhoffer did. As computing power came online, he wrote one of the first trading algorithms in the 1970s. George Soros gave him money to invest. Niederhoffer's personal wealth, and the wealth under management, increased over the next two decades. The gimmick above was soon overexploited, but Niederhoffer kept devising new ways to beat the market. He was done in by an indicator more unusual than the off-dollar trades: cigarette butts.

Niederhoffer wanted to invest in Southeast Asia. He delegated a friend, Steven Keeley, to scope out the region. Keeley was a veterinarian. He had a theory that a nation's economic health could be divined from the length of discarded cigarette butts. When people were feeling wealthy, they left longer butts. Another leading indicator was the hygiene in houses of prostitution. After several months of fact-finding, Keeley reported that Thailand was A-OK. Niederhoffer invested, and in 2007 the Thai economy collapsed. He lost his clients' money and much of his own.

Can a nonprofessional outguess the market? The prospects for the amateur stock picker have probably never been worse. Small investors are outgunned by the high-speed algorithms that account for about half of today's trading (and which haven't been doing that well themselves lately). Professionals who devise new ways to predict the market's movements with greater-than-chance accuracy can often profit from that. The profit taking in turn tends to eliminate the predictability. Thus many market inefficiencies vanish almost as soon as they are discovered and become known. This is how the market polices itself and remains almost completely efficient.

There are a few inefficiencies that have persisted despite being generally recognized. They are based on trader psychology that is presumably unlikely to change, and they are difficult or impractical for the professionals to arbitrage away. Some are hot hand effects.

In the NBA the hot hand is a mirage. In the financial markets it can be a self-fulfilling prophecy. Traders are predisposed to see trends in the noise of stock prices. When many traders come to believe that stocks are on a winning streak, they buy more stock, bidding up the prices. The shared fiction becomes a reality. As long as enough buyers believe that the market will keep going up, it will.

The cycle needn't stop there. A rising stock market makes consumers feel prosperous. They may buy more goods, boosting the economy and justifying further stock price increases. But eventually the house of cards collapses. Emotions cool, and stock valuations struggle to get any higher. A streak of market declines leads traders to see the slump as a grim portent. Many pull out of the market, forcing further declines. In this way hot hand and cold hand thinking help create bull and bear markets. That's been going on ever since there were markets and isn't likely to change in the foreseeable future.

One of the small investor's few advantages is time. He or she has the luxury of pursuing strategies that may play out over decades. That puts small investors in a different niche of the financial ecosystem from the star managers, hedge funds, and traderbots that must prove their worth every quarter. Individuals of moderate means are also likely to have much of their portfolios in tax-deferred retirement accounts. Trades within the account do not trigger taxes. That puts these individuals in a position to profit from the market's mood swings—*if* they've got the discipline to do it.

Discipline is very much the issue. The ongoing and well-concealed scandal of the investment industry is that average investors don't make anything like the "average" returns you hear about. It's not that market averages are a fiction. It's just that most people buy and sell at the wrong times. The more investors trade, the lower their realized return, on average. The shortfall goes by the name of the *behavioral penalty*. As a study by Brad Barber and Terrance Odean put it, trading is hazardous to your wealth.

The research firm DALBAR computed that the average stock investor in the period 1990 through 2009 underperformed the S&P 500 index by 5.03 percentage points a year. The reason investors underperformed is that they were trying to beat the market. Like a carnival game, it looks so easy. "People tend to be overconfident about their own abilities," said Teresa Ghilarducci, an economist specializing in investor behavior. "They tend to focus on the short term rather than thinking about long-term consequences. And they tend to think that whatever the current trend is will always be the trend."

That's hot hand thinking. Bryan Harris, an analyst at Dimensional Fund Advisors, reported that investors sold $266 billion of US stock mutual funds from March 2009 through June 2011. The selling peaked almost precisely when the market was at its bottom.

How do you tell when stocks are a good buy? It's not rocket science. The ultimate justification for stock prices is earnings. This is a truism of Economics 101. It hardly merits mentioning except that most investors don't believe it, or don't *act* as if they believe it.

From the investor's standpoint, a stock is a machine for producing earnings. Were you buying an apartment building as an investment, you'd ask how much rent it was producing. You would want to buy as much rental income as possible for your money. Corporate earnings are the stock market's rent. Any dividends will be paid out of those earnings. Earnings not paid out may be reinvested in the company, increasing the value of shares.

Take a corporation's earnings per share and divide it by the share price. This is the price-to-earnings (PE) ratio. It's the standard, quick-and-dirty measure of how attractive the stock is as an investment. A PE of around 15 is typical. When the PE is low, the investor is getting a lot of earning power for not so much money. When the PE is high, the investor is paying a lot for a trickle of income.

There are plenty of reasons why a stock's PE may be high or low. When a company's earnings are growing rapidly, its PE is usually high, and this might make sense. When a company is in a declining industry or has financial problems, its PE may be low, and this also could be reasonable.

You can compute PE ratios for a market index like the Dow Jones Industrial Average (of thirty blue-chip stocks) or the S&P 500. The S&P 500 index covers the broad American stock market, and there are scores of index funds tracking it. Historically, the median PE for the S&P 500 (or an S&P 500 index fund) has been around 16. It has varied wildly, though. At times it's been 30 or more; other times it's been in the single digits.

This *doesn't* make sense. The S&P 500 is all of America's big companies averaged together. Even in boom times, the whole S&P 500 can hardly merit the valuation of a growth stock. In the worst of times, it doesn't deserve the low PEs of a doomed company. Yet that's the way the market works. Stock prices, and PEs, are a lot more volatile than corporate earnings are.

To be sure, index earnings sometimes *do* fall off a cliff. In 2009 the S&P 500's earnings fell to less than a tenth of where they'd been before the subprime mortgage crisis. This was due to banks and other companies writing off a mountain of bad debt all at once. After the purge, earnings promptly bounced back. The market is supposed to take a long-term outlook and price stocks according to the whole future stream of earnings. But investors, like everyone else, believe in the representativeness of small samples. PE valuations have too much to do with the latest news cycle, the latest quarter, and the last few years.

Yale economist Robert Shiller devised a better way of gauging stock market valuation. It's the current S&P 500 price divided by a ten-year moving average of earnings. This has the merit of smoothing out business cycles and much of the duplicity in corporate earnings reports—for there are cycles of candor as well as profit. A ten-year average of corporate earnings is about as truthy as these things get.

Shiller's idea wasn't entirely new. At least as far back as 1934, pioneering value investor Benjamin Graham recommended using five to ten years of earnings in computing PE ratios. Graham was talking about PEs of individual stocks, but the notion could equally apply to indexes. Shiller's Cyclically Adjusted PE ratio (aka the CAPE ratio, the Shiller PE ratio, or the PE 10) is computed by dividing the current S&P 500 value by the average of the past ten years' earnings of the S&P companies. Shiller adjusts those past earnings for inflation. In that way the ratio's value is comparable to a regular PE.

A first reaction might be that Shiller has thrown the baby out with the bathwater. The name of the game is to predict *future* earnings. Why bother with the past? Surely we can forecast earnings.

Don't bet on it. The best way to demonstrate that astrology is nonsense is to compare predictions. When different astrologers have different forecasts for Libra, they can't all be right. Well, the best way to show that earnings forecasts are of dubious value is to compare the predictions of Wall Street analysts. These forecasts are often alarmingly different and biased toward optimism. One Federal Reserve Board study found that analysts' average expectations for the current year's S&P 500 earnings were too high in nineteen out of twenty-one years (from 1979 to 1999). Just like investors, analysts are too obsessed with the current trend. Shiller's ten-year PE enforces a big-picture perspective.

What if S&P earnings rise dramatically over the ten-year period? It's not going to happen. A few smart and lucky companies will have skyrocketing earnings; the broad market indexes won't. Remember, that hot technology company is cannibalizing the market of older companies that are in the index, too. When you subtract the fake growth of inflation, the real, averaged-out S&P earnings don't change much over ten years. They haven't in the past, anyway.

The Standard & Poor's 500 index is a fairly recent invention, inaugurated in 1957. It is intended to track the 500 largest companies, by market value, publicly traded in the US stock market. Shiller backtracked and projected what 500 companies would have been in the S&P index, had it existed before 1957. He used earnings reports to reconstruct the ten-year PE back to January 1881. Here's a chart of it.

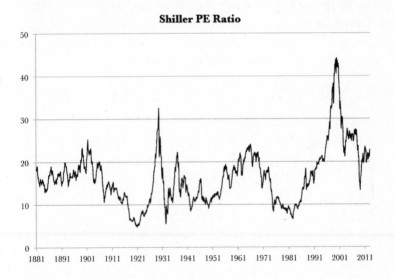

Shiller PE Ratio

It is hard to explain the huge variations as reasonable changes in the outlook for future earnings. Look at the rises to the big peaks in 1929 and 2000, and the equally insistent drops afterward. These were famous stock market bubbles driven by hot hand beliefs.

Shiller found that his backward-looking ten-year PEs have considerable power in predicting future returns. This is demonstrated in the chart below. Every dot represents a month, from January 1881 through January 1993. The dot's position is determined by that month's ten-year PE value (on the horizontal axis) and the return that an investor would have achieved had he invested a lump sum in the S&P 500 stocks that month and held that investment for twenty years (this return on the vertical axis). These are average annual returns over the twenty-year-period, adjusted for inflation. It's assumed that dividends are reinvested, but this does not account for commissions, management fees, or taxes, all of which can vary a good deal. (To save words, hereafter all quoted returns will be adjusted for inflation, and *PE* will mean Shiller's ten-year PE.)

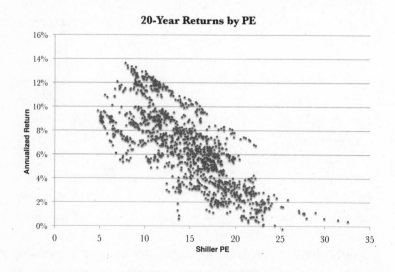

20-Year Returns by PE

The dots are not scattered all over the chart. Instead, the dot cloud forms a diagonal swath from upper left to lower right. That means that future market returns are predictable, albeit with a good deal of noise. The most important conclusion: The lower the PE when a long-term investor enters the market, the higher that investor's likely return.

This is true even though the great mass of investors pay no attention to ten-year PEs and have no awareness of how predictable their collective actions are. This predictability also exists despite the fact that many smart traders were and are trying to take advantage of it. In an all-wise market, investors should have bid up the prices of stocks during those low-PE periods, nullifying the advantage of buying at those times. Investors also should have shunned stocks during high-PE periods, lowering prices and increasing returns. The result would have been a straight horizontal line of dots or (more realistically) a fuzzy horizontal dot cloud. I will show you a chart like that in a moment. But that's not what we see here. The diagonal dot cloud shows that there's a penalty for buying at high PE and a bonus for buying at low PE.

The average of the twenty-year returns is 6.58 percent after inflation. This is in line with the "average" stock return values touted by those who want to sell you stocks and mutual funds. When those values aren't adjusted for inflation, and usually they aren't, the average is around 10 percent.

There is only one dot with a negative return. An investor unlucky enough to have jumped into the market in June 1901 (at a PE of just over 25) would have lost buying power. After twenty years of inflation, the average return would have been -0.24.

Every other twenty-year period eked out a positive real return, and most beat the returns that could have been achieved with bonds. (Typically, the safest bonds have offered a real return of a little over 2 percent.) Many of the dots represent periods that spanned the 1929 crash and the Depression. Those investors still came out ahead. This fits in with the credo that stocks are not that risky for the long-term investor willing to stay the course. A very few of the periods achieved real returns over 12 percent. All those charmed spans started with a low PE.

Today's investors have every right to feel cursed. They have had few opportunities to buy at average PEs, much less low ones. In mid 2013 the Shiller PE was around 23. The average real return at that valuation is something like 2 percent over the coming twenty years. *Never* has the twenty-year stock market returned as much as 3 percent annually (after inflation) when the PE was 23 or higher.

Many investors would say that a 23 PE is not all that high. It's *not* that high in the experience of anyone born after the mid-1970s. Forget the "lost decade." There's a lost generation of stock investors who have never had a decent shot at making so-called average stock market returns.

The correlation between PE and return makes perfect sense. Why don't most investors believe it?

Opposite is another chart of return versus PE. This time it's the return over a one-year period, after buying the S&P stocks at a given PE.

The dot swarm is now horizontal. An investor's prospects at PE 30 aren't much different than at 10. This is what you'd expect of an efficient market in which investors price in everything known and guessable about future earnings. There is no free money to be had by investing at low PE for a one-year holding period.

The PE's effect on returns comes with a time lag. That's unfortunate because most of us have trouble making good decisions when effects do not immediately follow causes. High PEs are bad for you, like sugary drinks are bad for you, but it may take decades for that to become apparent. During bull

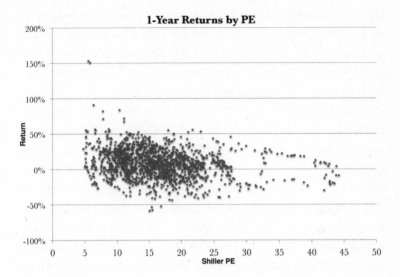

markets, investors want to do what feels good at the moment. They join the crowd and buy the stocks that are supposedly making everyone rich. The chart of one-year return doesn't reveal a problem with that. Some buying months had positive returns even when the PE was over 40. The most obscenely overvalued markets may extend their winning streak another year. It's only when you look at much longer periods that returns correlate with PE.

"One might have thought that it is easier to forecast into the near future than into the distant future," Shiller wrote, "but the data contradict such intuition." Investors, traders, and analysts are trying to predict the wrong thing: the market's next minutes, weeks, and quarters. Most are banging their heads against a brick wall. Certainly the small investor is.

There are long regimes where investors pay scant attention to PE valuations. These periods are terminated by the mass epiphany that stocks are over- or underpriced. Once the market starts correcting, the pendulum usually swings through the mean and keeps going. It may take a decade or more for this process to come to completion. That pummels the twenty-year returns when stocks are bought at high PEs, and augments returns when investing at low PEs.

The effects of buying at high or low PE can persist much longer than twenty years. Those promoting stock investments often quote an "average" return from 1920 to the present. This sounds so reasonable because, without the need of anyone pointing it out, we all recognize that the period includes the 1929 crash, the market's worst catastrophe. Not everyone realizes that PEs were at rock bottom in 1920, dipping below 5. The PE is currently almost five times that. That PE increase alone adds about 1.7 percentage points a year to an "average" return calculated from 1920 to the present. Whenever you hear someone bragging about great returns, it's a safe bet that he was riding a PE cycle up.

"Long-term investors would be well advised, individually, to lower their exposure to the stock market when [the PE] is high, as it has been recently, and get into the market when it is low," Shiller wrote in 2005. This observation may seem incontestable. Yet the reaction to the notion of the small investor outguessing the stock market has been schizophrenic.

On the one hand, a legion of high-visibility experts talks as if it's *easy* and *routine* to "time the market." When valuations are high, you "take money off the table." When valuations are low, "stocks are on sale" and it's a great time to buy. Pundits are usually not talking about Shiller's long-term changes but rather about the market ups and downs happening all the time, even on a daily basis. They propose trading a lot. Many of these experts are sponsored by brokers or mutual funds.

Paul Samuelson memorably expressed the opinion of many economists. "Suppose it was demonstrated that one out of twenty alcoholics could learn to become a moderate social drinker," Samuelson said. Then the wisest course would be to pretend that it wasn't so. "You will never identify that one in twenty, and in the attempt five in twenty will be ruined." In Samuelson's view, friends shouldn't let friends try to beat the market. Even if it's possible, they are more likely to lose than to profit from the attempt. As we've seen, there is ample evidence for that proposition.

Lately the behavioral penalty has been co-opted by the mutual fund industry to promote buy-and-hold investing. They're not entirely motivated by the public good. Fund managers collect fees only while investors own their funds. It's easier to justify high fees for stock funds than fixed-income funds. Therefore, the fund industry is reluctant to admit that there might be times when it's not worth owning stocks. They have concocted bogeyman stories to scare investors into buying-and-never-selling.

One of the favorite pitches is that most of the stock market's long-term return is due to a few halcyon days that post big gains. You don't know when those days will be; ergo, you have to be fully invested all the time. Take the ten largest daily percentage gains for the Dow Jones index. Had you been invested in Dow stocks, you could have almost tripled your money (a 195 percent gain) in just ten days.

A reasonable response is *So what?* Here's a statistic they don't offer. Take the ten worst days for the Dow. You could have lost over two-thirds of your wealth (a 68 percent loss) in just ten days.

Seven of the ten "best" days came after the 1929 crash and in the ensuing chaos, through early 1933. The treasure chests are mixed in with the landmines.

Thoughtful investors realize there are times when the stock market isn't very attractive relative to the alternatives. In December 1999 the market achieved its highest-ever ten-year PE, 44.20. The earnings yield—the maximum the S&P companies could have paid in dividends, had they decided to distribute every penny of their earnings—was a miserable 2.3 percent. Meanwhile, Treasury bonds were paying 6 percent. *Duh.* A sane long-term investor would have favored virtually risk-free bonds over risky stocks. At that valuation, stocks were very risky. Less than three years later, the S&P 500 had shed almost half its value.

Daily changes are noise. Market tops and bottoms are noise. The regular investor can't predict them and shouldn't try. The mistake is in thinking that the investor can't predict *anything.* Given the evidence that market returns are moderately predictable over decades, the long-term investor should make use of that.

The ten-year PE is not unique in its forecasting power. There are many other ways of assessing fundamental value, and they all work, to a greater or lesser degree. You can look at S&P 500 dividend yields, asset value, or a ten-year moving average of the index itself. All have substantial predictive power (and their predictions correlate reasonably well with those of the PE10). Shiller's main point is that the underlying value of America's corporations does not change too much or too quickly. It's emotion-driven stock prices that get out of line.

There are two good reasons for an investor to favor Shiller's PE as a predictor of return. One is that the economic case for the importance of earnings is especially compelling. The other is that the Shiller PE is easy to look up on the Web.

A number of workable trading systems using PEs have

appeared in books and the financial press. Ben Stein and Phil DeMuth's 2003 book, *Yes, You Can Time the Market!* describes several of them. In one you make an annual determination of whether the market is overvalued or undervalued, using a moving average of S&P 500 PE ratios (Stein and DeMuth favor a fifteen-year term rather than Shiller's ten-year frame). You add to your stock fund holdings only in years when the market is undervalued. Otherwise, you bank that year's contribution to your portfolio, awaiting a better buying opportunity. When favorable valuations return, you don't buy in all at once (for that would probably be at a PE only a little lower than average). Instead, you buy in gradually, at a rate of twice your intended annual contribution, as long as valuations remain below average.

This system is simple and well tailored to the saver who adds money to a retirement account each year. It guarantees that all stock funds are bought at lower-than-average valuations. That alone is enough to boost returns. For a twenty-year holding period, a typical gain is about half a percentage point a year.

The Stein-Demuth system works entirely by deferring stock purchases. It makes no assumptions about market tops and bottoms, and it's about as stress- and regret-free as a market outguessing system can be. One limitation is that it works on new contributions only, not on capital you may already have. Someone who wants to get the most value from the PE's predictive power needs to be willing to sell as well as buy. Let's look at ways to do that.

Warren Buffett said that the first rule of making money is to not lose money. A realistic goal is to use PEs to exit the US stock market during most of the biggest plunges. These generally happen when PEs are high.

Here's the simplest PE-based system of all. You invest in a low-cost S&P 500 index fund, buying low and selling high (in PE terms). When the ten-year PE hits a specified high value (the sell trigger), you sell and put the proceeds in a low-cost fixed-income fund (offering the return of ten-year US Treasury bonds, let's say). You stay in the bond fund until the PE hits a particular low value, the buy trigger. Then you buy back into the stock fund, and the cycle repeats. To make things as easy as possible, I'll assume that you're very busy and can check the PE—and trade when indicated—only once a month.

I tested all the plausible whole-number pairs of buy and sell limits, computing the compound return that could have been realized over the period January 1881 to January 2013. In each case the portfolio started 1881 (when the ten-year PE was 18.47) fully invested in stocks.

The table below shows the most interesting part of the results. Sell trigger values are at top, and buy trigger values are on the left. Each cell within the table gives the average real annual return, for the corresponding pair of sell and buy thresholds, over the entire 132-year period. Returns are adjusted for inflation but not for trading expenses, management fees, or taxes.

	16	17	18	19	20	21	22	23	24	25	26	27	28	29	30	31	32	33
5	3.00%	3.04%	3.05%	3.16%	3.20%	3.26%	3.39%	3.41%	3.69%	3.73%	3.81%	3.81%	3.92%	3.92%	3.96%	3.96%	3.99%	6.17%
6	3.66%	3.75%	3.80%	3.96%	4.07%	4.15%	4.32%	6.03%	6.38%	6.86%	7.23%	7.27%	7.40%	7.43%	7.54%	7.54%	7.62%	6.17%
7	4.30%	4.42%	4.51%	4.68%	4.80%	4.91%	5.12%	6.89%	7.28%	6.99%	7.12%	7.16%	7.29%	7.32%	7.43%	7.43%	7.50%	6.17%
8	4.03%	4.15%	4.25%	4.42%	4.53%	4.64%	4.85%	6.61%	7.01%	6.78%	7.02%	7.05%	7.19%	7.22%	7.33%	7.33%	7.40%	6.17%
9	4.93%	5.90%	6.05%	6.32%	6.69%	6.86%	7.08%	6.75%	7.14%	6.74%	7.02%	7.05%	7.19%	7.22%	7.33%	7.33%	7.40%	6.17%
10	5.46%	5.46%	5.62%	5.88%	6.26%	6.42%	6.64%	6.38%	6.77%	6.46%	6.80%	6.83%	6.97%	7.00%	7.11%	7.11%	7.18%	6.17%
11	5.71%	5.72%	5.88%	6.14%	6.52%	6.68%	6.90%	6.69%	7.09%	6.81%	6.80%	6.83%	6.97%	7.00%	7.11%	7.11%	7.18%	6.17%
12	5.65%	5.53%	5.68%	5.94%	6.32%	6.49%	6.71%	6.44%	6.83%	6.66%	6.64%	6.68%	6.82%	6.85%	6.95%	6.93%	7.03%	6.17%
13	5.59%	5.42%	5.61%	5.91%	6.04%	6.20%	6.42%	6.19%	6.58%	6.43%	6.53%	6.57%	6.70%	6.73%	6.84%	6.84%	6.91%	6.17%
14	6.09%	6.07%	6.43%	6.42%	6.29%	6.52%	6.76%	6.63%	7.13%	6.93%	7.07%	7.10%	7.24%	7.27%	7.38%	7.38%	7.43%	6.71%
15	5.96%	6.07%	6.28%	6.26%	6.15%	6.37%	6.62%	6.55%	7.05%	6.86%	7.02%	7.05%	7.19%	7.22%	7.33%	7.33%	7.40%	6.66%
16		3.67%	5.95%	6.02%	6.19%	6.28%	6.52%	6.46%	6.96%	6.86%	6.80%	6.83%	6.97%	7.00%	7.11%	7.11%	7.18%	6.58%
17			5.42%	5.67%	5.90%	6.13%	6.42%	6.21%	6.71%	6.63%	6.61%	6.65%	6.78%	6.81%	6.92%	6.92%	6.99%	6.51%
18				5.62%	5.91%	6.23%	6.55%	6.41%	6.63%	6.60%	6.61%	6.65%	6.78%	6.81%	6.92%	6.92%	6.99%	6.51%
19					5.77%	6.08%	6.46%	6.34%	6.58%	6.48%	6.55%	6.59%	6.72%	6.75%	6.86%	6.86%	6.93%	6.51%
20						6.10%	6.45%	6.48%	6.32%	6.43%	6.55%	6.59%	6.72%	6.75%	6.86%	6.86%	6.93%	6.51%

The average real return of the S&P 500 stocks and their precursors during this period was 6.23 percent. Any cell containing a value higher than 6.23 percent marks a strategy that would have beaten the market. In fact, most of the strategies shown did outperform the market.

I've crossed out the cells in the lower left corner, as they represent policies that clearly make no sense (buying higher and selling lower, in PE terms). The other cells are colored as a heat map. The region of light-shaded cells on the left, in the topmost row, and at upper far right shows strategies that would have returned less than a buy-and-hold S&P 500 portfolio. The white cells are strategies that beat the market by up to a percentage point a year, and the medium-shaded cells at upper and center right outperformed the S&P index by at least 1 percent a year. The highest return was 7.62 percent, the result of buying at 6 and selling at 32.

Would it be wise to adopt a policy of trading at 6 and 32? No, not unless you can replay the last century. The chart's returns are noisy. There is much cell-to-cell variation, owing to luck in trading at a particular crest or trough in the historic record. The 6 and 32 limits happened to call the bottom and top of the 1920s bull market rather closely. This would have been profitable enough to spike returns even when averaged over our 132-year period.

No one should expect that kind of luck. Given that the future won't be exactly like the past, you should pay more attention to the general pattern of returns. Picture yourself tossing a dart at the chart, unable to control the exact cell you hit. Where would you aim, to have the best chance of landing in a cell with a good return?

It would be unwise to aim for the "best" return, at 6/32, as it's adjacent to cells that underperformed the market. A not-so-accurate dart thrower would be better off aiming for somewhere in the right center of the chart. Let's say you picked 13 and 28. That would have earned a return of 6.70 percent, beating the stock market by 0.47 percentage points a year.

If that doesn't sound like anything special, take a look at this chart. It shows the (hypothetical!) growth of a $1,000 portfolio invested since 1881. A buy-and-hold investment in the S&P stocks would have grown to an inflation-adjusted $2,932,724. A buy-low, sell-high portfolio, with PE limit values of 13 and 28, would have grown to $5,239,915.

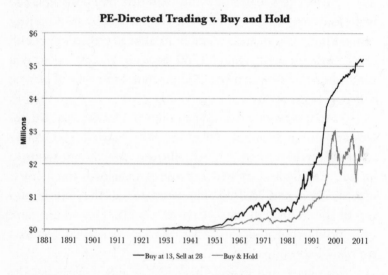

PE-Directed Trading v. Buy and Hold

—— Buy at 13, Sell at 28   —— Buy & Hold

The return is only half the story. Look at how smooth the upper line is, compared to buy-and-hold, over the past twenty years. A PE-directed investor would have sold out of stocks in January 1997, sparing herself a couple of agonizing crashes. She would have been in safe, steady fixed-income investments through January 2013. The PE investor's superior return is due entirely to avoiding losses.

The maxim is that risk and return are trade-offs. To get more return, you have to accept more risk. The historical data says that downside risk goes up with PE, just as long-term return goes down with it. By exiting the market during the least profitable times, you also skip some of the riskiest times.

In fact, all the returns in the table are more appealing when you factor in risk. As long as you manage to buy into the stock market at a low PE and sell at a higher one, you're almost certain to realize a greater-than-"average" stock return. The buy and sell trigger pairs that underperformed the market did so because they had too much downtime in bonds. Say you had picked 8 and 22 as your limits. This would have averaged only a 4.85 percent return. You might think that was a dud. But with those limits, the PE-directed portfolio would have been in stocks only 37 percent of the time. It beat the market while it was in stocks and offered the safety of fixed-income invest- ments the rest of the time. By risk-adjusted return, that's not so bad.

To top the S&P 500's return, you need to be more selective about limit values. The historical record suggests that this is not too difficult to do. Many pairs of buy and sell thresholds would have beaten the market by half a percentage point a year.

Most trading schemes have you trade a lot to eke out a minuscule advantage. With this system you hardly trade at all. Had you used 13 and 28 limits, you would have made only three trades in the past 132 years. You would have sold out of stocks in July 1929, three months before the crash, and bought back in in September 1931. Then you would have sold out of the market in January 1997, before the dot-com crash. In retrospect these actions look almost psychic.

These three timely moves would have avoided horrific losses, thereby beating the market handsomely over a 132-year period. But notice that a trader who began using the buy-low, sell-high system in the mid-1930s could have spent an entire investing lifetime without ever getting a trading signal or benefiting from the system in any way! On the other hand, had you been in the market in 1997, or 1929, you would have appreciated the system's guidance.

There is a more powerful way to make use of PEs. The self-fulfilling nature of hot hand beliefs often creates momentum. Stocks will keep going up (or down) for a while. An index fund investor can take advantage of that with a trick similar to a *trailing stop order.*

Traders of individual stocks may place a standing order to sell a stock when it drops below a specified price. Say you own Apple and it's trading at $420. You're going on an Antarctic cruise (no Internet connection south of Tierra del Fuego) and can't stand the idea that you might come back to find that the stock has dropped sharply. You could put in a stop loss order for $380 a share. This tells your broker to sell Apple if and when it dips below $380.

A stop loss order is insurance. As with any type of insurance, you hope you won't need it. It limits your losses when something bad happens. In the case of a decline in Apple stock, the broker will likely be able to sell at a little below $380.

A stop loss order can be more sophisticated. It's possible that Apple may shoot up first and then plunge, all while you're incommunicado. You'd like to get some of the upside action. With a trailing stop order, you tell the broker to sell whenever the stock price drops 10 percent (or any percentage you name) from a high. The high is the stock's maximum price during the time the order is in effect.

Example: Apple is selling at $420 when you place the trailing stop. The next day it rises to $428. That resets the maximum. Thereafter the broker will sell only if Apple drops 10 percent from that new high-water mark of $428. Should the stock continue to rise without much of a pullback, the maximum price will ratchet upward. Maybe it's a roller-coaster couple of weeks and Apple surges to $483 before crashing down to $392. The broker would attempt to sell at a price 10 percent below the high. You could return from the Antarctic to find you've scored a nice profit—even though Apple is down from where it was when you left.

The index fund investor can create a do-it-yourself trailing stop, using PEs. As before, you choose a pair of PE values as buy and sell thresholds. The difference is that you don't trade the instant the threshold is reached. You keep a record of the highest level the PE has reached since the sell threshold was crossed and sell whenever it drops X percent below that running high. I'll continue to assume that you check the ten-year PE only once a month.

For buying back in, it's the reverse. Once the PE sinks below the buy limit, you keep a record of its lowest monthly value. You buy back into the market the first month in which the current PE is at least X percent above the running low.

Stock traders typically set trailing stops at 10 to 30 percent. There is reason to keep X small. You will be selling at a discount of at least X percent from the peak, and buying at least X percent above the market's bottom. The trade-off is that when X is very small, regular month-to-month volatility will quickly trigger a trade. You want a less itchy trigger finger—a larger X—in order to piggyback on any momentum that might cause valuations to move beyond the threshold.

As it turns out, the precise value of X was not too crucial. Here is a table of returns for a 6 percent trailing limit, over the period 1881 to 2013.

	16	17	18	19	20	21	22	23	24	25	26	27	28	29	30	31	32	33
5	3.37%	3.42%	3.41%	3.41%	3.57%	3.57%	3.57%	3.57%	3.79%	3.79%	3.91%	3.91%	3.91%	3.91%	3.91%	3.91%	3.91%	6.24%
6	3.93%	3.98%	3.98%	3.98%	4.13%	4.13%	4.13%	5.88%	6.10%	6.95%	7.22%	7.22%	7.22%	7.22%	7.22%	7.22%	7.22%	6.24%
7	4.32%	4.37%	4.37%	4.50%	4.66%	4.66%	5.20%	6.97%	7.20%	6.93%	7.22%	7.22%	7.22%	7.22%	7.22%	7.22%	7.22%	6.24%
8	4.23%	4.28%	4.28%	4.41%	4.57%	4.57%	5.11%	6.88%	7.11%	6.93%	7.22%	7.22%	7.22%	7.22%	7.22%	7.22%	7.22%	6.24%
9	5.09%	6.14%	6.14%	6.27%	6.73%	6.73%	7.29%	7.08%	7.31%	6.93%	7.22%	7.22%	7.22%	7.22%	7.22%	7.22%	7.22%	6.24%
10	6.18%	6.14%	6.14%	6.27%	6.73%	6.73%	7.29%	7.08%	7.31%	6.93%	7.22%	7.22%	7.22%	7.22%	7.22%	7.22%	7.22%	6.24%
11	6.57%	6.53%	6.53%	6.67%	7.12%	7.12%	7.68%	7.48%	7.71%	7.33%	7.22%	7.22%	7.22%	7.22%	7.22%	7.22%	7.22%	6.24%
12	6.49%	6.37%	6.37%	6.51%	6.96%	6.96%	7.52%	7.48%	7.71%	7.33%	7.22%	7.22%	7.22%	7.22%	7.22%	7.22%	7.22%	6.24%
13	6.60%	6.37%	6.54%	6.70%	6.96%	6.96%	7.52%	7.48%	7.71%	7.33%	7.22%	7.22%	7.22%	7.22%	7.22%	7.22%	7.22%	6.24%
14	7.04%	6.90%	7.25%	6.86%	6.96%	6.96%	7.55%	7.50%	7.93%	7.78%	7.67%	7.67%	7.67%	7.67%	7.67%	7.67%	7.67%	6.68%
15	6.03%	7.14%	7.13%	6.77%	6.96%	6.96%	7.55%	7.50%	7.93%	7.78%	7.67%	7.67%	7.67%	7.67%	7.67%	7.67%	7.67%	6.68%
16		7.19%	7.23%	6.90%	7.23%	6.95%	7.54%	7.50%	7.93%	7.77%	7.67%	7.67%	7.67%	7.67%	7.67%	7.67%	7.67%	6.68%
17			6.69%	6.45%	6.91%	6.63%	7.22%	6.89%	7.31%	7.16%	7.06%	7.06%	7.06%	7.06%	7.06%	7.06%	7.06%	6.68%
18				6.77%	7.08%	6.80%	7.39%	6.95%	7.31%	7.16%	7.06%	7.06%	7.06%	7.06%	7.06%	7.06%	7.06%	6.68%
19					6.83%	6.83%	7.43%	6.95%	7.21%	7.16%	7.06%	7.06%	7.06%	7.06%	7.06%	7.06%	7.06%	6.68%
20						7.52%	7.49%	7.08%	7.21%	7.16%	7.06%	7.06%	7.06%	7.06%	7.06%	7.06%	7.06%	6.68%

I'm using the same range of buy and sell values as before, and the same heat-map shading. There are more threshold pairs beating the market by 1 percent and even 1.5 percent (the darkest shading, in the center). Once again, the individual cells matter less than broad patterns. In this case, the highest returns—14, 15, or 16 to buy and 24 or 25 to sell—form a bull's-eye, surrounded by other high returns. A dart thrower's reasonable aiming point might be 15/24. It returned 7.93 percent in this period, beating the S&P 500 by 1.70 percentage points a year.

These thresholds are less extreme than those of the simpler buy-low, sell-high system because you're not necessarily trading at them. When there is momentum, the trailing limit trick can often hitch a ride. This also has the effect of producing a few more trades. That helps ensure that the system will produce an advantage in the investor's lifetime.

Let me now justify the trailing stop value of 6 percent. Here is a chart showing how returns varied with X. I'm holding 15 and 24 constant as the buy and sell triggers. All the trailing stop values through 20 percent performed respectably, though choices from 3 to 11 percent did best. Six percent had the highest return, barely.

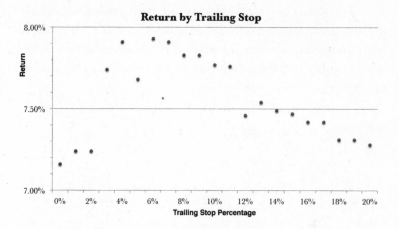

Return by Trailing Stop

You can likewise vary the checking interval. Checking the PE just once a year—and trading if called for—would have produced a respectable return of 7.46 percent. That a monthly or yearly checking regimen performed so well may come as a shock to mobile device addicts who check the market multiple times a day. A lot can happen in a month, and that was true even in slower times. The market dropped 26 percent in October 1929. But it had dropped 11 percent the previous month. Someone selling on a 6 percent drop would have gotten out before the crash and sold at a price about 11 percent off the peak.

Pretend an ancestor of yours started with a $1,000 US stock investment in January 1881 and that capital was completely invested with a PE momentum system ever since, using 15 and 24 as the limits. The system would have sold out of the stock market four times and bought back in four times. That's eight trades in 132 years, or an average of about one trade every seventeen years. A typical investor can expect several trades in a lifetime.

Below is a chart of the ten-year PE with shaded bars marking the times when a 15/24 momentum investor would have been invested in the stock market. The unshaded strips represent periods when the system would have been in fixed-income investments.

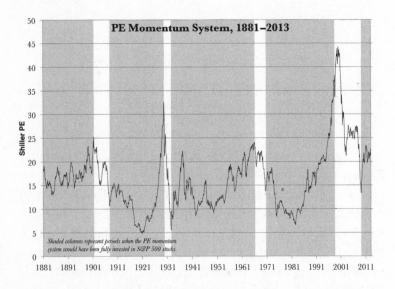

Over short time frames, changes in the ten-year PE are almost all due to changes in stock prices. The chart's steep declines in PE correspond to steep declines in stock prices. The momentum system skipped the 1929 crash and both crashes of the 2000s with remarkable timing. It sold near the top of the 1901 and 1966 bubbles, though it bought back in before the ultimate low.

Here's a chart of portfolio value. These are real gains after allowing for the diminishing dollar (but not transaction costs, management fees, and taxes). During this 132-year period an investment in ten-year US Treasury bonds might have turned an initial $1,000 into $18,704, inflation adjusted. I do not chart that because the line would hug the axis so closely as to be indistinguishable from it.

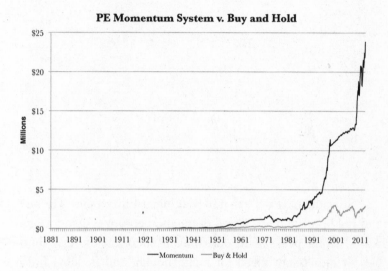

PE Momentum System v. Buy and Hold

A buy-and-hold stock investor in the S&P 500 and its precursor companies would have turned $1,000 into about $2,932,653. An investor using the PE momentum system to switch between stocks and bonds would have realized $23,836,362. That's over 8 times the wealth of a buy-and-hold investor.

Nobody invests for 132 years. Let's look at something a little easier to relate to, the twenty years from January 1993 to January 2013. This time we start with $1,000 in 1993. A bond investment would have grown to $1,617 in real terms. A buy-and-hold stock investment would have risen to $3,173. The PE momentum system would have ended up with $5,517.

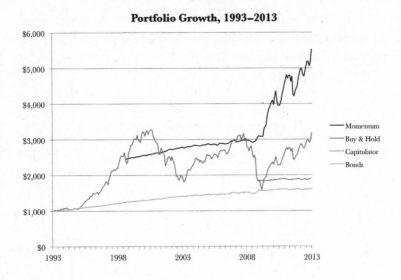

Portfolio Growth, 1993–2013

It would have done that by making just two trades. The buy-and-hold portfolio was ahead of the momentum system for brief periods at the peaks of the dot-com and subprime mortgage bubbles. It didn't stay ahead for long, though, and it didn't finish ahead. The buy-and-holder weathered two horrific declines. In the first, the stock portfolio lost 43 percent of its value. In the second, it lost 50 percent. (These figures may be different from what you've heard, as they account for reinvested dividends and inflation.)

At the bottom of the market's second plunge, in March 2009, the stock portfolio's value was nearly tied with that of the bond portfolio. That's one demonstration that stocks do not always outperform bonds over fairly long periods.

The dotted line labeled "Capitulator" represents the possible fate of someone who considered himself a buy-and-hold investor but who was spooked by the second big plunge in a decade. Exasperated by weeks of declines, the capitulator threw in the towel. He sold, vowing never to invest in stocks again.

The capitulating investor was lucky enough to sell somewhere above the very bottom. Still, as the dotted line shows, the capitulator ended up with less than the strict buy-and-hold investor. This is the behavioral penalty.

Investors have been told that the booms and busts of recent years are unprecedented. Really, booms and busts are two of the few things that haven't changed. A 50 percent drop in the market is not an anomaly. The long-term investor should have a strategy in place for dealing with such declines, rather than hoping to come up with something in the heat of the moment. This is an area where intuition is all too fallible.

Nobody should stake everything on US stocks. Small investors are advised to build a portfolio of low-cost funds investing in bonds or Treasury bills, inflation-indexed bonds (TIPS), American and foreign stocks, and commercial real estate. The PE momentum system is to be applied only to that part of your portfolio allocated to US stocks (ideally, an S&P 500 fund). Some may prefer to apply it only to part of their US stock allocation. If you can't bear the thought of ever being completely out of the US market, you might use it for half your allocation, or any fraction you like.

To recap, here's how the system works. Put a reminder on your calendar, once a month, to check the ten-year PE. (One source is at www.multpl.com, where you click on "Shiller PE"). As long as the PE remains below 24, you do nothing.

The first month that the PE moves above 24, make a note of the PE value. Don't sell anything yet. Each month afterward, record the latest PE value. You sell only on a downturn. When the current month's PE is at least 6 percent less than the highest monthly value since it rose above 24, sell your US stock index fund (or whatever fraction is being managed with this system) and put the money in safe fixed-income investments. Since you'll probably have a permanent allocation to fixed income as well, you'll need to keep a record of how much is the stock fund proceeds.

Example. The Shiller PE is above 24 when you check in June. By November you've got this list:

> June, 24.03
> July, 24.60
> August, 24.41
> September, 27.45
> October, 27.32
> November, 25.53

The highest value in the list is 27.45, for September. The current (November) value is 25.53, which is more than 6 percent short of the 27.45 maximum. That means you should sell.

Note that there were also pullbacks in August and October, but neither was big enough to trigger a sale. In August the highest value on the list was 24.60 for July (obviously you didn't then have the values beyond August). The August pullback was only 1 percent from the July maximum and should not have triggered a sale.

You remain parked in fixed-income investments until you get a buy signal. This will usually take several years. Keep checking the PE monthly. When it first dips below 15, note the month and PE. Each month thereafter, add the latest PE value to the list. Eventually there will be an upturn. When the current month's PE is at least 6 percent above the recent low value, buy back into the stock index fund, using the proceeds of the fixed-income investments you bought at the previous sell signal (plus reinvested interest).

With that the cycle renews. You go back to waiting for a sell signal. Meanwhile, reinvest dividends and capital gains distributions, and keep making contributions. All reinvestments and new contributions go to the current allocation.

A well-informed (and disciplined) investor can make adjustments for interest rates and other factors that we haven't considered. In recent years interest rates on fixed-income investments have been extraordinarily low by historic standards. That makes bonds less attractive as an alternative and presumably makes higher PE valuations less risky. You might therefore move the 15 and 24 thresholds up a bit. But for those who don't trust their instincts, the 15 and 24 limits would have worked well in recent decades without any adjustments.

Can someone using a PE momentum system expect a similar advantage going forward? No, that would be unrealistic for a couple of reasons. The familiar caveat is that the future could be different from the past, perhaps in ways we can't envision. This applies to any trading system, including having no system at all.

There is also a subtler issue. A trading system can be "overfitted" to the data. Economist and money manager David J. Leinweber supplied a classic example. He searched UN statistics to determine that the best predictor of S&P 500 performance was...butter production in Bangladesh.

The connection was, of course, just a coincidence. Leinweber's point was that not all that correlates is gold. While no one would be so daft as to use butter production as a buy signal for stocks, it's not always easy to tell what's a useful predictor. It's been seriously or semiseriously proposed that hemlines, sunspots, and the political party in the White House predict stock market returns.

It's best to favor systems offering a believable economic

reason for their outperformance. How much you pay for earnings affects how much you can expect to realize from dividends and capital appreciation, and how attractive bonds are as an alternative. This is true even without the also-reasonable supposition that PEs that go up must eventually come down.

It would be asking too much to expect that the limit values that were optimal for the past 132 years would be exactly optimal for the coming decades. Even so, a look at the table of returns shows that not-quite-optimal limits can beat the market while reducing risk.

Ideally, you'd want to apply a similar strategy to other volatile parts of your portfolio: developed market funds, emerging market funds, and funds investing in real estate investment trusts (REITs). Like the S&P 500, they have shown wild swings in PE valuation. Unfortunately, it's not easy to look up ten-year, inflation-adjusted PEs for these investments, or to find the historical earnings needed to calculate them.

In the absence of earnings data, a ten-year, inflation-adjusted moving average of price can be a helpful benchmark. Anyone comfortable with spreadsheets can compute that. A current price exceeding 150 percent of the ten-year moving average is high. You should scale down your return expectations accordingly—and may want to trim your allocation as well. It would be realistic to restore the allocation when the price dips below the ten-year average.

When an investing system really works, people adopt it. Widespread adoption usually reduces or nullifies the benefit. What if PE-based trading systems become popular?

PE ratios have been a standard measure of valuation since the early twentieth century. The Shiller PE is now part of the education of any earnest investor. Yet most people don't act on what PEs are telling us. Investors continue to have short memories and believe that the recent past foretells the future.

Above all, the PE momentum system demands *patience*. It involves a few extra trades in an investor's lifetime, and they may be spaced decades apart. You have to stick with the PE-checking regimen through years of inactivity. You have to ignore the "new era" apologists who pop up like mushrooms in the loam of every overvalued market. Few investors have that kind of staying power. But that may boost the likelihood that the system will continue to work for those who stick with it.

Recap: How to Outguess the Stock Market

• When the Shiller PE is high, future stock market returns are likely to be low. Investors should defer buying stock funds when the PE is high and wait for better opportunities.

• For better returns yet, investors can sell stock funds when the PE is sufficiently high. A simple system is to sell when the Shiller PE hits 28 and buy back into the market when it hits 13.

• For still better returns, take advantage of hot hand momentum. When the Shiller PE rises above 24, check the market monthly and sell whenever the market falls 6 percent or more from a recent high. Keep the proceeds in fixed-income investments. Then, when the Shiller PE falls below 15, check the market monthly and buy back into the market whenever the PE rises 6 percent or more from a recent low.

• By sitting out the market's most turbulent times, these systems reduce risk, and that may be as important as the extra return.

Epilogue: Fortune's Wheel

I asked Thomas Gilovich whether any basketball coaches had accepted the hot hand as an illusion. His answer was an emphatic no. He said he'd been able to convince gamblers — but not coaches and players. He did report one small victory. After many years of arguing, he had devised a line of questioning that helps basketball fans understand his point.

Gilovich: "So you play basketball, right? Have you ever had the hot hand?"

Fan: "Yes!"

· "Isn't it great when you have that?"

"Oh, absolutely. It feels like you can do no wrong. The basket seems big!"

"At the same time it's thrilling, do you find there's this fear or anxiety…that creeps up the back of your spine into your skull? You think, this is so wonderful, I don't want it to come to an end?"

"Oh yeah, I know what you mean!"

"It's particularly anxiety-producing because you know it

could come or go at any moment. And you can't predict when that's going to happen."

"Yeah!"

Gilovich concludes: "Well, *that's* what we're saying."

Our inability to recognize or produce randomness is the most invisible of problems. Randomness is like air, all around us and never noticed until the gale hits. We are not prepared to connect our difficulty with randomness to the real world of missed tennis serves, bad passwords, and Ponzi schemes.

The economic costs are massive. Sports bets lost on misplaced faith in winning streaks must account for a few billion out of the guesstimated $300 billion wagered on US football, basketball, and baseball annually. Consumers' out-of-pocket losses due to easily cracked passwords are said to be running about $5 billion a year in the US alone. These amounts in turn are dwarfed by the losses of the hundreds of millions of homebuyers and investors throughout the world, all chasing hot streaks that aren't there. Accept the claim that average investors underperform the stock market by five percentage points a year, and any back-of-the-envelope estimate of the toll is stupefying. In 2011 the value of the global stock market was put at $54 trillion. If $20 trillion of that is active investors and funds catering to them, a 5 percent penalty would come to $1 trillion a year. That rivals the gross domestic products of Mexico and Australia.

In some quarters these implications are beginning to be appreciated beyond the psychology lab. Economists are recognizing the importance of hot hand perceptions in driving markets. Practitioners of predictive analytics tease predictability out of their petabytes, often revealing how rote our arbitrary choices are. People like Mark Nigrini have convinced businesspeople and governments of the value of randomness psychology in detecting fraud. Yet in most ways knowledge of our fraught relationship with randomness has yet to filter down to the general public.

Gilovich's little catechism for basketball fans works because we do appreciate, at a gut level, that the lucky streaks we believe in are fragile. They vanish like smoke. This view is enshrined in folk wisdom as the wheel of fortune. Medieval Europeans pictured a literal wheel, spun capriciously by the blindfolded goddess Fortuna. Kings and beggars and everyone else were attached to the wheel's rim. The wheel's turns could lower the status of the high and mighty, or raise the humble to glory. The message was not merely that fate changes but that it runs in streaks that seemingly can't be random. A succession of catastrophes follows an age of good fortune. When it rains, it pours.

The *Carmina Burana,* a bawdy anthology of medieval poems and drinking songs, contains this lament.

> *Fate—monstrous*
> *and empty,*
> *you whirling wheel,*
> *you are malevolent,*
> *well-being is vain*
> *and always fades to nothing*

Today we are better able to appreciate the mysteries of randomness and human choice on an intellectual level. Our emotions and intuitions haven't changed much since the so-called Dark Ages. To understand the misperception of randomness is to gain power, not over fate but over ourselves. Fortuna keeps spinning her wheel, and no one gets out of the game.

Acknowledgments

A few years ago I wrote a book called *Fortune's Formula: The Untold Story of the Scientific Betting System That Beat the Casinos and Wall Street*. Quite a few of the people I interviewed for that book brought up Claude Shannon's passion for building unusual machines. Several mentioned the outguessing machine as a particularly ingenious creation. Thanks to all who did so; you are the ultimate inspiration for this book.

I've had the privilege of drawing on the expertise, assistance, and memories of an unusually fascinating group. David Hagelbarger was helpful in putting together the story of the outguessing machines and sketching the Bell Labs milieu. He supplied contacts, photographs, his original publication, and other documents. Ariel Weinberg of the MIT Museum graciously retrieved Shannon's outguessing machine from storage so that I could see and photograph it.

Mark Nigrini is not only a proponent of using Benford's law to catch bad guys; he is the foremost historian of Frank Benford's influential idea. This book is indebted to his research into Benford's life and the applications of his law.

Special thanks also go to Tom Adams, Nick Berry, John Brockman, Daryl Fisher, Bernard Geoghegan, Thomas Gilovich, Ted Hill, Larry Hussar, Daniel Kahneman, Sean Sears, Barbara Tversky, the staff of the UCLA Research Library, and Darryl Wolgemuth.

Notes

Epigraphs

v "It is clear that one thing": Coupling 1950, 84.

v "[The] power of accurate observation": The full quote referred to the fashion for real objects as stage props on the London stage of the 1890s: "Pasteboard pies and paper flowers are being banished from the stage by the growth of that power of accurate observation which is commonly called cynicism by those who have not got it." Shaw was writing in *The World*, July 18, 1894.

v "A good magician": Sept. 13, 2012, Twitter post on @danguterman.

Prologue: The Outguessing Machine

3 Required to wear neckties; 400 °C, assistant left vinyl gloves in oven: David Hagelbarger interview, Nov. 27, 2012. Lucky 1989, 51, gives a slightly different account.

3 Read and think: David Hagelbarger e-mail Nov. 21, 2012. He read *The Design of Switching Circuits,* published 1951, by William Keister, Alistair E. Ritchie, and Seth H. Washburn.

3 Article on a computer composing music: Coupling 1950.

4 A year before Cage's experiments: Christian Wolff gave Cage a copy of the *I Ching* in 1951.

4 "One may, for instance": Coupling 1950, 84.

5 "The strategy of the machine": Hagelbarger 1956, 3.

6 "Did I put on a red tie this morning?": Lucky 1989, 53.

6 "No scientist or engineer will fail to recognize": Lucky 1989, 53.

7 "You should do something on that": Gertner 2012, 196.

7 Founding document: Harvard psychologist Howard Gardner called it "possibly the most important, and also the most famous, master's thesis of the century."

7 "told me I was married to a brilliant, brilliant man": Gertner 2012, 121.

7 "A Mathematical Theory of Communication": Shannon 1948.

8 "We hope that research in the design": Shannon 1955, 448.

8 Short film about Theseus: Gertner 2012, 140. As far as I can tell, the film is not presently on YouTube.

9 Lego block version of ultimate machine: See www.youtube.com/watch?v=gKsP4vuTg2c

9 "My characterization of his smartness": Gertner 2012, 143.

9 Story about EEG machine: Lucky 1989, 53.

10 65 percent success: See chnm.gmu.edu/digitalhistory/links/pdf/chapter6/6.19b.pdf

10 "discussed from the game theoretic angle": Shannon 1953.

10–11 Hirzebruch and outguessing machine: Schroeder 1992.

11–12 Description of mechanical scorekeeper: See Shannon 1953 and Lucky 1989, 53.

12 "To give an idea of how much intellectual activity": Hagelbarger 1956, 3.

14 "The three machines were plugged together": Shannon 1955, 452; Hagelbarger 1956, 4.

14–15 "Why build such a machine": Hagelbarger 1956, 1–2.

15 "It is possible, if not probable": Hagelbarger 1956, 3.

16 "It is extremely difficult to carry out": Shannon 1953.

17 Stanford Research Institute and psychic research: See Wikipedia entries for "SRI International" and "Stargate Project."

17 "My daughter got this in the mail": Duhigg 2012.

18 "I had a talk with my daughter": Duhigg 2012.

19 Visa predicts divorces, default rates: Ayres 2006, 36.

19 "With the pregnancy products": Duhigg 2012.

20–21 UPS initial public offering prices: See money.cnn.com/1999/11/10/companies/ups/.

20–21 Mark Madoff story: Tim Reynolds, interview, January 19, 2011.

1 The Zenith Broadcast

27 McDonald's yacht, checked suits, gin, and pistachio ice cream: "Zenith" in *Time*, June 29, 1936.

27 Interest in pirate gold: "McDonald v. the Adenoidal" in *Time,* Feb. 4, 1946.

27 WATCH ABSENCE OF PEOPLE ON STREET: "Zenith" in *Time,* June 29, 1936.

27–28 Zenith radios in movies: Zenith had a particularly close relationship with MGM and Columbia studios. The Three Stooges short in which Curley gets hit with a Zenith is "Punch Drunk." See Cones, Bryant, Blankinship 2003, 188–192; also the discussion at www.antiqueradios.com/forums/viewtopic.php?p=981751.

28 *DEVELOPED IN PARAPSYCHOLOGY LABORATORY AT DUKE UNIVERSITY:* The cards regularly turn up on eBay with photos.

29 "the brief rage of women's clubs": "Radio Patterns and Peepholes" in *Time,* Sep. 5, 1938.

29 MacDonald invited Rhine aboard yacht: Horn 2009a, 60.

29 "nothing stops a crowd on a street": Horn 2009a, 61–62.

30 Day and time of Zenith show: The most complete sources for details of the show are Cones, Bryant, Blankinship 2003 and Goodfellow 1938.

30 "a program so DIFFERENT": Cones, Bryant, Blankinship 2003, 184.

30 "The broadcasts of The Zenith Foundation have been planned": Cones, Bryant, Blankinship 2003, 184.

31 "*Narrator.* It is best to write down your impression": Goodfellow 1992, 130.

31 Woolworth's sold out of ESP cards: Horn 2009a, 62.

31 150,000 decks printed: Horn 2009a, 63.

32 Fifteen weeks, over a million responses: Goodfellow 1992, 130.

32 10,000,000,000,000,000,000 to one: Goodfellow 1992, 140.

33 Goodfellow's description: Bechtel-Wherry and Womack 2009, 17.

33 McDonald canceled the show: The Cones, Bryant, and Blankenship book says the last broadcast was March 27, 1938. Goodfellow gives results through January 2, 1938.

33–34 "pricked Telepath McDonald's iridescent bubble": "Radio Patterns and Peepholes" in *Time,* Sep. 5, 1938.

34 "full of loopholes": Horn 2009b.

34 Problems with ESP cards, B.F. Skinner demonstration: Horn 2009a, 62–63.

34 "Rhine and Goodfellow keep me supplied": Horn 2009b.

39 Thornton Fry's interest, ESP machine, Rhine's visit: Horn 2009a, 192.

39 "Mr. Townsend, do you know": Chapanis 1999, 139.

39 Design of kitchen stove controls: Chapanis 1999, 202–203.

40 "Use all the numbers": Chapanis 1995, 1350.

41 "more random": Chapanis 1995, 1355.

41 17, 28 percent accuracy: These figures are derived from those in Table 5 in Chapanis 1995, 1359.

43 Chapanis was spy: Chapanis 1999, 226.

43 "persons not acquainted with mathematics": Reichenbach 1949, 153.

43 "there is no way of combining details": Wagenaar 1972, 69.

44 Favored letters common in English: Rath 1966, 100–101.

44 Hill homework assignment: Hill 1998.

47 90 percent success rate: Maue 250.

2 How to Outguess Rock, Paper, Scissors

50 "The client was very serious about this": Vogel 2005.

51 "There was some discussion": Vogel 2005.

52 $17.8 million: Auction prices are quoted inclusive of the auction house commission. The paintings went for $15.9 million plus a 12 percent commission.

53 "I went in scripting only my first throw": Sean Sears interview, Nov. 19, 2012.

54 "I didn't worry about what I was going to do": Interview on *CBS Morning News,* Oct. 27, 2008. www.youtube.com/watch?v=ecNuYjHl1I8.

54 Monaco wears dark sunglasses: See www.mtvu.com/shows/spring-break/rock-paper-scissors/rps-contestant-jonathan-naco-monaco/.

54 Hand tells: In 2012 the University of Tokyo unveiled an RPS-playing robot, Janken, that works entirely by hand tells and has a 100 percent win rate. Its machine vision is able to recognize the human sign as it's being formed and then respond with the winning countersign in one millisecond.

55 Lacan's classroom experiment: Geoghegan 2011, 191n.

55 "If I was behind, I would play": Sean Sears interview, Nov. 19, 2012.

55 RPS outguessing apps on the Web: There's a good one on the *New York Times* site, www.nytimes.com/interactive/science/rock-paper-scissors.html. It offers two modes, "novice" and "veteran." "Novice" starts playing randomly and gradually learns to exploit your unconscious biases. "Veteran" incorporates statistics on 200,000 previous games to give it a head start.

56 Preference for rock enhanced: See Walker and Walker, 101–102, a semifacetious treatment that claims a 90 percent success rate!

3 How to Outguess Multiple-Choice Tests

57 Educators told to vary location of right answer randomly: See Haladyna, Downing, Rodriguez 2002, for an overview of professional thinking about how multiple-choice exams should be constructed.

59 *Physical Geology* quiz: This is a true-false quiz accompanying chapter 17, online at highered.mcgraw-hill.com/sites/0072402466/student_view0/chapter17/true_or_false_quiz.html.

61 "none of the above" answers right 65 percent of the time: Quizzes for *Physical Geology* by Plummer, McGeary, and Carlson.

61 Longest answer is most likely to be correct; see, for instance, the University of Minnesota's "How to Be Test Wise" at www.sass.umn.edu/pdfs/111%20StudySkills/Exams/Objective%20Exams/How%20To%20Be%20Test%20Wise%20%20C%204.5.7.pdf.

61 "To turn right, you should be in": www.dol.wa.gov/driverslicense/practicetest.html.

62 A word used to describe a noun: Burton, Sudweeks, Merril, Wood 1991, 21.

63 Rated multiple-choice strategies: For each test, I determined how often a strategy would have succeeded when applied to the applicable questions and divided its success rate by the expected rate for random guessing with that number of choices. I then averaged the relative success rates among all the tests. The averaged result was greater than 100 percent for each effective strategy (190 percent for picking "none of the above" or "all of the above" answers). The benchmark, random guessing, would be rated 100 percent. I subtracted that from each strategy's value to get the improvement (90 percent for "none of the above"–style answers).

65 Won't give the question: In case you're curious, the question is

Choose the word or set of words that, when inserted into the sentence, best fits the meaning of the sentence as a whole.

Barbara McClintock's systematic examination of corn demonstrated the transposition of genes, a finding that overturned entrenched beliefs and proved that ------- study may produce brilliant insights and ------- change.

This was "Question of the Day" for September 25, 2012 on the College Board website, sat.collegeboard.org/practice/sat-question-of-the-day?questionId= 20120925&oq=1.

66 "distractors": Haladyna, Downing, Rodriguez 2002, 317.

67 Pick most familiar answer: This is known as favoring "cognitive fluency." Daniel Kahneman talks about using it on a driver's written exam in Kahneman 2011, 62.

4 How to Outguess the Lottery

68 New Jersey introduced pick-number lottery: Thaler and Ziemba 1988, 172.

70 "if the system were good and this became well known": Chernoff 1981, 172.

71 7 is most popular pick: Thaler and Ziemba 1988, 169; Ziemba, Brumelle, Gautier, Schwartz 1986.

71–72 Fortune cookie wins: See www.lotterypost.com/news/112702; Garcia 2005.

72 *Lost* numbers played in lottery: See Wikipedia entry for "Mega Millions."

72 Least-played numbers: Ziemba, Brumelle, Gautier, Schwartz 1986.

77 "Dynasty" could use system: MacLean, Ziemba, Blazenko 1987; Thaler and Ziemba 1988, 169.

77 Almost never pays off while you're drawing breath: This idea is given mathematical form in the "Kelly criterion" of John L. Kelly, Jr. See Poundstone 2005.

77 "I figure you have the same chance": This appears in many Internet quote archives. See www.goodreads.com/quotes/85215-i-figure-you-have-the -same-chance-of-winning-the.

5 How to Outguess Tennis Serves

78 "There was one opponent who would serve to my backhand": Fisher interview, Oct. 15, 2012.

78 "rhythm": Fisher interview, Oct. 15, 2012.

78 Fisher read about outguessing machine: Fisher 2004.

79 "It's very easy to become one-dimensional": Walker and Wooders 2001, 1522.

6 How to Outguess Baseball and Football

83 60 percent of major-league pitches are fastballs: These are calculated from the figures in Kovash and Levitt 2009. Somewhat different percentages are given in Weinstein-Gould 2009, 6.

83 Study of 3 million major-league pitches: Kovash and Levitt 2009.

85 .001 OPS worth 2.16 extra runs: Fox 2006, cited in Kovash and Levitt 2009.

7 How to Outguess Soccer Penalty Kicks

87 University of Amsterdam psychologists in a bar: Vedantam 2001.

87–88 Rules said goalie can't move until the kick: Chiappori, Levitt, Grose-close 2002, 1140.

88 90 percent chance of score: Chiappori, Levitt, Groseclose 2002, 1141.

88 Studies of soccer penalty kicks: Chiappori, Levitt, Groseclose 2002; Palacios-Huerta 2003.

88 Van Breukelen, Lehmann crib sheet: See Wikipedia entry for "Penalty Kick."

88–89 Humans look right; influences design of supermarkets: Poundstone 2010, 150.

8 How to Outguess Card Games

90 1982 experiment at Northwestern University: O'Neill 1987.

93 Hess experiment with pinup picture: Hess 1965, 46.

93 "interesting possibility…": Hess 1965, 53.

9 How to Outguess Passwords

95 Klingon name site may harvest passwords: Nick Berry interview, Jan. 8, 2013.

95 Stolen passwords sell for $20: Perlroth 2012.

95 1 percent of passwords can be guessed in four tries: Weir, Aggarwal, Collins, Stern 2010, 168. This statistic refers to passwords of seven characters or more.

96 Program claims it can check 2.8 billion passwords a second: See www .elcomsoft.com/eprb.html#gpu.

96–97 "Simply, people can no longer": Schneider on Security blog, June 17, 2005. www.schneier.com/blog/archives/2005/06/write_down_your .html.

97 RockYou.com passwords compromised: Siegler 2009.

99–100 Twitter hacking: Zetter 2009.

102 "Protect the hell out of it": Berry interview, Jan. 7, 2013.

103 Palin, Romney accounts hacked via security questions: Palmer 2012.

104–105 Berry's most-used PINs: Scherzer 2012.

10 How to Outguess Crowd-Sourced Ratings

108 "the first number that comes to mind": Kubovy and Psotka 1976, 291.

108 "the first number that comes to mind": Kubovy and Psotka 1976, 293.

109 "The subject is placed in a paradoxical situation": Kobovy and Psotka 1976, 294.

109 "the unique position of being…": Kubovy and Psotka 1976, 294.

110 "School 'Fine,' U.S. Teens Report": www.theonion.com/articles/school -fine-us-teens-report,236/.

11 How to Outguess Fake Numbers

112 "I went to the library that night": Nigrini interview, Sep. 21, 2011.

114 Newcomb discovered same law earlier: Newcomb 1881.

114 "That the ten digits do not occur": Newcomb 1881, 39.

114 piggybacked on the fame of Bethe physics paper: See Goudsmit 1977.

116 "is really the theory of phenomena": Benford 1938, 572.

118 Chapanis made bar charts: Chapanis 1995, 1352.

120 "was the anti-Benford": Nigrini interview, Sep. 21, 2011.

121 Bought IRS tax return packages; use of VAX computer: Nigrini interview, Sep. 21, 2011.

122 One of Nigrini's first believers: Nigrini interview, Sep. 21, 2011.

122 "Bingo, that means fraud": Berton, 1995.

125 Team of crooks with pooled data make fraud harder to detect: Nigrini interview, Sep. 21, 2011.

126 "It wasn't the first digits that caught her": Nigrini interview, Sep. 21, 2011.

126 Fast-food manager made up sales; no number ending in 00: Nigrini, talk at Saint Michael's College, April 1, 2008.

12 How to Outguess Manipulated Numbers

130 Insurance salesman who changed receipts: Nigrini interview, Sep. 24, 2011; also Nigrini 2012, 172.

131 "This is usual for government": Nigrini interview, Sep. 24, 2011.

133 SEC charges against Health Maintenance Centers: Complaint: SEC v. Health Maintenance Centers, Inc., filed in U.S. District Court, Seattle, Jan. 17, 2002. See www.sec.gov/litigation/litreleases/comp17335.htm.

136 "Well, thank you very much": Kneale 2009.

137 Enron bump: See Nigrini 1993.

137–138 AIG and AOL TimeWarner losses: Nigrini 2012, 209.

139 5 percent criterion is arbitrary: It's based on the probability of a normally distributed variable exceeding the mean by two standard deviations.

140 IRS use of digit analysis: See Berger and Hill n.d., 2.

140 "The income tax agencies of several nations": *New York Times*, August 4, 1998.

141 Random audits resumed in 2011: See www.michaelplaks.com/irs-problems/random-audits.

141 Inland Revenue finding: Nigrini interview, Sep. 21, 2011; Nigrini 2012, 79.

142 Tax evasion based on tax-table steps: Nigrini 2012, 193–6. Nigrini used tax data from 1978, when a typical tax step was $7.

143–144 Sobyanin study of Russian elections: Sobyanin and Suchovolsky 1993.

144 magic black box: Deckert, Myagkov, and Ordeshook (n.d.).

145 "There has been fraud of course": Quoted in Deckert, Myagkov, and Ordeshook (n.d.), 4, from *Moscow Times*, Sep. 9, 2000.

146 Argument about crooks' knowledge of Benford's law: Nigrini 1993.

13 How to Outguess Ponzi Schemes

148 "I…was successful at the start": Henriques 2011.

149 "When everyone is running around like a chicken": Lux 2000.

150 Split-strike conversion strategy; experts couldn't duplicate returns: Bernard and Boyle 2009.

150 123 Procter & Gamble calls reported versus 20 traded: Patterson 2010, 63.

153 "concerned about lack of transparency": Chew 2009.

153 Threat to Madoff investors: Whitehouse and Decambre 2008.

154 Fairfield Sentry returns less Benford-like than S&P 500, stocks: See discussion of this in Nigrini 2012, 259–265.

156–157 Madoff golf scores: Rampell 2008. All the scores had 8 as the first digit, and the most common was 84, which occurred six times.

14 In the Zone

161 "He was a rough player": Barbara Tversky interview, July 8, 2008.

162 "You're in a world all your own": quoted in Tversky and Gilovich 1989a, 16.

162 "I went to talk to Amos about it": Gilovich interview, Oct. 28, 2012.

163 "The Hot Hand in Basketball": Gilovich, Vallone, Tversky 1985.

164 "Who is this guy?": quoted in Gilovich 1993, 17.

164 "There are so many variables involved": quoted in Gilovich 1993, 17.

165 "Please tell the stat man to get a life": Gilovich interview, Oct. 28, 2012.

165 Hebrew University hot hand study: Neiman and Loewenstein 2011; Matson 2012.

166 Hot hand is not *always* a myth: McFall, Knoeber, and Thurman 2009.

166 "When your whole life is telling you one thing": Gilovich interview, Oct. 28, 2012.

169 Si Stebbins arrangement: Si Stebbins was the stage name of William Coffrin, an American vaudeville magician, acrobat, and clown who died in 1950. See Schiffman 2005, 268.

170 "The beeps are coming in bursts": Pinker 2011.

170 "To the untrained eye": Feller 1968. The randomness of the London Blitz figures in Thomas Pynchon's *Gravity's Rainbow*.

170 "Who are you going to believe": said in *Duck Soup* (1933).

170 Run of twenty-six blacks at Monte Carlo: See Wikipedia entry for "Gambler's Fallacy."

171 "People's intuitions about random sampling": Tversky and Kahneman 1971, 105.

174 Predicted future occupations: Kahneman 2011, 6.

174 Influential 1972 paper: Kahneman and Tversky 1972.

175 Cite Zenith experiments: Kahneman and Tversky 1972, 436.

176 "unlike the situation with elephants": Lopes 1982, 630.

177 "Does belief in the hot hand matter for economics?": Camerer 1989, 1257.

15 How to Outguess Basketball Bracket Pools

178 "Buttons" the guinea pig: Behrens 2010.

178 Rivals Super Bowl betting: Kaplan, Garstka 2001 notes that about $80 million was wagered on the Final Four in 1998, an amount comparable to reported Super Bowl bets.

180 No #1 team has lost to a #16 team in twenty-five years: Butler 2010.

181–182 "The authors of this paper": Kaplan and Garstka 2011, 370.

183 Three top-performing brackets won 21 percent of games: Adams, "A Study of Two Pools."

184 Too many choose #1 team: Butler 2010.

184 Metrick study of twenty-four pools: Metrick 1996.

185 "In spite of the publicity": Tom Adams e-mail, Jan. 16, 2013.

185–186 60 percent of Chicago brackets money losers: Niemi, Carlin, and Alexander 2008, 44.

186 "People tend to pick upsets early": Butler 2010.

187 "I live in a Big Ten town": Butler 2010.

188 "The pool was disbanded and then reorganized": Tom Adams e-mail, Jan. 16, 2013.

188–189 "Last year the pool organizer": quoted in Tom Adams e-mail, Jan. 16, 2013.

189 "No matter how successful you are": Mather 2011.

16 How to Outguess Office Football Pools

191 Charles K. McNeil invented spread betting: Wikipedia entry, "Spread betting."

192 Levitt suggests that bookies maximize profits: Levitt 2004.
193 51.1 percent of NFL underdogs won: See www.onlinegambling.com/
     sports/american-football/betting-on-underdogs.htm.
193 betting on a home team increased 3.15 percent: Paul, Weinbach, Hum-
     phreys 2011, 10.
194 57.7 percent of the time: Levitt 2004, 235.
194 53.3 percent of the time; NCAA and NBA statistics: The 53.3 percent is
     computed from 46.7 percent, the fraction of games won by visiting
     favorites. See Levitt 2004, 236.
194–195 Looked at NFL games from 1985 to 2008: Wever and Aadland 2010.
196 Three-quarters of bettors pick favorites: Levitt 2004, 236.

17 How to Outguess Oscar Pools

202 SAG "best actor" won Oscar, too: Whipp 2012. I've updated the statistic to
     reflect Jean Dujardin's dual win in 2012 and Daniel Day-Lewis's in 2013.
204 Academy voters 77 percent male, 94 percent white: Horn, Sperling, and
     Smith 2012.

18 How to Outguess Big Data

208 Primary and secondary offers: forteconsultancy.wordpress.com/2011/03/
     31/stopping-churn-in-its-tracks — proactive-retention-strategies-for
     -mobile-operators/.
209 "Real-time consumer insights": See Neustar Information Services website,
     www.neustar.biz/infoservices.
209 "pinpoints a caller's location within feet": Neustar's white paper, "Jenny
     Craig Overcomes Complex Store-Locator Technology Needs." www
     .neustar.biz/information/docs/pdfs/casestudies/jennycraig
     _locator_casestudy.pdf.
209 Neustart scores consumers from phone numbers: Singer 2012 (which
     refers to the company by its previous name, TARGUSInfo).
209 "Knowing the bottom is more important": Singer 2012.
210 Google Voice; *67 does not work with toll-free numbers: See
     productforums.google.com/forum/#!category-topic/voice/getting
     -started — tips — tricks/AoEwD7udhAU.
212 "Why don't you just give me these prices in the store?": www.vons.com/
     ShopStores/Justforu-FAQ.page?#answer_3.
212 Vanek switched between Starbucks and Dunkin' Donuts coffee: Clifford
     2012.

213 Abandoned shopping cart strategy: Tuttle 2012.
213 Best Buy, Home Depot: Gladstone 2012.
213 65 percent of shopping carts abandoned: Gladstone 2012.

20 How to Outguess Home Prices

220 Phoenix, Las Vegas gains; Case's worry: Lazo 2013.
223 Friday listing sold for 99.1 percent of asking price: Tanaka 2013.

21 How to Outguess the Future

224 Close to $400 billion: Plunkett Research estimates $391 billion for 2012. See
      www.plunkettresearch.com/consulting-market-research/industry
      -and-business-data.
224 "Each year the prediction industry showers us": Sherden 1998, 5.
225 "We reach the point": Tetlock 2005.
225 Prediction tournament: "How to Win at Forecasting: A Conversation with
      Philip Tetlock," edge.org/conversation/win-at-forecasting.
225 "mechanized 'hugging booths'": 2006 predictions, archived on www
      .faithpopcorn.com.
225 "a surge in popularity": 2006 predictions, on www.faithpopcorn.com.
226 "will turn battlefield decisions": 2011 predictions, on www.faithpop
      corn.com.
226 "As the cost of genetic modification": 2006 predictions, on www.faithpop
      corn.com.

22 How to Outguess the Stock Market

232 "I criticized all those who had concluded": Cassidy 2007.
233 Floor trader could predict price movements: Niederhoffer and Osborne
      1966, 897.
235 "Professional traders will recognize these rules": Niederhoffer and Osborne
      1966, 914.
235–236 Keeley told Niederhoffer to invest in Thailand: Cassidy 2007.
236 Half of today's trading: Steinert-Threlkeld 2013.
237 Trading is hazardous to your wealth: Barber and Odean 2007.
237 DALBAR study on average investors: Richards 2010.
237–238 "People tend to be overconfident": Nocera 2012.
238 $266 billion in mutual fund redemptions: Harris 2001.

240 Five to ten years of earnings: Graham and Dodd 1934, 452.
240 Analyst projections too high in nineteen years out of twenty-one: Sharpe 2002, 637.
245 "one might have thought": Shiller 1996.
246 "Long-term investors would be well advised": Shiller 2005, 187.
247 "Suppose it was demonstrated": Bogle 2007.
247 Almost tripled money in ten best days: This is computed from the record gains on the *Wall Street Journal*'s site at online.wsj.com/mdc/public/page/2_3024-djia_alltime.html.
249 Half a percentage point a year: This is estimated from figures and charts in Stein and DeMuth 2003, 37–42.

Epilogue: Fortune's Wheel

268 $300 billion: This figure is taken from Light, Rutledge, Singleton 2011, which gives $255 to $300 billion as the size of the illegal football, basketball, and baseball betting market. *Legal* sports bets are a drop in the bucket. In Nevada they came to $2.8 billion in 2010.
268 $5 billion: This is a Federal Trade Commission estimate from a 2003 survey. I would imagine the figure is higher today. See www.ftc.gov/opa/2003/09/idtheft.shtm.
268 $54 trillion: Roxburgh, Lund, Piotrowski 2011, 13.
269 "Fate—monstrous and empty": See Wikipedia entry for "O Fortuna."

Bibliography

Adams, Tom (n.d.) "A Study of Two Pools." www.poologic.com/study.htm.

Associated Press (2005). "Rock paper scissors settles auction house battle." May 5, 2005.

Ayres, Ian (2007). *Super-Crunchers*. New York: Bantam.

Barber, Brad M., and Terrance Odean (2007). "Trading Is Hazardous to Your Wealth: The Common Stock Investment Performance of Individual Investors." *Journal of Finance* 55, 773–806.

Bar-Eli, Michael, Simcha Avugos, and Markus Raab (2006). "Twenty Years of Hot Hand Research: Review and Critique." *Psychology of Sport and Exercise* 7, 525–553.

Bechtel-Wherry, Lori J., and Kenneth Womack (2009). *Penn State Altoona*. Mount Pleasant, SC: Arcadia Publishing.

Behrens, Andy (2010). "NCAA bracket update: We all lost to a guinea pig." Yahoo! Sports, Apr. 28, 2010. sports.yahoo.com/fantasy/blog/roto_arcade/post/NCAA-bracket-update-We-all-lost-to-a-guinea-pig?urn=fantasy,237132.

Belkin, Lisa (2002). "The Odds of That." *New York Times,* Aug. 11, 2002.

Bender, Edward A. (n.d.). "Betting on Football Pools." math.ucsd.edu/~ebender/87/pools.ps.

Benford, Frank (1938). "The Law of Anomalous Numbers." *Proceedings of the American Philosophical Society* 78, 551–572.

Berber, Bernd, and Alexandra Scacco (2012). "What the Numbers Say: A Digit-Based Test for Election Fraud." *Political Analysis* 20, 211–234. files.nyu.edu/bb89/public/files/Beber_Scacco_ElectionFraud.pdf.

Berger, Arno, and Theodore P. Hill (n.d.) "Benford's Law Strikes Back: No Simple Explanation in Sight for Mathematical Gem." digitalcommons .calpoly.edu/cgi/viewcontent.cgi?article=1074&context=rgp_rsr.

Bernard, Carole, and Phelim Boyle (2009). "Mr. Madoff's Amazing Returns: An Analysis of the Split-Strike Conversion Strategy." www.northernfinance .org/2009/program/papers/233.pdf.

Berton, Lee (1995). "He's Got Their Number: Scholar Uses Math to Foil Financial Fraud." *Wall Street Journal,* Jul. 10, 1995.

Breiter, David, and Bradley Carlin (1997). "How to Play Office Pools If You Must." *Chance* 10, 5–11.

Brooks, Caryn (2011). "How to win your office pool without really trying (sort of)." Reuters, Feb. 25, 2011. blogs.reuters.com/reuters-money/2011/02/25/ how-to-win-your-office-pool-without-really-trying-sort-of/.

Brown, William O., and Raymond D. Sauer (1993). "Does the Basketball Market Believe in the Hot Hand? Comment." *American Economic Review* 83, 1377–1386.

Browne, Malcolm W. (1998). "Following Benford's Law, or Looking Out for No. 1." *New York Times,* Aug. 4, 1998, F4.

Bui, Kha (2011). "Das Benford'sche Gesetz." Working paper, Max-von-Laue Gymnasium, Koblenz, Germany.

Bullock, Nichole (2012). "US corporate bond yields hit record low." *Financial Times,* Feb. 15, 2013. www.ft.com/intl/cms/s/0/0a3cad02-57f7-11e1-ae89 -00144feabdc0.html#axzz1mawRD46e.

Burton, Steven J., Richard R. Sudweeks, Paul F. Merrill, and Bud Wood (1991). "How to Prepare Better Multiple-Choice Test Items: Guidelines for University Faculty." Provo, Utah: Brigham Young University Testing Services.

Butler, Sarah Lorge (2010). "NCAA Brackets: How to Win Your March Madness Pool." CBS News, Mar. 12, 2010. www.cbsnews.com/8301-505123_162 -51403055/ncaa-brackets-how-to-win-your-march-madness-pool/.

Camerer, Colin F. (1989). "Does the Basketball Market Believe in the 'Hot Hand'?" *American Economic Review* 79, 1257–1261.

Campbell, John Y., and Robert J. Shiller (1998). "Valuation Ratios and the Long-Run Stock Market Outlook." *Journal of Portfolio Management,* Winter 1998, 11–26.

Cassidy, John (2007). "The Blow-Up Artist." *New Yorker,* Oct. 15, 2007.

Chapanis, Alphonse (1953). "Random-number Guessing Behavior." *American Psychologist* 8, 332.

——— (1995). "Human Production of 'Random' Numbers." *Perceptual and Motor Skills* 81, 1347–1363.

——— (1999). *The Chapanis Chronicles: 50 Years of Human Factors Research, Education, and Design.* Santa Barbara: Aegean Publishing.

Chernoff, Herman (1981). "How to Beat the Massachusetts Numbers Game." *Mathematical Intelligencer* 3, 166–172.

Chew, Robert (2009). "Madoff's Banker: Where Was JPMorgan Chase?" *Time*, Mar. 25, 2009. www.time.com/time/business/article/0,8599,1887338,00.html.

Chiappori, P.-A., S. Levitt, and T. Groseclose (2002). "Testing Mixed-Strategy Equilibria When Players Are Heterogeneous: The Case of Penalty Kicks in Soccer." *American Economic Review* 92, 1138–1151.

Clifford, Stephanie (2012). "Shopper Alert: Price May Drop for You Alone." *New York Times*, Aug. 9, 2012.

Cones, Harold, John H. Bryant, and Martin Blankinship (2003). *Zenith Radio, the Glory Years, 1936–1945: History and Products*. Altgen, Penna.: Schiffer Publishing.

Coupling, J. J. (1950). "Science for Art's Sake." *Astounding Science Fiction*, Nov. 1950, 83–92.

De Bondt, Werner, and Richard H. Thaler (1985). "Does the Stock Market Overreact?" *Journal of Finance* 40, 793–805.

Deckert, Joseph, Mikhail Myagkov, and Peter C. Ordeschook (n.d.). "The Irrelevance of Benford's Law for Detecting Fraud in Elections." www.vote.caltech.edu/sites/default/files/benford_pdf_4b97cc5b5b.pdf.

DeStefano, Joseph, Peter Doyle, and J. Laurie Snell (2003). "The Evil Twin strategy for a football pool." www.math.dartmouth.edu/~doyle/docs/twin/twin.pdf.

Duhigg, Charles (2012). "How Companies Learn Your Secrets." *New York Times*, Feb. 16, 2012.

Falk, Ruma (1981). "The Perception of Randomness." In *Proceedings, Fifth International Conference for the Psychology of Mathematics Education*. Grenoble, France.

Fama, Eugene (1991). "Efficient Capital Markets, II." *Journal of Finance* 46, 1575–1617.

Feller, William (1968). *An Introduction to Probability Theory and Its Applications*. New York: Wiley.

Fisher, Daryl (2004). "Serving up the unpredictable." *ADDvantage*, Jul. 2004. www.addvantageuspta.com/default.aspx?act=newsletter.aspx&category=ADDvantage&menuitemid=344&MenuGroup=ADD-depts&NewsLetterID=484&&AspxAutoDetectCookieSupport=1.

Garcia, Michelle (2005). "Smart cookie brings good fortune to 110 in Powerball." *Washington Post*, May 12, 2005.

Gardner, Martin (1975). *Mathematical Carnival*. New York: Knopf.

Geoghegan, Bernard Dionysius (2011). "From Information Theory to French Theory: Jakobson, Lévi-Strauss, and the Cybernetic Apparatus." *Critical Inquiry* 38, 96–126.

Gilovich, Thomas (1993). *How We Know What Isn't So: The Fallibility of Human Reason in Everyday Life*. New York: Free Press.

Gilovich, Thomas, Robert Vallone, and Amos Tversky (1985). "The Hot Hand in Basketball: On the Misperception of Random Sequences." *Cognitive Psychology* 17, 295–314.

Gladstone, Beth Pinsker (2012). "Abandon online shopping cart, reap discount?" Reuters, Jun. 7, 2012.

Golden, Daniel (2009). "Cash Me If You Can." Portfolio.com, Mar. 18, 2009.

Goodfellow, Louis D. (1992). "A Psychological Interpretation of the Results of the Zenith Radio Experiments in Telepathy." *Journal of Experimental Psychology: General* 121, 130–144. A reprint of the 1938 article.

Goudsmit, S. (1977). "Pitfalls in elementary probability." *Proceedings of the American Philosophical Society* 121, 188–189.

Graham, Benjamin, and David L. Dodd (1934). *Security Analysis*. New York: McGraw Hill, 1934.

Hagelbarger, D.W. (1956). "SEER, A Sequence Extrapolating Robot." *IRE Transactions on Electronic Computers*, Mar. 1956, 1–7.

Haladyna, Thomas M., Steven M. Downing, and Michael C. Rodriguez (2002). *Applied Measurement in Education* 15, 309–334.

Hämäläinen, Heikki, Iiro Honkala, Simon Litsyn, and Patric Östergard (1995). "Football pools—A game for mathematicians." *American Mathematical Monthly* 102, 579–588.

Harris, Bryan (2011). "Learn About Passive Index Funds Strategy." www.indexingblog.com/2011/11/06/lessons-in-mutual-fund-flows.

Heller, Nathan (2012). "Listen and Learn." *New Yorker*, Jul. 9, 2012.

Henriques, Diana B. (2011). "The Lasting Shadow of Bernie Madoff." *New York Times*, Dec. 10, 2011.

Hill, Theodore P. (1988). "Random number guessing and the first digit phenomenon." *Psychological Reports* 62, 967–971.

——— (1998). "The First Digit Phenomenon." *American Scientist* 2.

——— (1999). "The Difficulty of Faking Data." *Chance* 12.3, 27–31.

Horn, John, Nichole Sperling, and Doug Smith (2012). "Oscar voters overwhelmingly white, male." *Los Angeles Times*, Feb. 19, 2012.

Horn, Stacy (2009a). *Unbelievable: Investigations into Ghosts, Poltergeists, Telepathy, and Other Unseen Phenomena, from the Duke Parapsychology Laboratory*. New York: HarperCollins.

——— (2009b). "ESP Games and Academic Politics" (blog post). *Unbelievable*, Oct. 18, 2009. www.echonyc.com/~horn/unbelievable/?p=1275.

Hsu, E.H. (1948). "An experimental study on 'mental numbers' and a new application." *Journal of General Psychology* 38, 57–67.

Kahneman, Daniel (2011). *Thinking, Fast and Slow*. New York: Farrar, Straus and Giroux.

Kahneman, Daniel, and Amos Tversky (1972). "Subjective Probability: A Judgment of Representativeness." *Cognitive Psychology* 3, 430–454.

Kaplan, Edward H., and Stanley J. Garstka (2001). "March Madness and the Office Pool." *Management Science* 7, 369–382.

Keller, Maryann (2000). "Getting a Premium Over List Price." *Automotive Industries,* May 1, 2000.

Kneale, Klaus (2009). "How Do You Control CEO Rage?" Forbes.com, Jul. 10, 2009. See www.forbes.com/2009/07/10/ceo-anger-management-ceonetwork-leadership-outbursts_slide_2.html.

Kovash, Kenneth, and Steven D. Levitt (2009). "Professionals Do Not Play Minimax: Evidence From Major League Baseball and the National Football League." National Bureau of Economic Research Working Paper 15347. www.nber.org/papers/w15347.

Kubovy, Michael, and Joseph Psotka (1976). "The Predominance of Seven and the Apparent Spontaneity of Numerical Choices." *Journal of Experimental Psychology: Human Perception and Performance* 2, 291–294.

Lavietes, Stuart (2002). "Alphonse Chapanis Dies at 85; Was a Founder of Ergometrics." *New York Times,* Oct. 15, 2002.

Lazo, Alejandro (2013). "Home price rise fuels fear of boom mentality." *Los Angeles Times,* Jan. 30, 2013.

Leinweber, David J. (1998). "What's the Stock Market Got to Do with the Production of Butter in Bangladesh?" *Money,* Mar. 1998.

Levitt, Steven. (2004). "Why are gambling markets organized so differently from financial markets?" *Economic Journal* 114, 223–246.

Light, Glenn, Karl Rutledge, and Quinton Singleton (2011). "Betting on the U.S. Market: A Discussion of the Legality of Sports Gaming Businesses." UNLV Center for Gaming Research Occasional Paper Series 12. gaming.unlv.edu/papers/cgr_op12_light_rutledge_singleton.pdf.

Lopes, Lola L. (1982). "Doing the Impossible: A Note on Induction and the Experience of Randomness." *Journal of Experimental Psychology: Learning, Memory, and Cognition* 8, 626–636.

Lucky, Robert W. (1989). *Silicon Dreams: Information, Man, and Machine.* New York: St. Martin's.

Lutz, Mary Champion, and Alphonse Chapanis (1955). "Expected Locations of Digits and Letters on Ten-Button Keysets." *Journal of Applied Psychology* 39, 314–317.

Lux, Hal (2000). "The Secret World of Jim Simons." *Institutional Investor,* Nov. 1, 2000. faculty.fuqua.duke.edu/~charvey/Teaching/BA453_2006/II_On_Jim_.pdf.

MacLean, Leonard, William T. Ziemba, and George Blazenko (1987). "Growth versus Security in Dynamic Investment Analysis." University of British Columbia, Faculty of Commerce and Business Administration, mimeograph.

Massey, Cade, and Richard H. Thaler (2010). "The Loser's Curse: Overconfidence vs. Market Efficiency in the National Football League Draft." Working paper, ssrn.com/abstract=697121.

Mather, Victor (2011). "2011 N.C.A.A. Tournament: How to Win a Pool That Rewards Upsets." *New York Times*, Mar. 14, 2011.

Matson, John (2012). "The Not So Hot Hand." *Scientific American*, Feb. 2012, 16.

Maue, Rick (2000). *The Book of Haunted Magick*. Pittsburgh: Deceptions Unlimited.

McCool, Grant (2011). "Ex-Madoff trader admits faking records since 70s." Reuters, Nov. 21, 2011. news.yahoo.com/ex-madoff-trader-admits-faking-records-since-70s-203324439.html.

McFall, Todd A., Charles R. Knoeber, and Walter N. Thurman (2009). "Contests, Grand Prizes, and the Hot Hand." *Journal of Sports Economics* 10, 236–255.

Metrick, Andrew (1996). "March Madness? Strategic behavior in NCAA basketball tournament betting pools." *Journal of Economic Behavior & Organization* 30, 159–172.

Miller, George A. (1956). "The Magical Number Seven, Plus or Minus Two: Some Limits on Our Capacity for Processing Information." *Psychological Review* 63, 81–97.

Mlodinow, Leonard (2009). "The Triumph of the Random." *Wall Street Journal*, Jul. 16, 2009.

Moody, Reginald F. (2010). "Taking Tips from Zenith's Legendary Eugene McDonald, Jr.: Getting Public Relations and Advertising to Say 'I Do.'" *Public Relations Journal* 4, 1–15.

Morrissey, Janet (2011). "Retiring Without a Home Loan." *New York Times*, Nov. 10, 2011.

Neiman, Tal, and Yonatan Loewenstein (2011). "Reinforcement learning in professional basketball players." *Nature Communications* 2:569, DOI: 10.1038/ncomms1580.

Nelson, Douglas L., Cathy L. McEvoy, and Thomas A. Schreiber (1998). "The University of South Florida word association, rhyme, and word fragment norms." www.usf.edu/FreeAssociation.

Newcomb, Simon (1881). "Note on the frequency of use of the different digits in natural numbers." *American Journal of Mathematics* 4, 39–40.

Newmark, Evan (2010). "Mean Street: Crash—The Machines Are in Control Now." *Wall Street Journal*, May 6, 2010. blogs.wsj.com/deals/2010/05/06/mean-street-crash-the-machines-are-in-control-now/.

Niederhoffer, Victor, and M.F.M. Osborne (1966). "Market Making and Reversals on the Stock Exchange." *Journal of the American Statistical Association* 61, 897–916.

Niemi, Jarad B., Bradley P. Carlin, and Jonathan M. Alexander (2008). "Contrarian Strategies for NCAA Tournament Pools: A Cure for March Madness?" *Chance* 21, 39–46.

Nigrini, Mark J. (1993). "Can Benford's Law Be Used in Forensic Accounting?" *Balance Sheet,* Jun. 1993, 7–8.

——— (1996). "A Taxpayer Compliance Application of Benford's Law." *Journal of the American Taxation Association* 18, 72–91.

——— (2005). "An Assessment of the Change in the Incidence of Earnings Management Around the Enron-Andersen Episode." *Review of Accounting and Finance* 4, 92–110.

——— (2012). *Benford's Law: Applications for Forensic Accounting, Auditing, and Fraud Detection.* New York: Wiley.

Nocera, Joseph (2005). "$100 Billion in the Hands of a Computer." *New York Times,* Nov. 20, 2005.

Nocera, Joe (2012). "My Faith-Based Retirement." *New York Times,* Apr. 27, 2012.

Palmer, Brian (2012). "Your Pet's Name vs. Where You Met Your Spouse." *Slate,* Jun. 7, 2012. www.slate.com/articles/news_and_politics/explainer/2012/06/mitt_romney_email_hack_which_password_recovery_questions_are_most_secure_.html.

Pätäri, Eero J. (2009). "Do Hot Hands Warm the Mutual Fund Investor? The Myth of Performance Persistence Phenomenon." *International Research Journal of Finance and Economics* 34, 117–139.

Patterson, Scott (2010). *The Quants.* New York: Crown Business.

Paul, Rodney J., Andrew P. Weinbach, and Brad Humphreys (2011). "The Belief in the 'Hot Hand' in the NFL: Evidence from Betting Volume Data." University of Alberta Working Paper 2011-16.

Perlroth, Nichole (2012). "How to Devise Passwords That Drive Hackers Away." *New York Times,* Nov. 7, 2012.

Pinker, Steven (2011). *The Better Angels of Our Nature: Why Violence Has Declined.* New York: Viking.

Pinkham, Roger S. (1961). "On the Distribution of First Significant Digits." *Annals of Mathematical Statistics* 32, 1223–1230.

Poe, Edgar Allan (1845). "The Purloined Letter." xroads.virginia.edu/~hyper/poe/purloine.html.

Poole, Kate (2011). "Analytics Industry Expected to Grow, Advance in 2011." *EContent,* Jan./Feb. 2011. www.econtentmag.com/Articles/News/News-Feature/Analytics-Industry-Expected-to-Grow-Advance-in-2011-73911.htm.

Poundstone, William (2005). *Fortune's Formula: The Untold Story of the Scientific Betting System that Beat the Casinos and Wall Street.* New York: Hill and Wang.

———— (2010). *Priceless: The Myth of Fair Value (and How to Take Advantage of It)*. New York: Hill and Wang.

Ramos, Sophia (2009). "The Size and Structure of the World Mutual Fund Industry." *European Financial Management* 15, 145–180.

Rampell, Catherine (2008). "Madoff: As Consistent a Golfer as He Was an Investor." *New York Times,* Dec. 19, 2008.

Rath, Gustave J. (1966). "Randomization by Humans." *American Journal of Psychology* 79, 97–103.

Reichenbach, Hans (1949). *The Theory of Probability*. Berkeley: University of California Press.

Richards, Carl (2010). "Investors Are Still Behaving Badly." *New York Times,* Aug. 5, 2010.

Ross, Bruce M. (1955). "Randomization of a Binary Series." *American Journal of Psychology* 68, 136–138.

Roxburgh, Charles, Susan Lund, and John Piotrowski (2011). "Mapping global capital markets 2011." McKinsey & Company, www.cfr.org/economics/mckinsey-global-institute-mapping-global-capital-markets-2011/p25592.

Salsman, Richard M. (2004). "The Cause and Consequences of the Great Depression, Part 1: What Made the Roaring '20s Roar." *Intellectual Activist,* Jun. 2004.

Scherzer, Lisa (2012). "Cracking Your PIN Code: Easy as 1-2-3-4." Yahoo! Finance, Sept. 21, 2012. finance.yahoo.com/blogs/the-exchange/cracking-pin-code-easy-1-2-3-4-130143629.html.

Schiffman, Nathaniel (2005). *Abracadabra!* Amherst, NY: Prometheus Books.

Schroeder, Manfred (1992). *Fractals, Chaos, Power Laws: Minutes from an Infinite Paradise*. New York: W.H. Freeman.

Shannon, C.E. (1948). "A Mathematical Theory of Communication." *Bell System Technical Journal,* Jul. and Oct. 1948, 379–423; 623–656.

Shannon, Claude (1953). "A Mind-Reading (?) Machine." Bell Laboratories memorandum, Mar. 18, 1953.

———— (1955). "Game-Playing Machines." *Journal of the Franklin Institute* 250, 447–453.

Sharpe, Steven (2002). "Re-examining Stock Valuation and Inflation: The Implication of Analysts' Earning Forecasts." *Review of Economics and Statistics* 84, 632–48.

Sherden, William A. (1998). *The Fortune Sellers: The Big Business of Buying and Selling Predictions*. New York: John Wiley.

Shiller, Robert J. (1996). "Price-Earnings Ratios as Forecasters of Returns: The Stock Market Outlook in 1996." www.econ.yale.edu/~shiller/data/peratio.html.

———— (2005). *Irrational Exuberance* (second edition). New York: Broadway Books.

Siegler, M. G. (2009). "One of the 32 Million With a RockYou Account? You May Want to Change All Your Passwords. Like Now." Techcrunch.com, Dec. 14, 2009. techcrunch.com/2009/12/14/rockyou-hacked/.

Singer, Natasha (2012). "Secret E-Scores Chart Consumers' Buying Power." *New York Times*, Aug. 19, 2012.

Sobyanin, Alexandar and V. Suchovolsky (1993). "Elections and the Referendum December 11, 1993, in Russia." Report to the Administration of the President of the RF, Moscow.

Spencer-Brown, G. (1957). *Probability and Scientific Inference*. London: Longmans, Green.

Stein, Ben, and Phil DeMuth (2003). *Yes, You Can Time the Market!* New York: John Wiley.

Stein, Mark A. (1993). "'Evil Twin' Helps Even the Odds in Office Betting Pools." *Los Angeles Times*, Apr. 17, 1993.

Steinert-Threlkeld, Tom (2013). "High-Frequency Trading Less Profitable, Less Prevalent." TradersMagazine.com, Mar. 1, 2013. www.tradersmagazine.com/news/high-frequency-trading-less-profitable-prevalent-110953-1.html.

Tanaka, Sanette (2013). "The Best Day to List a Home Is..." *Wall Street Journal*, Feb. 8, 2013.

Tetlock, Philip. *Expert Political Judgment: How Good Is It? How Can We Know?* Princeton: Princeton University Press, 2005.

Thaler, Richard H., and William T. Ziemba (1988). "Anomalies: Pari-mutuel Betting Markets: Racetracks and Lotteries." *Journal of Economic Perspectives* 2, 161–174.

Time (uncredited) (1936). "Zenith." *Time*, Jun. 29, 1936.

——— (1938). "Radio Patterns and Peepholes." *Time*, Sep. 5, 1938.

——— (1946). "McDonald v. the Adenoidal." *Time*, Feb. 4, 1946.

Tuttle, Brad (2012). "The Passive-Aggressive Way to Haggle Online: Abandon Your Shopping Cart." *Time*, Sep. 27, 2012.

Tversky, Amos, and Thomas Gilovich (1989a). "The Cold Facts about the 'Hot Hand' in Basketball." *Chance* 2, 16–21.

——— (1989b). "The 'Hot Hand': Statistical Reality or Cognitive Illusion?" *Chance* 2, 31–34.

Tversky, Amos, and Daniel Kahneman (1971). "Belief in the Law of Small Numbers." *Psychological Bulletin* 76, 105–110.

——— (1974). "Judgment under uncertainty: Heuristics and biases." *Science* 185, 453–458.

——— (1983). "Extensional Versus Intuitive Reasoning: The Conjunction Fallacy in Probability Judgment." *Psychological Review* 90, 293–315.

Varian, Hal (1972). "Benford's law." *American Statistician* 26, 65.

Vendantam, Shankar (2011). "Under Pressure, Soccer Goalies Tend to Dive Right." "All Things Considered" story for NPR, Aug. 2, 2011. www.npr

.org/2011/08/02/138922339/under-pressure-soccer-goalies-tend-to-dive -right.

Vogel, Carol (2005). "Rock, Paper, Payoff: Child's Play Wins Auction House an Art Sale." *New York Times,* Apr. 29, 2005.

Wagenaar, W.A. (1972). "Generation of Random Sequences by Human Subjects: A Critical Survey of Literature." *Psychological Bulletin* 77, 65–72.

Walker, Douglas, and Graham Walker (2004). *The Official Rock Paper Scissors Strategy Guide.* New York: Simon & Schuster.

Walker, Mark, and John Wooders (2001). "Minimax Play at Wimbledon." *American Economic Review* 91, 1521–1538.

Weatherall, James Owen (2013). *The Physics of Wall Street.* Boston and New York: Houghton Mifflin Harcourt.

Weinstein-Gould, Jesse (2009). "Keeping the Hitter Off Balance: Mixed Strategies in Baseball." *Journal of Quantitative Analysis in Sports* 2, article 7.

Weir, Matt, Sudhir Aggarwal, Michael Collins, and Henry Stern (2010). "Testing Metrics for Password Creation Policies by Attacking Large Sets of Revealed Passwords." web.cs.wpi.edu/~cshue/cs525/papers/passwords_revealed -weir.pdf.

Wever, Sean, and David Aadland (2010). "Herd Behavior and Underdogs in the NFL." www.uwyo.edu/aadland/research/nflbets.pdf.

Whipp, Glenn (2012). "Oscar predictions: We call the four acting races." *Los Angeles Times,* Feb. 25, 2012.

Whitehouse, Kaja, and Mark Decambre (2008). "Bernie's Bravado: Madoff's Desperate Acts to Save Fund from Implosion." *New York Post,* Dec. 18, 2008. www.nypost.com/p/news/business/item_e2ldeTLlP2nP7lNqcIDpWK;jsess ionid=FF247983DD3AB6226FE22DBBF90CAF71.

Wiles, Joel (2006). "Mixed Strategy Equilibrium in Tennis Serves." Duke University honors thesis. econ.duke.edu/uploads/assets/dje/2006_Symp/Wiles.pdf.

Zetter, Kim (2009). "Weak Password Brings 'Happiness' to Twitter Hacker." Wired .com, Jan. 6, 2009. www.wired.com/threatlevel/2009/01/professed-twitt/.

Ziemba, William T., Shelby L. Brumelle, Antoine Gautier, and Sandra L. Schwartz (1986). *Dr. Z's 6/49 Lotto Guidebook.* Vancouver and Los Angeles: Dr. Z Investments.

Index

About the Author

WILLIAM POUNDSTONE is the author of thirteen previous books, including *Are You Smart Enough to Work at Google?*, *Fortune's Formula*, and *How Would You Move Mount Fuji?*. He has written for the *New York Times*, *Harper's*, *Harvard Business Review*, and the *Village Voice*, among other publications, and is a frequent guest on TV and radio. He lives in Los Angeles. Follow Poundstone on Twitter (@WPoundstone) and learn more at his website, home.williampoundstone.net.